EYUP A(

COMEDY AND TRAGEDY

1982-2010

Bobby Knutt

Buy our books online at www.aldbooks.co.uk

Printed and published by:
ALD Print Limited
279 Sharrow Vale Road
Sheffield S11 8ZF

Telephone 0114 267 9402
E:mail a.lofthouse@btinternet.com

ISBN 978-9-01587-85-2

First published September 2010

Copyright: Robert Wass July 2010

Cover picture by Glendane Photography, Wombwell, Barnsley.

CONTENTS

Foreword 1
1. Battleships & Booze, The Falklands 1982 2
2. It's a Madhouse 39
3. All Creatures Great & Des O'Connor 42
4. The Mile High Club 45
5. Sun City & My First and Last Joint 50
6. Triumphs & Disasters in South Africa. 53
7. Knutty on Safari 58
8. The Ladie's Bicycle Saddle Sniffing Club 65
9. Fairy Glitterclit 71
10. Paula 76
11. Donna 79
12. The Gypsy's Prophesy 87
13. Sad Pantomime 91
14. Mile High Proposal. 93
15. Biffer & Ben 95
16. What Goes Round Comes Round 97
17. Pumping Iron & Tony Toms. 102
18. The Tale of 33 Coffin Dodgers 110
19. The Best Day of My Life 112
20. Angela 119
21. Lance Edwards 127
22. Four Trees for Charity 130
23. Cottages & Cornwall 134
24. The Strange Tale of the Vanishing Egg 139
25. I Belt a World Class Superstar 142
26. The Trouble With Cars Is 147
27. Pumping Iron & Spare Tyres 154
28. Ladder Of Swords. 159
29. My Heroes 162
30. Mother Goose 167

31. Clouds On The Horizon. 173
32. Courts & Committee Men 178
33. Bob's Your Uncle and Fanny's Your Aunt 182
34. Unhappy New Year 188
35. Death In Germany 191
36. A Summer of Woe 198
37. I Miss an Entrance. 203
38. Buckingham Palace 205
39. The Life of a Struggling Actor 209
40. Panto With Mother. 213
41. Knutty on the Square 218
42. Heartbeat 218
43. Brian Glover's T Shirt. 223
44. Delia Knutt & The Missing Postman 228
45. Knutty's Soap Box. 230
46. Dingling in Emmerdale 235
47. My One and Only Screen Kiss 241
48. I Become The Gaffer. 242
49. Knutty The Panto Baddie 244
50. The Tragedy of Mike Kay 247
51. The Unexpected Guest. 250
52. Tony Capstick 257
53. A Life On The Ocean Wave. 267
54. Camembert, Bouillabaisse & Peril At Sea 280
55. Lost Luggage. 285
56. Airport Security 290
57. Stormy Seas 294
58. I Have A Stroke. 301
59. What's Round The Corner? 306
60. It Doesn't Get Any Easier 309
61. It's Goodnight From Me...... 313
62. More Knutty Recipies. 314

Foreword

Welcome to the world of Bobby Knutt, comedian, actor, raconteur, gourmet and now author.

I have watched in the wings as the honourable Knutty made the transition from clubland comic to brilliant writer of humour.

He has his own unique style of writing with complete openness and honesty. He pulls no punches especially with his language and his likes and dislikes are described in graphic detail. If you are easily offended with down to earth, tell it how it is tales and you don't like to laugh, read no further.

Witness if you will his trysts with the Gemini twins aided and abetted by Ronnie Hilton. Laugh out loud at his spat with Roger de Courcey and his alter ego Nookie Bear. Sympathise with the tragedy of advancing years and ill health but warm to a generously talented man who simply likes the world to laugh with him.

His exquisitely crafted humour is displayed with a relish reminiscent of an era of comedy which has kept the world laughing for as long as I can remember. His story of his experiences cruising the Baltic with a passenger he describes as a "shit encrusted numpty" is a joy. If you can imagine being a guest at a gourmet dinner with great friends, grog, terrific banter, laughter to the point of crying with a guaranteed "lie in" the next day, this is would be an equal to this reading experience.

When people ask me about this book I will say it was written by one of my greatest pals and I am grateful to have witnessed so much of its history.

Thank you Knutty for the privilege of writing the foreword but, most of all, thank you for your friendship.

Stephen D. Smith M.B.E.

Battleships & Booze, The Falklands 1982

If you read my first book, which became incomplete as soon as I'd finished it, the story took you up to the end of 1981 and you'll have gathered I'd had a pretty successful career as a comedian, actor, radio and TV personality and latterly, pantomime performer. I'd been married and divorced twice, my first two wives having totally different temperaments, and was now living with a dancer twelve years my junior. I've always been a man who loved the ladies which I confess was the chief reason for the breakdown of my two marriages. Paula, my girlfriend was a beautiful gentle girl from a very wealthy family on the East coast in Skegness. She often used to go off for a couple of months, dancing on the cruise ships and as I explained in book one, she didn't mind me having the odd little dabble with another lady as she knew I could never go that long without a fettle. It's not anything I'm particularly proud of, but it's just how I was at that time in my life. I was young, extremely fit and my saddlebags were always full. Paula used to say, "As long as you don't go falling in love with anyone, it's OK".

It was the early eighties, a time of great prosperity and Maggie Thatcher. I was working seven nights a week and needed to as I was paying off the taxman from an in-depth tax investigation the year before which concluded with me owing him nineteen thousand pounds. I'd managed to gather together fourteen thousand from savings and the sale of my beloved Austin Healey 3000 but I was still five grand short so I went into overdraft to pay him off. I was also paying out a fair old whack in maintenance so I couldn't really have a rest. It was work, work, work. I was still in Coronation Street back in 1982 so my profile was sky high as far as the public was concerned and my fees reflected that popularity.

I didn't do a summer season in '82 and was quite disappointed when Johnnie Peller failed to secure one. John was my personal manager and sole agent, we'd been together about ten years and I looked upon him as best friend, mentor and father-figure. He was very Jewish and was highly thought about within the Jewish fraternity in my home town of Sheffield. He was also my business partner in our health studio and gym which was called "Intashape". I was a mad keen weightlifter in those days and built like a brick shithouse, that was then, you should see me now, thanks to my great love of good food and wine, I'm a big fat bastard. On hindsight, I'm so glad that a summer season didn't come in for that year, for had it done, I wouldn't have been able to embark on one of the greatest adventures of my life.

When the Argentinians invaded the Falklands on April 2nd 1982, I, like most of my fellow countrymen was angry about it but I think it's true to say, however, that no one expected it to escalate into the full blown conflict that it became. Choose what ever anyone thinks about Margaret Thatcher, I totally believe that her Churchillian rallying during those early days of the trouble encouraged the whole of Great Britain into a patriotic fervour, the intensity of which had not been felt since the Second World War. Within a matter of days, our forces were mobilized and sent to the bottom of the world to defend a tiny outpost of our depleted Empire that most Brits had never even heard of, or cared about.

The ferocity of the Falklands War came right into our homes via the TV news coverage and made us all realise what our lads were going through as the Exocets destroyed our ships and killed our servicemen. There were those among us who disagreed with the conflict saying why should we send a force down there to defend a couple of Islands way down in the arsehole of the world. Maggie told them that the Falklands were just as much a part of Gt Britain as the Isle of Wight or Cornwall and I for one agreed with her. Thank God it was a short engagement and within three months the war was over but we still lost over 250 men.

In late July I got a call from JP (Johnnie Peller) asking if I fancied going to the Falklands for a month to entertain the troops down there. I was over the moon at the offer and accepted immediately, I didn't even ask what the fee was. I had a call later that day from the chap at Combined Services Entertainment (CSE) to fill me in on the details of the trip. I was to top the bill and host the show; there would be a comedy double act called Roger Idiot and Celia plus a three girl singing and dancing group called "Dream". There was no backing band so all the backing had to be on tapes. I decided to take my own sound system and both my guitars so I could sing my soldier songs and play the Shadows as well. I put two 15k dumb-bells in a strong bag so I could work out on the trip. We were to fly from RAF Brize Norton to Ascension Island then pick up a ship which would take us down to the task force zone. I was very excited about going on the tour and started boning up on my military gags as I'd not done any troop work for quite a while.

I arrived at Brize Norton on Monday the 9th August. My baggage consisted of two PA speakers plus the amp to drive them, an echo chamber, a tape deck, a big 100w Fender guitar amp, two guitars and my suitcase. As well as this lot I had my sports bag with the two 15k dumb-bells in it. I met the other members of the gang and we were to be known as "Operation Showboat". Roger and Celia were a very experienced club act and very funny both on and off stage. The three girls were young, attractive and typical of the girls that were doing what my Paula was doing, all tits and feathers. I was surprised to find the TV cameras there to interview us along with the local Radio Oxford mob. The three dancers were absolutely over the moon at the thought of being on the News at Ten and they happily preened and posed at the presenters' every request to do so. Roger Idiot was a wiry little chain smoker who looked more like a market barrow boy than a comedian but he was great company and we became close pals. We were all invited to a drinks reception with the station commander and treated like visiting royalty. This first day was going exceedingly well up to now with this ego-boosting treatment by the hierarchy and then I was brought down to earth with a bang. I was requested to go outside and see the NCO who was responsible for loading the VC10 which was to transport us all to Ascension. I was escorted by this huge man with lots of stripes and decorations on his chest to the loading area where the kit bags of over two hundred squaddies had just been stowed on the plane. Nearby was the luggage and equipment belonging to "Operation

Showboat". What with all my stuff plus the props, costumes and suitcases of the other five members of our party, it amounted to quite a load. We were met by this officious little jobsworth whose first words were "You can't put that lot on the plane, it's full". We've all met this self-important overzealous little arsehole in one form or another. He's the man in the flat cap and brown smock with a bad limp who patrols the works car park and only knows one sentence which is "You can't park there, I say you can't park there". He's the traffic warden that pounces thirty seconds after your ticket has expired. He's the twat at the airport check-in desk that tells you your bag is one kilo overweight and charges you for it. I looked at the Warrant Officer who was accompanying me and said "Do you want to tell him or shall I". The chap was a good four inches over six feet and was the RAF equivalent of a Regimental Sergeant Major. His back was ramrod straight and you could see your face in the toecaps of his boots and he strode smartly up to the baggage handler and told him to make room for our gear. The NCO insisted that there was no room for it at which point my shiny friend barked at him to stand to attention. Having entertained the troops on many an occasion in the past, I was fully aware of the power that the RSM possessed on a military base. He was God almighty and even the CO would treat him with the utmost respect. What amused me most about the next few moments was not so much as *what* he said to the NCO, but *how* he said it. He started off quietly but gradually rose to a crescendo which must have frightened the shit out of the fellow. It went as follows.

"Now listen up because I'm only going to say it once, this lad here and his party are going out to entertain our lads who've been fighting and dying in the Falklands. This is his fucking gear and without his fucking gear he won't be able to entertain the fucking lads will he. I don't give a flying fuck if you have to unload the whole fucking aircraft and re-pack it but if you don't get that fucking gear on board I'll have you square bashing till you're a fucking pensioner. NOW FUCKING JUMP TO IT!!!!"

"Yes Sir, right away Sir, I'll see to it Sir"

The RSM turned smartly and winked at me saying "We can rejoin the CO's reception now Sir, if you'll kindly follow me". We were later told that it was time to board the aircraft and my adventure was about to begin. We were to fly to Ascension via a refueling stop at Dakar in Senegal then board the "Norland" which was a North Sea ferry that had been commandeered by the war office. I'd only ever flown as far as Majorca on a BAC One Eleven so this long flight was to be a new experience for me. The VC10 was in my opinion the most beautiful aircraft ever built and to actually fly on one was a dream come true. On military aircraft, the seats face the back of the plane as opposed the front and there were over two hundred randy squaddies all gawping at our three lovely blonde dancers as we climbed aboard. The whispering giant took off into the blue without a bump or a vibration and quite soon afterwards the stewards came round with chicken and two veg to keep us going. All RAF flights are dry, the only drinks available are water and soft drinks but good old Roger had stowed a bottle of vodka in his hand luggage so we watered down the orange juice with it. I asked if it was possible for me to go up into the cockpit and they gladly obliged. They allowed me to stay in the cockpit while we landed which was an experience that money couldn't buy. The captain and co-pilot were a right pair of gung-ho tally-ho types who made me feel really welcome in their inner sanctum. Everyone had to disembark the aircraft while refueling took place in Dakar. We were all made to stay within a cordoned off area on the tarmac for two hours and the temperature was up in the high nineties. I experienced my first ever mosquito bite that day and my arm swelled up like a balloon.

The flight on to Ascension was made shorter by Roger's stash of vodka and once more I went up onto the flight deck to meet the new aircrew who'd taken over in Dakar. The pilot had a huge handlebar moustache and looked like he should have been flying Spitfires. He'd also seen me on Coronation Street and was really chuffed when I gave him a signed photograph for his kids. They also let me stay in the cabin while we landed but it was far more exciting as it

VC10 at Brize Norton

Knutty the pilot

was dark. As we approached Ascension Island it appeared as a tiny pin-prick of light in the distance but gradually increased in size until the runway came into view. Flying Officer Kite put the VC10 down as gently as you'd put a baby in a cot; I hardly felt the wheels touch the tarmac. It was 11-30pm and the first part of my epic trip was over.

We were taken straight from the aircraft onto a helicopter and it made the short journey to the Norland where we were dropped off onto the makeshift heli-pad which took up most of the stern deck of the vessel. The ship seemed to be in chaos with military personnel running here there and everywhere but none of them seemed to give a shit about us. I can only assume it was the presence of the four girls that eventually attracted the attention of a passing officer who enquired who we were. We told him we were Operation Showboat so he asked us to follow him; he took us to the Officer's Mess. We were all desperately tired but gladdened to find a bar with a friendly barman. The officer informed us that we were not allowed to purchase drinks at the bar as we didn't have an account, nor were we officers. He then told the barman to give us whatever we wanted and put it on his tab. His name was Lt Commander Ian Hughes and he was the Navy man in overall charge of the ship since it had been commandeered by the military. He was a proper gent and we became very firm friends for the whole of the trip. He had the largest capacity for alcohol of any human being I've ever met, and that includes up to the present day. He was a portly, ruddy faced man who spoke with the poshest Oxbridge accent I'd ever heard but that in no way deferred him from being "One of the Lads". He came back to join us about half an hour later and informed us that we weren't expected until tomorrow so there must have been a cock-up somewhere along the line. It was now nearly 2am and we were all dead on our feet in desperate need of sleep. Ian left us again to return shortly with the good news that he'd managed to secure two cabins for us, a four berth and a two. Roger and I shared the two berth while the girls had the four. This was a miracle as the ship was packed like a sardine can with two thousand squaddies, some of whom were sleeping in the corridors. Ian told us that we could use the mess for all our dining arrangements and he'd see us for breakfast. I think I must have got off to sleep at about 3am and at 6am the tannoy system woke me up plus the bells and buzzers and hooters were deafening so it was impossible to sleep. I'd started to have a shower before I realised that my towels were in my case which I'd not seen since Brize Norton. I used the bed sheet to dry myself and went up to the mess. There weren't many people in there but I got myself a full English and a mug of tea. I was just about finished when a geezer came in, took one look at me and asked me who I was and what was I doing there. He had on a uniform but it was nothing like Ian's and was definitely not Royal Navy.

"I'm having a cup of tea mate", I replied.

"You are NOT my mate, and you are not allowed in this mess".

I told him that Lt Commander Hughes had given me and my party permission to use the mess and that we were Operation Showboat.

"I'm the Captain of this vessel and I say who dines in this mess so get out now".

He'd really rubbed me up the wrong way and it was too early in the morning for diplomacy and submission to authority. I wasn't going to let this pompous twat overstep his jurisdiction by being just plain fucking rude, when I'd been given permission to be there.

"Now you listen to me MATE!! Me and my party have come all the way down here to entertain the soldiers for less than half our normal fees, we've hardly slept for forty eight hours and we are hungry. If you can't go to a bit of bacon and egg and a cup of tea after all we've been through, you can stick the fuckin' job up your pompous arse you arrogant twat". I don't think anyone had ever spoken to him like that in all his years in the merchant navy and his face was turning purple. I got up and walked straight into Ian Hughes who'd heard the whole altercation. He immediately informed the Captain or rather the "Master" of the Norland that he indeed had given me and my party permission to use the mess and seeing as how the new Master was joining the ship in less than half an hour, there wasn't much use in pursuing the matter further. The

9

man huffed and puffed a little then stormed off. Ian congratulated me on my standing up for myself and added that the Master had had a bug up his arse ever since he (Ian) had boarded the ship at the start of the war. What had upset the old man was the fact that although he was the Master of the vessel, since it had been commandeered by the Royal Navy, Ian was in overall command of her.

When the others had finally risen from their pits, I suggested we explore the ship and find the various "Mr Fixits" who would make our lives a little easier on the journey south. The girls weren't the least bit interested on going on my reccy so Roger and I set off. Seeing as how it was now the day we were supposed to actually join the ship, I sought out the cabin fixer. He'd got some paperwork which confirmed our being there and quickly allotted us our correct cabins. We were only supposed to have two between us but when I informed him that Roger and Celia were a married couple, he did a bit of juggling and I ended up with one to myself, as did Roger and Celia and the three girls shared a four berth. Our bags had still not arrived on board so I was feeling pretty scruffy having worn the same pants and socks for three days. I went up on deck and ran into Ian again who introduced me to the new Master who'd just come on board, his name was Bob Lough and he was a twenty four carat geezer. He asked if we were all comfortable and his gentlemanly concern really touched me as he invited us all up to his cabin for drinks at lunchtime. He was a total opposite to the other officious bastard whom I'd encountered earlier on at breakfast.

The Norland was a hive of industry as Chinooks swept in and out dropping off supplies which were all being stored on the car decks. Our bags and my equipment finally arrived so I got my cabin squared away and stowed my guitars on the opposite bunks. The girls immediately unpacked their bikinis and went up to sun-bathe onto the bridge deck which had been allocated by Captain Bob as our own personal rest and relaxation area. As they draped themselves temptingly on their towels, I noticed that the Chinooks were now flying in over the bows of the ship instead of the stern so

10

as to get a glimpse of the sort of sight they'd not seen for many a long month. I suspected they'd all be wanking themselves silly that night.

When I returned to my cabin I was greeted in the corridor by one of the most memorable characters I've ever met in my whole life. He introduced himself as Wendy and that he was my cabin steward. I later found out that good old Ian had granted us all temporary Officer Status which not only allowed us into the mess but also afforded us a steward. Wendy was the campest Queen I'd ever met in my life, and you can imagine, I'd met a few in my game. He was from Hull and was resident on the Norland, it was his home. He'd volunteered to stay on and had been down in the task force zone during the whole of the conflict. I should imagine the thought of being billeted with two thousand hairy-arsed men-at-arms would have sweetened the cup for him. He told me what a time he'd had with all it's ups and downs but was really upset that on the way back from the Falklands, a mob of drunken squaddies from Two Parachute Regiment had smashed up his beloved old upright piano and now he couldn't play for the lads. Apparently, his sing-songs were legendary and one of the engineers had managed to patch up his piano as best he could but it was still way out of tune. He told me that he was the girl on the ship who could get *anything at all* and whatever I wanted, I just had to ask. He totally refused to acknowledge that he was of the male gender and although the rules strictly forbade him to wear anything other than his immaculate steward's whites, I knew he'd have felt a lot more at home in a frock. His ability to acquire anything was soon demonstrated when I asked him if there was any chance of some orange juice. He said there wasn't any actual orange *juice* on board, but he'd do his best. I swear to you, within ten minutes he'd reappeared at my door, struggling with a whole case of fresh oranges and a battered old aluminium jug which had a capacity of about two litres.

"You'll have to squeeze 'em with your hands Love cause I couldn't nick a press, that naff Queen who calls herself a chef always locks her cupboards up. Anyway, look at those muscles; you'll have no

Operation Showboat

Missed again

trouble squeezin' an orange Dear Heart". He was priceless, although the chef was a man, he referred to him as "She", inferring to me that he also batted for the other side.

We were invited into the officer's quarters that night for a drink in the 2nd engineer's cabin. We were obviously quite a novelty to these guys and our popularity increased more every day. I took my big "Ovation" twelve string guitar with me and we had a major sing-song and lots of booze. Everyone got as pissed as farts and my fingers were sore from playing for about two hours. I awoke early the next morning thanks to the cacophony of bells buzzers and hooters so I went up to the mess for bacon, eggs and Anadins. I felt like there was a miner playing the "Flight of the Bumblebee" on the back of my eyeballs with a lump hammer. I *never* get hangovers because all my drinking life I've had this wonderful built-in safety mechanism which has always prevented me from getting them. Before I can drink enough booze to cause a bad head, I *always* fall asleep. I'm always the one that's fast asleep on the sofa while everyone else is still up enjoying themselves. On this occasion, the company and the guitar and the atmosphere had kept me awake and allowed me to consume more booze than I normally did so there I was, feeling like shit. I thought a workout might clear my head so I took my dumb-bells up onto the bridge deck hoping it would clear my head. It made me feel worse, to the extent that I nearly threw up.

I wandered down to back of the car deck where some of the lads were fishing. If you read my first book, you'll remember that I was a mad-keen angler in my much younger days. The lads were catching red mullet and an ugly looking little bleeder called a black sea-piranha, it had rows of needle like teeth like a pike. One of the lads caught a flying fish; it had wing-like pectoral fins which enabled it to glide over the surface of the sea like a bird. I really enjoyed chatting to the crew that was dangling their lines over the stern of the Norland and they said they were really looking forward to our first show.

We'd been taking on supplies for the whole of the three days that

Capt. Bob Luff - Me - Ian Hughes

Me and the Admiral

I'd been on the ship and finally at 4-30pm on the Wednesday, we sailed for the task force zone. Our party was invited to the sergeant's mess at 8-00pm for a darts and dominoes evening. I've *never* been a pub goer and I've always found darts and dominoes to be mind-numbingly boring so I went under sufferance. To add to the night's misery, the beer was in short supply so it was rationed until the storekeepers could find the new supply. The water was also rationed because the purifier had broken down so showers were banned until it was fixed. The sergeant's mess was also the large lounge where we were to be doing our shows for the lads and it was right in the bows of the ship where any movement would be felt more than anywhere else. At around 8-30pm, we hit what was described as a "Light Swell". The bloody thing was going up and down like a yo-yo and started to feel really ill. I'd only ever been sea-sick on one occasion before and that was on a fishing coble out of Bridlington harbour when I was eighteen. There's only one cure for sea-sickness..... LAND. I left the mess as I wanted to avoid the embarrassment of throwing up in front of everyone and ran to my cabin. As soon as I lay down, I started to feel better. I fell asleep shortly after and didn't awake until 9am the next day so I must have needed the rest.

I've never been superstitious but our first show on board The Norland was to be Friday the thirteenth at 8-30pm. Roger and I set up all the gear and did a sound check and it was perfect. The tapes were all tried and set up to play and we were all very excited about doing the show. At around 4-30 the ship started rocking and rolling and by 6-30 we'd hit a force eight storm. We had to secure all the sound system and the amps but we were determined that the show would go on. At 8-20 little Carol was sick as a dog but she stoically chose to remain with us. The room was packed to the back doors with ship's crew and officers plus as many of the squaddies we could squeeze in. The ones who couldn't get in were promised a special stag show with just me and Roger in a couple of night's time.

I went on to a rousing cheer from the lads and my first gag was as follows.

"I call my Mother-in-law the Exocet, I know she's coming but there's fuck-all I can do to stop her". They clapped and cheered and I could do no wrong after that. I put the girls on in their scanty outfits and you can imagine the reaction, they went berserk and it was definitely eyes down for a full trouser. Roger and Celia tore the bollocks off 'em and nobody seemed to notice the ship pitching and rolling like a cork. I closed the show then we all did a sing song for the finale which had them up on their feet for a very long standing ovation. I must confess, I was crying my bloody eyes out as the lads clapped, cheered and chanted for more. We'd done three hours between us and I was starting to feel the movement up there in the bows of the ship but we'd been invited up to Captain Bob's cabin for a nightcap so off we went. He was over the moon with the way we'd been received by the lads and from then on we were treated like superstars.

The next day we were invited up on to the stern deck to fire the SLR rifle. The targets were bags of rubbish which had been tossed off the back of the ship. You'd never get away with that nowadays thanks to the environmental laws regarding disposal of waste at sea. I was a pretty good shot when I was in the Army Cadets as a lad and I fired at Bisley in the inter-county championships but I didn't come anywhere. On this occasion I hit sod-all and was very disappointed at my efforts, the lads took the piss unmercifully. A while later that same day we were briefed by an RAF pilot on helicopter safety procedure. He really cheered us up by referring to them as "Dangerous Beasts" but not to worry as they'd only lost one with twenty six killed when a short sighted albatross flew into the rear rotor. He then showed us our "Goon Suits" which were compulsory clothing when travelling in a military helicopter over the sea. It's a bright orange rubberised suit with elasticated seals at wrists, neck and ankles. I was chosen by the instructor to demonstrate the wearing of the suit and I looked and felt a right twat with it on. Considering the temperature of the South Atlantic Ocean, I thought to myself that should I be unfortunate enough to end up in the drink, this suit would keep me alive long enough to die of exposure. The worst thing about wearing the suit was the heat which it generated so the minute I was zipped up I started sweating so much that my normal clothes underneath the suit were absolutely drenched.

Later that afternoon I was invited to shoot again on the stern deck and this time I redeemed myself by aiming more carefully and obliterating the rubbish bags with a couple of well placed tracer bullets. It was all very manly stuff and I was enjoying every second.

The next night was our stag show and I was a bit nervous as I never worked blue in my normal shows. Roger was in his element as he was a popular stag comic in the Nottingham area but he helped me out considerably with some gags. The show stormed the lower ranks who were by far in the majority; we just took the piss unmercifully out of the officers who were always referred to as "Ruperts and Rodneys". We also got very, very pissed because the lads just kept on bringing drink after drink up to the stage. By the end of the night I had vodka coming out of my ears. The best thing about that night for me was the collection we organised for a new piano for Wendy. The lads gave generously and we ended up with over three hundred quid. Wendy sobbed like a baby when we presented it to him at the end of the show.

As we sailed further South the weather got increasingly colder which put paid to the sunbathing with the girls and I was starting to feel very randy as I'd not had a fettle since before I left England and my saddlebags were filling up. I was quite attracted to one of the trio, her name was Carol. She was a petite doll of a girl with a lovely figure but although she consented to visit my cabin for a drink or two, she wouldn't let matters progress further than a snog and a grope because she was "courting strong". It only increased my frustration to the extent that I would have fucked a frog if I could have stopped it jumping.

The day came when we had to leave the Norland and begin our tour of the task force zone, entertaining on board the various ships which were patrolling the area. We were invited for a farewell drink in Captain Bob's cabin before the choppers came to lift us off onto our first ship. It was only 11am and there we were, drinking Bacardi and Cokes, I was in serious doubt as to whether my liver would survive the trip. At noon we were told to get into our goon suits as the Sea Kings were on their way to pick us up. I was comforting little Carol about the prospect of a helicopter journey as she was near to tears with fright. The two Sea kings appeared over the horizon and swooped down onto the stern deck of the Norland. There was only room for one at a time so the first one landed and picked up all our gear then as it flew off; the second one came in for Operation Showboat. The two pilots got off to welcome us and the girls were wetting their knickers when they recognized the familiar features of one of them. HRH Prince Andrew stood there large as life and began helping the ladies on board his machine. We were all strapped in and off we went. I was a little sad at leaving the Norland, especially as all the crew and most of the squaddies were lining the decks and cheering their hearts out at us. It became easy to understand how sailors became much attached to their ships as if they were alive.

The helicopter journey from Ascension airport to the Norland had taken no more than two or three minutes but this trip was much longer. There was no chance of any conversation as the noise inside the chopper was unbearable and I was very grateful for the ear defenders. After a while, the ships of the task force came into view, it was a grand sight after seeing nothing but empty ocean for so long. I was then suitably gobsmacked at my first ever sight of HMS Invincible. A bloody great Leviathan ploughing through 25 foot waves like she was on Endcliffe Park boating lake. Her deck was lined with Sea Harriers as they'd moved them up top to make room for our show in the hangar deck. HRH put the Sea King down like a feather and we got out onto the deck, God it was windy. We were taken to a certain spot on the deck and told to stand still; suddenly we started sinking into the ship. We were standing on a giant lift which was used to transport the aircraft from the hangar to the flight-deck. The hangar was like something out of a James Bond film; it was huge with lots of sailors running around doing their

The Goon Suit   *Bridge on Invincible*

Supper with Prince Andrew

No you can't have one

Me and Roger Idiot

various tasks.

We were taken straight to our quarters where we could freshen up prior to meeting Captain Jeremy Black. I couldn't believe my good fortune; I'd been allocated the Admiral's cabin. He was berthed on the flag-ship which was HMS Bristol so his cabin was vacant. It was like a palace, bathroom, shower, carpets and furniture, it made me feel very grand. Captain Black was a proper gentleman and made us so welcome with drinks in the officers ward room. His career ended up with him becoming the First Sea Lord, he was no mug. Roger and I went down to set up the gear in readiness for the first show which was scheduled for 2-30pm. The crew had built us a huge stage about five feet high with Union Jacks pinned all the way round it. I'd performed in some unusual places during my career, but this hangar on board an aircraft carrier in the freezing South Atlantic surely won the first prize. There were six hundred junior ranks in for the show, all very young and I'm afraid, a wee bit thick. The comedy went reasonably well but the lasses stole the show as you would expect. The sailors hooted and whistled and cheered their every number and it was so bloody good to know what a difference we were making just by being there.

More drinks in the ward room after the show, it was much busier now and the young officers were all jostling for position to get as close to our four young ladies as possible. I must admit, they were looking absolutely gorgeous with their full make-up and best dresses on. Then it was *their* turn to battle for position as HRH came into the room. The Captain introduced us all to him and he immediately put us all at our ease by requesting that we call him "H". This was his nick-name in the service so we obliged. I found him to be a really nice lad who, regardless of his position in life due to his birth, was eager to be treated as one of the lads.

The second show on board Invincible was something I'll never forget as long as I live. The lads were literally climbing the walls, hanging like monkeys from whatever spot they could secure for themselves. They were sitting on the wings of the few Harriers remaining in the hangar; they were perched atop helicopters and

The Invincible Show

Dig the white flares

intertwined in the netting which seemed to festoon every wall. The Captain and all the ship's officers in their best dress-whites occupied the first few rows of the seating area with the lesser ranks behind them. The reception we received was beyond our wildest expectations. I did a couple of Royal gags and HRH was honking with laughter as were all his mates. When I sang "The Band Played Waltzing Matilda" which is a very moving anti-war song about the Gallipoli landings in 1916, you could hear a pin drop. The only source of live music was my twelve-string guitar but we bashed out the most amazing Finale which had every man in the room up on his feet clapping, cheering and in a lot of cases, crying. We did "Sailing" by Rod Stewart, "Land of Hope and Glory", "Rule Britannia" and finished up with the National Anthem. I promise you dear reader, as I sit writing this and reliving it as though it was only yesterday, I have tears streaming down my cheeks.

The whole day had been so memorable and it ended with us all in the ward room for a steak supper and yet more drinks. Prince Andrew asked me if I'd mind getting my guitar as he wanted me to sing Waltzing Matilda again. He allowed us to have our photographs taken with him. I'd recorded Waltzing Matilda so I promised to send him a copy. It got a laugh when I asked him where he lived; he just replied "Send it to Mummy's house". I still have the letter he sent me thanking me for the record.

The next morning before we left for our next ship, we had an invitation to join the Captain on the bridge, the girls weren't that bothered but me and Roger lapped it up. I saw a couple of Sea Harriers take off and couldn't help but realise how lucky I was just to be there witnessing all these amazing sights and sharing the company of these remarkable men. I was loving every aspect of the trip, except for one, those bloody awful goon suits which we had to wear for every helicopter ride. We were also told to wear warm clothing underneath the suits so I had on long Johns, my camouflage jacket and trousers, or my "Can't see me suit" as I called it. I'd won it off an infantry sergeant a few years before in a drinking contest in Belfast. He'd fancied a flowery shirt I was wearing so I

Gerrem off

You can't get away from 'em

offered to swap him for his jacket and trousers. We compromised with a vodka drinking contest with winner takes all. He collapsed before me so I got his outfit. The moral to this tale, never try and out drink comics or musicians.

As well as all the clothes I've just mentioned, I also had on a thick sweater, I was going to be warm alright. I was helped into the goon-suit and we started out on what seemed like a three mile hike through corridors, up stairs then more corridors and more stairs. The temperature below decks on the carrier enabled you to be comfortable in a T shirt, but with all the clobber that I was wearing, I felt I was being poached alive. The sweat was literally running down my back like a waterfall and my clothes were drenched. When we finally arrived onto the flight-deck, a bitingly cold wind hit us and went straight through all the layers of clothing to practically freeze the damp under-garments which we were wearing. I cannot properly describe how cold it was down there in the Falklands. I'd experienced cold winters at home in my beloved North of England but I'd never felt anything like this. It seemed to attack any part which was exposed to the elements so I felt like my face was being bitten off.

The first chopper arrived and took off the girls and the equipment while Roger and I volunteered to await the next one. HRH came and invited us into a flight shack to keep warm, he thanked us for all our efforts and stayed chatting to us until our transport arrived a short while later. I remembered one of my dear old Mother's sayings when it was cold, she'd say "Bloody Hell! My hands feel like a bit of frozzen hen-shit". That's just how I felt on the deck of the Invincible on that day so long ago.

We were on our way to appear on the HMS Southampton which was a destroyer far smaller than Invincible. We were to do the show in the small hangar on the stern of the ship. As on Invincible, the lads had gone to so much trouble to try and build us a stage and considering the space available, they'd worked wonders. The sailors piled in and "Wallop", we did it again. They were crammed in like sardines and they cheered us for what seemed like forever. It was definitely lump-in-the-throat time when they all sang The Saints go Marching In to us. After the show came the compulsory visits to the various messes for drinks with the ascending ranks aboard the vessel. I was thinking that my liver was going to resemble a pickled gherkin when I got home. Had I known what was to happen shortly afterwards, I would have had a lot more booze than I normally did. We were having our farewell drinks in the officer's ward room when a chappie came in to inform us that HMS Bristol, our next ship, had run into rather rough seas and could we send a member of Operation Showboat along with the equipment so they could set it up and secure it safely for the show. Bristol was the flag ship and the Admiral was on board so the show *had* to go on. Seeing as how all the equipment was my own personal property, I volunteered to go along. It was on with the fucking goon suit again and I was led up onto the heli-pad on the stern. They'd sent a Lynx helicopter which is about as big as a Ford Escort. All the gear including my precious guitars was stowed aboard and off we went. The pilot had given me a helmet with an intercom attached so I could hear what he said. The journey was about a hundred sea miles to the flagship which was heading at full speed for Barclay Sound where the sea was much calmer than out in the open ocean. As I gazed out of the window of the Lynx, I couldn't really form an impression of how rough the sea was as I had no perspective to allow me to do so. Things became very clear when I caught first sight of the Bristol bashing through the waves like a huge Behemoth and being tossed around like a cork. The waves were crashing right over the bridge wings and her stern was coming way out of the water, affording me the sight of her screws turning. I said to the pilot, "You're never gonna try and land on that are you?" he replied "We've got to mate, we can't go back to Southampton, she's hit worse seas than this". He then asked me if I was OK. I said "Don't worry if I'm OK, I'm not flying the fuckin' thing, ARE YOU OK???" "Yeah, don't worry; hold tight, I'm going in now".

He gradually flew lower until he was hovering just over the heli-pad, when I think of what he was doing to maintain this manouevre in these horrendous conditions with such calm and self-assurance, I realised I'd be 99.9% safe. I just told myself to relax and enjoy a moment which only happens once in a lifetime. The idea was for him to allow for the rising and falling of the ship which was at the same time ploughing forwards at full speed, and drop the Lynx on board as gently as possible. Unfortunately for us, he mis-judged it by a split second and he put it down just as the stern of the Bristol was on her way back up. The force with which the little helicopter hit the deck was immense. I thought my spine had come up into my skull and one of the struts holding on the wheels gave way as we made contact with the deck. The Lynx tilted over slightly and he told me not to move until I was told to. He got out to inspect his aircraft which was now listing dangerously close to the ship's rail; he'd turned off the power so the rotors had thankfully stopped turning. He had a morose look on his face which seemed to say "Oh fuck! I've broken it". He came around and opened my door, the wind was howling and the spray was coming into the tiny cabin and drenching my precious amplifiers. A door opened in the small hangar and a seaman appeared, he threw me a length of rope with a carabiner on the end of it. I immediately put it round my waist and clipped it securely, it wasn't safe to walk even the short distance to the hangar without some form of safety line and he practically pulled me over to him. He told me to get below but I refused to budge until my gear had been taken off the Lynx. He could see I was deadly serious so he picked up a wall phone and almost immediately, two of his shipmates appeared as if by magic to unload my stuff. When it was safely stowed below decks I was taken down to the ward room to be greeted by a couple of real toffs. It had all happened so quickly that it had only just dawned on me that I'd just endured a very dangerous, life threatening situation and I'd not batted an eyelid. Don't get me wrong, I'm not professing to be brave or heroic, but the speed at which it had all occurred must have made me oblivious to the danger I was in.

The two officers helped me off with the goon suit and I stripped down to my jeans and T-shirt with their blessing, ignoring the dress code for the ward room. The posher of the two told me he had only one thing to say to me and that was "Hets orf". I wish I could express phonetically, in print, what he actually said to me, as I can remember every single word he said in his overpoweringly posh Oxford accent. He told me how proud the ships company was of our party for coming all the way down to the South Atlantic to entertain the "Cheps". He asked me what I wanted to drink so I requested a brandy and port as I felt I deserved it. He went behind the bar and passed me a bottle of Remy Martin and a bottle of Taylor's vintage port. "There you go old chap, they're for you with my compliments". What happened next was uncanny. While I was taking off the cover of the cork on the port bottle, he, assuming I was a smoker, lit up two cigarettes and seeing as how I'd got my hands full with the port, he stuck one between my lips. "Oh cheers Mate", I said, I took a drag of the cigarette as if I'd been smoking for years. The truth is, I'd stopped smoking four years previously in 1978 when I'd started seriously back on the weights and was very proud of the fact that I'd managed to do so having been a very heavy smoker. The fag made me cough and feel dizzy, but I thought to myself "Fuck it, *one* won't hurt me" so I smoked it. Oh what a silly lad I was, the demon known as nicotine lies dormant in reformed smokers, waiting to pounce like a persuasive little imp, telling us "Go on mate, one won't hurt you, it's only one little smoke, you've kicked the habit so you can have just the one now and again". Silly stupid fucking bastard that I was, I succumbed to the temptation of Messrs Benson and Hedges and although I felt guilty knowing I'd given in to that one small temptation, I knew it was just a one-off occurrence.

On the way home from Ascension on the VC10, I cadged a fag from Roger after an urge which I couldn't control.

"You don't smoke Knutty", he said.

"I know, but I just fancy the one". He obliged, and within a week of returning home, I'd bought my first packet of twenty. I soon crept up to forty a day and it took me another four years to summon up enough will-power to stop forever on New Years Eve 1986. To this day, I've never had another smoke.

They managed to repair the damaged Lynx in time for it to fly off and make room for the one carrying the rest of my gang. They didn't join me until the Bristol had reached Barclay Sound and the sea was indeed, relatively calm in comparison to what we'd just been through. We were to perform in the main crew mess, it was very small but once again, the lads had gone to enormous trouble to build us a stage and erect very effective stage lighting. The show did another burster once again and the Admiral, who was on the front row, nearly collapsed with laughter. At the end of the show, he came on stage and made a very moving speech in praise of our efforts then he presented us all with a plaque and an ash-tray formed from a brass shell case which had been polished and inset with a Falklands coin. I shared a tiny cabin with Roger, an officer and a Daily Telegraph reporter. I hardly slept a wink as we were right next to the forward bulkhead and it creaked and banged all bloody night.

We couldn't fly off the Bristol the next day as all the helicopters were grounded due to the bad weather. We had to transfer onto a little tug aptly named "The Yorkshireman". That was a barrel of fun, they tied a thick rope around our waists and lowered us down like sacks of spuds. We only had to steam round the bay to our next port of call, the "Rangatira". Ships have souls, I genuinely believe this to be true after having sailed on so many. The Norland was a happy ship, as were all the others which we'd performed on during our trip and they all seemed to say "Welcome Aboard" when we joined them. Rangatira, or Rangatraz as it was nick-named was a dismal forbidding floating shit-hole. The smell on board was staggering as it had a sewerage plant aboard. We had to board her via a rope ladder that was slung down from a door in the hull to the deck of the tug. The girls found this quite distressing as the tug wasn't very stable in the swell of the sea. The Rangatira was an accommodation ship for the soldiers waiting to go ashore but it also housed some of the scum of the merchant navy. They were awesome, dirty drunken tattooed Neanderthals and they made up the majority of the audience for our first show at 2-30pm. They started to let them in at 2-00 and they all had cans of beer or bottles of spirits with them, Roger and I were very uneasy about the outcome, plus the safety of the girls and the equipment. I went to find the man in charge of keeping order and he happened to be a Major in the 7th Gurkha Rifles and looked like he chewed spanners for his breakfast. The security on board was provided by the Gurkhas and they took no shit from anyone whatsoever. He told us not to worry and that besides his own lads he was going to persuade a few infantry sergeants to patrol the room. The Gurkhas were much feared by friend and foe alike as their ferocity knew no bounds.

Allow me to digress for a couple of true stories about these heroic little men from Nepal. I have many Gurkha friends as they are the only people that P&O Cruises will employ as security personnel on their ships. P&O are now my chief source of income but I'll get to that in my final chapter.

The Major and I got on famously during my brief stay on Rangatraz and over a few drinks later that night he told me of an incident that occurred during the Falklands conflict. He was on night patrol with a platoon of his Gurkhas when he received a coded message to reconnoiter a certain area to check for any Argentinian soldiers who might be lurking in their immediate vicinity. He sent out four of his little chaps who returned about two hours later. He asked "Are there any Argies out there?".

They each threw down several severed ears at his feet and the patrol leader calmly replied "Not now Major". The Argies soon learned of the Gurkhas' utter fearlessness and unmerciful ferocity which struck fear in their hearts. My other favourite Gurkha tale was told to me by Ian Hughes aboard the Norland one night. During it's time down there it was commandeered by the local top brass as a prison ship to house the many Argies who'd been captured or had surrendered. Towards the end of the conflict there were nearly two thousand prisoners on board waiting to be repatriated to their homeland at Puerto Madryn in Argentina. You can well imagine the logistics involved in feeding, housing and most of all securing two thousand angry Argies. The ship was like a tinder box waiting to go up as the prisoners became more unruly and threatening. The problem was solved by an enterprising officer who simply suggested placing a Gurkha at each end of each corridor. This worked like a charm as the Gurkhas sat sharpening their kukris, not a sound was heard from the terrified prisoners.

Our first show on Rangatira was just as I anticipated, they were noisy, unruly and rude. I had a heckler from Liverpool who wouldn't shut up no matter what I threw back at him. He was a merchant seaman, pissed as a fart and when the girls came on he got up and staggered towards the stage. I was getting ready to halt his progress when from nowhere this big sergeant appeared and took the scouser by the arm, he gently guided him out of the room to the cheers of the rest of the lads. I later learned that the goodly sergeant kicked the shit out of him before throwing him in the brig. I went for a kip before the second show but the cabin was like an ice-box and even though I was togged up in my long johns, trousers, sweater and ski jacket, I was still shivering. It was well below freezing outside and not much warmer inside. I bumped into the ship's doctor just before the second show and he said he had a spare cabin down in the sick bay if I wanted to use it. I went to have a quick look and was delighted to find it clean, roomy, equipped with a toilet and shower but best of all, it was warm.

I slept reasonably well that night and rose early for a hearty full English. All of us couldn't wait to get off this depressing piss-hole of a ship. We were anchored off Port Stanley and the buildings looked as if they'd been built with Lego bricks. They were all painted in bright colours, red, blue and yellow and every one without a single exception flew a Union Jack from a flag-pole. We were lifted off Rangatira straight onto HMS Birmingham for a 2-30 show in the rear hangar. It was exactly the same as HMS Southampton and we went for the customary drinks with the lower ranks, then finished up as usual in the officer's ward room. It was our last show and we were all pretty whacked out from the very tiring schedule we'd

At Nidge & Ron's for supper

Inside the Tumble Dryer

33

been subjected to. We were just looking forward to getting back onto the Norland and steaming north for home.

As we were preparing to don our goon-suits for the last time, an officer came in with a signal for Operation Showboat. Could we go to RAF Stanley and do one last show? Well, you can't refuse can you. We all agreed and a short while later a Wessex came to pick us up in threes and as darkness fell we were whisked over the minefields to the airfield. We touched down on dry land for the first time in what seemed like months, we were actually setting foot on the Falklands. The wind was howling like a banshee and the temperature was below freezing. We trudged across a field to what was our "Concert Hall". It was a large portable helicopter hangar. A sort of giant rubber tent similar to the marquees which you see in the parks at summer shows. It had an earth floor and a few benches had been scrounged for the upper ranks while the lads would just sit on the floor. They'd even built us a stage out of beer crates with a curtain hung nearby for us to change behind. The walls were vibrating and shaking as the force of the wind increased and the noise was so loud that we had the amps on as high as possible to counteract it. By far the worst thing that night was the cold, my hands were freezing and I wondered how I was going to play the guitars. I had on my long johns and a thermal undershirt over which I wore a black polo neck sweater which kept me reasonably warm, but my feet were dropping off. I honest to God don't know how the girls endured it in their skimpy costumes and strapless open shoes. The audience came in looking like snowmen and plonked themselves down on the floor to watch what was to be the most memorable show of my whole career even to the present day. As I was singing "The Band Played Waltzing Matilda" I nearly broke down because I spotted this big tough looking corporal on the front row crying his eyes out at the lyrics to that wonderful song. They were so bloody grateful that we'd come and done the show for them, we ended up with them giving us a standing ovation which I luckily captured on my camera.

A local married couple was standing at the back, they were to be

Bless 'em all

I've taken Port Stanley

our hosts for the night and on hearing we were coming ashore, had immediately volunteered to put us all up and feed us. He was a huge guy called Ron who sported a big bushy beard and his wife was just called Nidge. These two were very special people who'd settled in the Falklands five years earlier where Ron finished his time in the army. We packed the gear away and we all piled into a captured Argie Mercedes jeep which promptly delivered us to Ron's house. It was a large bungalow with a big smile on its face but best of all, it was warm. As we all trooped in the smell which emanated from the kitchen hit us. Nidge had got a bloody huge chunk of lamb roasting in the Aga which was surrounded by lots of roasting potatoes. Ron opened a bottle of navy rum and I thought I'd died and gone to heaven. I can't remember when I enjoyed a meal as much, the food was orgasmic and the company beyond compare. We discovered that Nidge had acted as a messenger for the army during the conflict and could have been shot if discovered. We polished off the rum and retired to bed; mine was a three quarter divan with a big duck-down duvet, I slept like a baby for the first time since I left home.

I was roused at 7-30 for breakfast and for the first time in ages, a mug of tea with *real* milk in it, after which I went outside for a nosey. It was the first time I'd seen the Island close-up in daylight, and what a day it was. It was a crisp clear cloudless morning and the snowcapped mountains looked amazing against the blue sky. Army personnel were buzzing past in Land Rovers and Lorries going about their business. I found the place to be very barren and I wondered why on Earth anyone would want to live there. We said a fond farewell to Ron and Nidge and donned our goon-suits for the very last time in order to board the incoming Sea King which was to transport us back to Norland.

We were welcomed back on board like lost children returning home, and the party given for us reflected it. We were carrying back about a thousand soldiers who'd been in the thick of it and were now returning home to their loved ones. Some were worse off for their experience. I was chatting to a young squaddie who was in a wheelchair with his foot heavily bandaged, he told me he had trench-foot. It's a very painful condition brought on by long immersion in cold water or mud and marked by blackening and death of the surface tissue. He was a smashing lad who bore his ailment with a steadfast stoicism which touched me greatly. I asked him what it was like out there and he explained what he'd gone through with a simple description of his experience. He said "Imagine going up onto Kinder Scout or Dartmoor in the middle of winter, digging a hole in the ground, and then living in it. That's what it was like mate".

We did another show for the lads on our way back and for the last four days the sun blazed down on us as we lay on the bridge deck relaxing. The night before we docked in Ascension, Captain Bob gave a special farewell dinner for us and once again the booze flowed copiously and the guitar made its final appearance for some bawdy songs. Wendy served us in his best whites and ended up sobbing his heart out at our leaving. I was by far a better man for having experienced the past few weeks with the extraordinary people who I'd met along the way.

We had an added bonus on the return flight from Ascension. Two hundred squaddies from 2 Para were due to fly back with us but they were delayed so missed the flight. The RAF quickly took out about a hundred seats from the VC10 and stowed some stuff which had to go back to Brize Norton. This left a large unoccupied floor space in the cabin so we found about thirty-odd pillows and arranged them into a sort of giant bed. We slept comfortably all the way to Dakar helped by the bottle of Vodka which Roger had snaffled from Wendy.

You may wonder how I've remembered the Falklands trip in such vivid detail. I kept a diary which I fortunately found hidden away in a desk drawer. I know I've dwelled a long time on the trip but in all my 47 years in show-biz, I've never experienced a more memorable, exciting excursion and I hope you didn't mind me sharing it with you.

From: Squadron Leader Adam Wise, M.B.E., R.A.F.

BUCKINGHAM PALACE

28th September, 1982.

Dear Mr Knutt,

      Prince Andrew has asked me to thank
you for your letter and for sending him the
record. He much enjoyed your show on board
HMS INVINCIBLE and is very grateful for your
efforts and those of your colleagues to
entertain the members of the Task Force.

      His Royal Highness was grateful for
your kind remarks about the photographs in
The Sun. He much appreciates your loyalty
in this matter.

Yours sincerely,

Adam Wise

Mr. Bobby Knutt

It's a Madhouse

After my third triumphant pantomime at the Sheffield Crucible I was disappointed to be told that they wouldn't be able to use me for a fourth year as they were doing Peter Pan and there wasn't a part in it for me. A new artistic director had taken over, her name was Clare Venables and she was definitely the "New Broom" sweeping clean. She wasn't the easy-going sort of boss that Peter James had been and her new way of doing things obviously made her unpopular in certain circles. For myself, I always found her honest and forthright in her dealings with me and she always said what she felt. She explained to me that the main male character in Peter Pan was Mr Darling who also doubled up as Captain Hook. She felt that the children of Sheffield, who'd got used to my lovable Knutty character, would never accept me as the villain, which Hook certainly was. She insisted that she still wanted to use me and offered me the lead role in an Alan Bleasdale play called "It's a Madhouse". It was scheduled for the autumn season of 1982 with three weeks rehearsal for a two week run and the money was shite. I accepted it though as I'd never done a straight stage play and knew it would be a new string to my bow. The director was an excellent actor himself called Kenneth Alan Taylor. The play was set over an eight hour shift on a ward in a mental hospital and I was cast as the male nurse, Eddie. Bleasdale was massive at the time as "Boys from the Blackstuff" was top of the ratings. I felt very slightly insecure for the first time in my career because Kenneth had played the part of Eddie in the past and the rest of the cast were a group of seasoned actors who'd all gone through various acting schools to acquire their diplomas. I comforted myself in the knowledge that my favourite actor in the world, James Cagney, had never had an acting lesson in his life.

As opening night approached I became more and more nervous and aware of every actor's nightmare which was forgetting his lines on stage. If you're doing a TV drama, drying up isn't a big problem because the director simply re-shoots the scene. Drying on live stage is unbearable because you can't ad-lib in a straight play like you can in a comedy. You just stand there wondering what comes next and feeling like a complete twat. We did two dress rehearsals then a public dress where the punters come in for half price in the hope that someone will fuck up. Everything went wonderfully well and my confidence was growing with each show we did. The opening night was packed and it went better than I could have ever expected. It was a very black comedy with some very moving moments in the story and the press loved it. I had to break down crying during one of the later scenes and I'm proud to say that I managed to muster real tears for every single performance. I was topping the bill but the show was stolen every night by a wonderful actor called David Ross. He played Ben, an old toothless, cackling, malevolent misogynist who'd been locked away by his daughter years before. The part was sent from heaven for an actor of David's calibre and he grabbed it with both hands. My character, Eddie was as firmly trapped as the inmates by a sexual skeleton in his cupboard {he was raped as a young soldier}, and it made the madhouse the only place he felt normal in.

It had some wonderful lines in the script, for instance, one of the inmates thought I was his mate Barry.

"Barry, Barry, where you going, Barry?"

"Out of my mind son".

"Can I come?"

I thoroughly enjoyed doing the play and loved the camaraderie of the other actors. I'm pleased to say that I never dried once during the whole run. I worked with David Ross again at the Crucible when he played dame in Dick Whittington. You couldn't get two parts as totally different as Ben and Sarah the cook, but he was just as bloody marvelous in the role. He's one of the unsung heroes of the British stage, every bit as good an actor as Anthony Hopkins, but who'll sadly remain unknown except to a minority of British theatre-goers who know his work.

Bobby Knutt is the actor's comedian and the comedian's actor. He belongs to that rare breed of professionals who are able to make that quantum leap from being a stand-up comic to dramatic actor and back again dependent on what is required.

Royston Mayoh. ITV Director.

It was soon time to return to the "Madhouse" that is pantomime and Christmas 1982 found me working for my dear old pal Duggie Chapman at Doncaster Civic Theatre doing a reprise of my first ever panto, "Little Red Riding Hood". In my first book, I told how I was introduced to the wonderful world of pantomime at Wakefield Theatre Club, matinees only. It was like being in a time warp at Doncaster, it was exactly the same script, and I must confess it was fucking awful, even by Panto standards. It even had lovely old Reg Cornish playing the same role as villager, scene shifter, dog act and dogsbody. He was, if you remember the first book, a really camp queen with the gentlest of natures. My girlfriend Paula was playing Principal Boy, the show was sold out and life was very sweet. During the run, I received a phone call from another old-school gentleman panto-booker, a chap called Slim Ingram. He wanted to know if I fancied doing Dick Whittington for him the following year at St Helens and Rotherham, three weeks at each. I wasn't that bothered as I knew them to be number three venues so I quoted him an over the top price thinking he wouldn't be able to afford it. He snatched my bloody hand off.

All Creatures Great & Des O'Connor

Not long after panto finished in early 1983, JP rang to say he'd got me on the Des O'Connor show. It was a very prestigious date and Des had veered away from the usual format of a variety show with top guests coming on and doing their acts. It was to be in the form of a chat show with the comfy settees and relaxed atmosphere. I was told that the format for the show which I would be doing was for Des to interview me, Jimmy Cricket and Mick Miller all at the same time. I thought to myself, "He's got some bottle, having three top pro comics on at the same time". Topping the bill on the show was an unknown American comedienne called Joan Rivers, her first time ever on British TV. I took my old school mate Mick Senior down with me for some company to keep me awake on the drive back home from London.

We got down to the studios in plenty of time and it was good to see Mick Miller again. We'd worked together years before on a radio series called "You've got to be joking". It was one of those corny Radio Two series which went out in the seventies at 7pm on a weekday evening. It was hosted by Cardew "The Cad" Robinson and featured three comics every week in a sort of "Us against Cardew" set-up. The regulars on the teams were me, Bernie Clifton, Tom O'Connor, Duggie Brown, Peter Wallis and Mick Miller. We had a lot of laughs doing it and Cardew was an absolute corker. He was, if you remember, a tall skinny, ugly looking sod with a beaked nose and buck teeth. His accent was unbelievably posh and he was a charmer in the Leslie Phillips mould. The uncanniest thing about him was his remarkable ability to pull crumpet. He turned up to every recording with a different girl on his arm, and they weren't munters, they were Miss Worlds. Mick and I had a good laugh reminiscing about the show.

Jimmy Cricket was enjoying current stardom with his "C'mere" catch phrase which was sweeping the country plus his wellies with L and R marked on them. I'd never met him before and he was a lovely quietly spoken fellow who I took an immediate liking to. The director of the show greeted us all and informed us that Des would be joining us shortly to explain the format of our contribution to the show. He also told us that all the questions were scripted and that we were not to veer away from the script, ad-lib or try and be funnier than Des. I thought to myself that you can make those sorts of rules when you're as big a star as Des was, still, hopefully it would still turn out funny after the editing. Des was going to allow Mick to do his hilarious "Wrestlers" mime; Jimmy was going to do his letter from his mammy and he wanted me to dish the dirt on Coronation Street, which I'd just recently been in. I think I pissed him off a little by refusing to do what he asked. I told him that I wasn't about to start slagging off fellow cast members when there was a chance I would be back in the programme. I found him to be a pretty cold fish and realised that it would be my last time on his show, I was right.

One of my favourite roles that I ever played was in the Christmas 1983 edition of All Creatures Great and Small. I was over the moon that I was going to be working in scenes with Robert Hardy, Christopher Timothy and Peter Davison. My role was that of a Josh, a barber who had the uncanny ability to read people's thoughts through their hair. I had some hilarious scenes with Christopher and we became firm pals but the highlight of the shoot for me was working closely with Robert Hardy. Oh what a wonderful actor he is, and what a gentleman. We shot it up in the Yorkshire Dales and I'd just bought a bright yellow E type V12 roadster in primrose yellow as my ragtop-runabout so the journeys were a pleasure.

It was completely different to any role I'd previously played and the director, Peter Moffat gave me a completely free reign to portray Josh in any way I chose. I decided to wear my old fashioned grandad spectacles and part my hair down the middle with lots of Brylcreem on it, I looked a right twat but it worked a treat and Josh was born. It was good to work with Peter Davison again; the last time had been in a Granada TV thriller called "Printout" where I played a hit-man who killed him. He's a nice guy and he was drooling over the E Type as he was, like me, a car freak. I was now

43

being cast in the better class programmes like "All Creatures" and my CV was starting to look pretty impressive.

When I cast Bobby Knutt to play in my production of "All Creatures Great and Small" I had never seen him before in a straight part, and was most impressed with the performance he gave. It was real and true, yet still with his wonderful underlying sense of comedy. He was a great person and a real joy to work with.

Peter Moffatt, Director B.B.C

The Mile High Club

In the autumn of 1982, my dear friend Marti Caine went out to South Africa for an extended season at Sun City in the province of Bophuthatswana. Sun City was the brainchild of Sol Koerzner, the South African billionaire. She got a bit of stick from the anti-apartheid brigade when they found out she was appearing there but it blew over eventually. Marti or "Mother" as I called her shared the same manager as me and had done for many years. Johnnie Peller, or JP as we called him, looked upon us as son and daughter and although we took the piss out of him unmercifully we both loved him like a second father. I remember one occasion years before in 1976 when Marti was chosen to do a big TV commercial launching "Limit" watches. At the same time, she and I were shooting the Marti Caine TV show down at Central TV in Birmingham. The actual corporate launch for the new watches was being held at the very posh four star Metropole Hotel at the new NEC. I was invited to go along and JP had arranged for us to dine in the extremely expensive restaurant on the Limit Watches account.

JP was a lovely kind generous man to people he loved or even liked, but in restaurants he could be a fucking monster. He'd complain about the least paltry thing and have waiters hating his guts. We were all chatting away at the table having a culinary treat when JP's face went white; he bent over his plate and spat out the contents of his mouth. He was having a salad and on disgorging it back onto his platter, there was a worm crawling around amongst the debris. Mother and I were dying to laugh but JP was getting ready to erupt so we managed to keep it in. He demanded to see the restaurant manager at once and when he arrived at the table, he gave him a right verbal seeing-to. There was steam coming out of his ears and the manager promised to waive the bill which only upset him more because we weren't paying anyway. When it all died down and calm was resumed, Mother said to JP, "Cheer up John, it could have been worse".

"Could have been worse!!" he repeated, "What could be worse than

45

spitting out a bloody worm onto my plate?"

She calmly replied, "Spitting out half a worm". I was honking with laughter but JP didn't see the funny side.

The Sun City show was an over-the-top extravaganza like the shows in Las Vegas with lots of topless dancers and spectacular scenery. Mother had just split with her husband Malcolm who'd run off with their best friend's wife and although she was putting on a brave face for the world, it was tearing her apart for she still loved him. This contract so many thousands of miles away would help her heal and get her life back.

She'd been out there about six months when JP asked me if I fancied going out to Johannesburg for a month to do cabaret at the Landrost Hotel which was part of Sun City Hotels. He said I could fly out a week early to watch Mother working so as to get an idea of what the South African audiences were like. I fancied a month in the sun, plus the money was good so I accepted the contract. The dates and flights were all fixed and I got down to Heathrow for the 6pm overnight twelve hour flight to Jo'burg. I'd checked in and was waiting in the departure gate to board the 747 when a very attractive blonde lady came across to me. I'd only just finished in Coronation Street a few weeks before and my mug was recognized almost everywhere I went. She politely asked if she could have my autograph for her mother who was an avid fan of the show. I'd still got some six by four hand-out photographs which Granada provided the cast with, free of charge. I gladly signed one for her and we started chatting. She looked to be in her early thirties and was a very classy looking lady. She told me that she was going out to Durban to see her husband who'd been away for nine months working on some project or other. I couldn't help thinking to myself, "Nine months eh, she'll be ready for it". She went on to say that they ran a small hotel in Blackpool which was doing very well. The time came to board the aircraft and she said she hoped to see me on the plane. I had requested a leg-room seat and was lucky enough to get one but unfortunately for me, it was right next to the middle bulkhead where the toilets were. The 747 was full up in my section which was steerage class. There were about a hundred and fifty pensioners on some sort of organized trip and most of them had clocked me as they got on the plane and I could hear the usual whispers of "It is him"

"Who?"

"Him off the telly"

"Who off the telly?"

"You know, him what's on Coronation Street".

"Well ask him then, ask him if he's him"

"I'm not askin' him, what if it's not him"

"I'm sure it's him"

All this is spoken in stage whispers as if I'm bleedin' deaf and can't hear what the silly old farts are saying. The first to pluck up courage comes up and says to me, "You're him aren't you?"

"Who do you mean?"

"*HIM*, you know! Him off the telly"

"Yeah, I'm him"

She goes back to her mate and says "It is him, I *told* you it was him" The word went all the way to the back of the plane, "It is him".

After a while, another coffin dodger comes up and asks "What's yer name? We've forgot yer name".

"Albert Fettlebuttock", I reply.

She tells her mate who says "See! I told you it were him didn't I".

We took off on time and the meal and drinks arrived at about 8pm after which a queue gradually formed of incontinent pensioners for the toilets next to my seat. As they passed, they all had a stare at me and a smile in some cases. I'd had about three glasses of wine with my meal and was now ready for the loo myself. There was a queue of maybe eight or nine passengers so I thought sod it I'll go through the curtain into club class and use theirs. I couldn't believe it, there was less than a dozen people sitting in this section of the aircraft. I went to their toilet which was in the forward bulkhead and as I returned down the aisle they were now facing me, and there she was, the blonde from Blackpool. She waved at me as I approached her and asked me if I'd like to join her for a drink. I said that I didn't think I could as I was in the back with the poor people. She summoned the steward who was working her section of the plane, he was a raving queen who, when she asked if I could join her for a drink, said I could sit there for as long as I liked. He brought me my preferred poison, a large port and brandy and she and I chatted away like old friends. The lights were dimmed as the screen came down for the film. This was way before the days of individual screens in the back of the seat, it was a bit like being at the cinema. We'd not been watching the film for long when she put her head on my shoulder, I've never been backward in coming forward in this situation so inside a few more moments we were groping each other for dear life and chewing each other's faces off. The camp steward was in his hidey-hole having his rest period and there was nobody at all sitting anywhere near us so we put the arm rests up and got cracking under the blanket. It wasn't planned nor was it expected, but by God it was fucking unbelievable. We didn't come up for air for about three hours and my assumption when I met her that she would be ready for it was the understatement of the year. It's twenty six years since that memorable assignation at forty thousand feet somewhere above the African continent, but I can remember every single second of it, every grunt and every orgasm, and there were a few of those I can tell you. The worst bit was trying to keep her quiet for she was a noisy moaner if you understand my meaning. The things we managed to achieve in that cramped space defied description. I'm proud to say that I am a fully paid up member of the mile high club thanks to that wonderful lady in club class.

I had to reluctantly return to my seat for landing and I didn't see her again until we were inside the terminal building. She'd been waiting for me and as I met her she gave me a business card with the address of her hotel in Blackpool and said to visit her if ever I was in the town. I did something at that moment which surprised even me. For a randy promiscuous bastard which is what I surely was at that time in my life, the chance of a super-fuck any time I was visiting Blackpool was difficult to refuse, but I did. I gave her the card back and said that what we'd done the night before on that 747 could never be surpassed by anything we could ever do in the future. It would always be the most exciting sexual experience of my life and trying to measure up to it again would only be a disappointing anti-climax. We parted company at the airport, I felt a bit like Trevor Howard in "Brief Encounter". I've obviously never seen her since, I don't even know her name, but I'll never, ever forget her.

I was embarking on a new adventure on the continent of Africa and little did I know what was in store for me.

Sun City & My First and Last Joint

I was met at Jo'Burg airport by a lovely lady who introduced herself as Melanie Millin, head of publicity for Southern Sun hotels. She was one of the smileyest people I'd ever met and joy seemed to emanate from her face like ectoplasm from a medium. She was Jewish, had a shock of auburn curly long hair and the biggest pair of Walters I'd seen in a long time. She spoke with a very strong South African accent and it took me a while to fully understand her every word but I soon mastered it and it wasn't long before I was mimicking her perfectly. She had appointed herself as my guide and guardian for the first part of my trip and she flew me up to Sun City in a private plane which made me feel very grand indeed.

We arrived at the palatial Sun Hotel where Marti was working and Melanie had booked me a suite, not a room, but a suite for the whole week. It was the most luxurious accommodation I'd ever been in but I was careful not to be at all impressed, I behaved as if it was what I was used to. She kept calling me "My Darling" and told me that whatever I wanted, I just had to ask. I thought "I wouldn't mind nestling my head between those gorgeous Walters"; little did I know that I would be doing just that a little while later. I rang Mother to let her know I'd arrived and we met up for a hug and a natter so we could fill each other in on all the gossip. I was due to open at the Landrost Hotel in seven days time so I'd have ample time to get an idea of what the SA audiences were like. Mother told me they were very strange, some nights she tore the bollocks off 'em and the next night she'd struggle for laughs. She wasn't actually doing *that* much patter as the show was a costume spectacular with lots of tits and feathers. I saw the show that same night and I was utterly gobsmacked. There was one scene in the show when a large pool containing thousands of gallons of water rose up from below stage and a huge mechanical octopus emerged to fight with one of the muscle-bound male dancers in a sort of "Tarzan" tribute.

During the next couple of days, JP arrived with his wife Marcia and their two sons Barry and David. He arranged for Marcia to visit the health spa for a full afternoon's pampering session while we went for a game of golf on the adjoining hotel course. I've not seen Barry or David for many years now and no doubt they've grown up to be a couple of nice guys, but when they were young boys, they were a pair of fucking monsters. Spoilt beyond imagination and in need of a bloody good hiding and believe me, there would have been no shortage of volunteers to dish one out.

We were about half way round the course which was in pretty good condition considering the shortage of water. JP hardly ever played so he was pretty crap and not giving me much of a game, not that I was exactly Nick Faldo. The monsters were running about like lunatics and making noise on the greens when I was trying to putt out. I could have cheerfully strangled them. JP hit another ball into the rough and the two little scamps ran to try and retrieve it like a pair of gun-dogs. The two black caddies wouldn't go anywhere near the rough and when JP told them to look for his ball they looked very fearful and said "No go in there Boss, many mambas in there, kill you quick Boss". JP went white and shouted at the top of his voice for them to come back immediately but true to form, they ignored him until he shouted that there were snakes in the long grass. I felt like shouting for them to keep looking as long as they liked.

One night during that week with Mother I went back to her dressing room after the show for a natter. I'd had quite a few drinks and I had a bit of a glow on. She said "Robert, (she either called me Wanker or Robert), I've got some really good shit, do you want to try it?" I told her I wouldn't know good shit from bad shit as I'd never tried it before. I knew that Mother used to partake of the odd joint or two and thoroughly enjoyed it. She never drank alcohol so she got her relaxation from her waccy baccy. It never seemed to do her any harm and she was always calm and serene as far as I was concerned. She talked me into it and rolled me a fat joint of whatever it was. She told me to take a deep drag and hold it down in my lungs for longer than you would a normal cigarette. I did as I was told and sat there waiting to feel all cool and tranquil. After the third drag, without any warning whatsoever, I projectile vomited all over her carpet, I didn't feel it coming on, it just happened. I felt a right twat, puking on my friend's floor and down her dressing table. I was unaware that cannabis and alcohol definitely don't mix and that was the cause of my problem. I have *never* had another try at any form of drugs in my whole life. I've got friends in the business who have done their brains and their money in on things like coke and cannabis. I have always been a quick learner and realised it definitely wasn't my cup of tea.

Triumphs & Disasters in South Africa

I'd been at Sun City almost a week and was basically no wiser on how to tackle the audiences. Mother was performing in a giant show-bar with spectacular special effects whereas I was to be working in an intimate cabaret room which seated around a hundred people. However, it had been a great experience, plus I was really relaxed now and chomping at the bit to get back on stage and feel the buzz. A couple of days before I was due to open in Jo'Burg, I had a call from Melanie asking me if I'd help her out at short notice by going to a very posh venue of theirs way out in the bush to entertain some people at a business convention. To her delight, I agreed and we flew off again in a private aircraft to this oasis of luxury out in the wild. I was pleasantly surprised at the polite behaviour of the audience because business conventions can be the kiss of death for a comic as they're usually pissed as farts and very noisy. I tore the bollocks off 'em and Melanie was over the moon, she bathed in the compliments and adoration from the punters and I was her new best friend.

Melanie invited me to supper after the show and I devoured a delicious steak with all the trimmings. The meat in South Africa is the best I've ever tasted anywhere in the world. We had a few glasses of wine together and not long after she invited me to her suite for a "nightcap". It was on my school report, "This boy is easily led". After my initiation into the "Mile High Club" on the flight over, this trip was turning out to be quite interesting. Melanie wasn't the most beautiful girl I'd ever been with, she was bordering on being slightly overweight, but her bubbly personality more than made up for what she lacked in the beauty-queen department. She was a very sexy lady, as are all Jewish girls, in my experience. She was a tigress between the sheets and I was as fit as a butcher's dog at that time in my life so I managed to keep her happy. I've been with a few Jewish girls in my life, and they are without doubt, in my experience, the sexiest things on God's Earth.

I opened at the Landrost on the Monday night. Marti was there, JP and Marcia were with her, Melanie was fussing around like a mother hen, the press was there and the room was full. I went on and from the opening gag I knew I was in trouble, they weren't an audience, they were a jury. There is nothing more unfunny than a comic who's dying, and I was dying beautifully. The first thing to go is your timing; you rush to get to the next gag in the desperate hope that it will get that first precious laugh. They made me feel about as welcome as a fart in a spacesuit and the more I tried for a laugh, the worse it got. I was dying with dignity and I realised I'd better come off before I started insulting the audience. I've got some very funny "Dying" lines but I didn't think *they* would get me out of the shit either. I came off to a smattering of sparse applause and all I wanted to do was crawl into a hole and die. It's impossible to explain to a normal person what it's like to die on your arse as a comedian. Mother came up and put her arm around me and said "Fuck 'em Robert, we've all died when we least expected it so just forget about it and you'll storm 'em tomorrow". She knew *exactly* what I was feeling at that moment because only another comedian possibly could. It's the worst feeling in the world, you've got every faith in your material because it's tried and tested and you know it's funny, then suddenly along comes this bunch of twats who refuse to laugh and you end up going down like a one-legged man in an arse kicking competition. If a singer goes on and they don't like his songs, they'll perhaps chatter a bit during his show, but he'll always get a round of indifferent applause at the end. With a comic it's poles apart from the singer, they don't actually *like* you, they resent your efforts to make them laugh and they actually dislike you.

The room quickly emptied after my show business funeral and I was left with JP, Marti and Melanie trying to console me. I knew I was funny, but an audience like I'd just had to contend with can seriously undermine your confidence and I was feeling very down. My opening night, with the press in the room had been a total disaster; I'd gone on full of confidence after having stormed them at the business convention in the bush a couple of nights before. The crowd on my opening night had made me feel about as welcome as a turd in a swimming pool and I just wanted to go home, the thought of another month in this fuckin' comic's graveyard was really depressing me. Melanie tried to console me later on but I wasn't even up for messing around so we just went to sleep.

The guy from the press was a vitriolic young queen and he gave me a right old slagging in the local rag. He was really evil, saying personal things as well as really slagging my act. Still, I consoled myself with the fact that the three most useless things in the world are a man's tits, the Pope's balls and a review in the Jo'Burg Times. Melanie was all over me the next day in an effort to cheer me up, but I was genuinely OK. I'd died before and I'd probably die again in the future, I was just disappointed that JP and Mother had been there to witness it. In the immortal words of Scarlett O'Hara in Gone with the Wind, "Tomorrow is another day". Melanie took me to lunch at a beautiful restaurant where the steaks were a culinary orgasm and a bottle of good Cape wine soon cheered me up. I was now in the mood to do to Melanie what I should have done the night before so we went back to the hotel for some "Afternoon delight".

I was now naturally feeling a little apprehensive about the show which I was to do on the second night. I was a little worried about the revue which the nasty little shirt-lifter had written in the local rag but I consoled myself with the fact that it was highly improbable that the hotel guests would have read it, and by tomorrow it would be toilet paper. JP was flying home that day so it would be the day after before I could report any improvement in my progress to him.

I went on that night and absolutely paralysed them, every gag got applause and the crowd was beyond my wildest expectations. I did over an hour and came off to long ovation. It was totally incomparable to the previous evening's catastrophe and Melanie was ecstatic, she ordered champagne which I reluctantly sipped as I can't stand the bleedin' stuff. I even got a nod of approval from the hotel manager, a rather taciturn German guy called Heinrich who wasn't the friendliest of characters. He had a very Teutonic manner about him and I remember thinking that all he lacked was a pair of dueling scars on his cheek to complete his surly, pompous attitude.

The rest of the week went just as well and the opening night was like a bad memory. The weather was wonderful and I was sunning myself by the hotel pool every day and using the gym which was pretty poorly equipped by my standards but at least I got to train every day.

I've always been pretty sensitive to people's vibes and I could tell that Melanie was really falling for me. She was fantastic company and I loved her to bits but I knew I could never be *"In Love"* with her, as sweet as she was. I'd spent the night at her flat a few times and loved her sparkling personality, she was educated, funny, articulate and most of all, very, very sexy and rules didn't exist when we were between the sheets. I knew that when the time came to leave for home it was going to be very tearful.

The next two weeks went just as I expected, the audiences were intermittently good and bad. Some nights the room would be full and on other occasions there would be so few in that it would have been quicker to run round and tell them a joke each. I remember one great night when I had a crowd of Cockneys in from London and I sang them "The Streets of London" by Ralph McTell. They went bloody wild so I carried on with a few more "buskers" and we had a great sing-song. I've never been able to read music but I have an uncanny gift of being able to pick up the right chords for just about any song you throw at me so I was able to play their numerous requests without much trouble.

Towards the end of the second week I was summoned to Heinrich's office and he informed me that the hotel was being taken over for the whole of the following week by about four hundred Italians on a big business convention, the conversation went as follows —

"Do you speak ze Italian language?"

"Not a word Mate"

"Vell in zat case you vill sing to zem".

His typically German bombastic approach to any situation had led him to believe that I could just cobble together a totally new act and entertain the Italian guests at the drop of a hat.

"Heinrich, I'm not a singer, I'm a comedian".

"I hef heard you singing ze ozzer night to ze people from London".

"That was a one off sing-along just busking their requests, I've got no music for the band, and I've got no repertoire of songs to sing".

"I vill sink about it zen and let you know".

"There's nothing to think about Mate, I can't go on to a crowd of eye-ties when I can't communicate with them, I'll die on my arse like on the opening night, and I'm not about to do that again".

I came out of his office and went straight to my room and phoned Melanie. She was a big wheel in the Sun Hotels company and I knew she'd help me out if she could. I explained the situation to her and she just said "Don't you worry my Darling; I'll sort it out and ring you back in a little while".

Knutty on Safari

Melanie rang me back about an hour later and the joy in her voice told me everything was going to be OK.

"Robert my darling, I have sorted out your problem and you are to have the whole of next week off on full pay. Furthermore, on Sunday lunchtime, you and I are flying up to Mala Mala game reserve for a week's safari. It's all booked; we will have a week together in paradise. Mala Mala was the most exclusive and the most expensive game reserve in the whole of South Africa. The charges were two hundred pounds a day, per person. She reassured me that it was all on the company and not to even think about the cost. She asked me if I'd take my guitar along so I could sing to her outside the cabin. I was immediately very excited about the prospect of a safari out in the bush and equally happy about getting one over on Heinrich who by now I'd nick-named Himmler.

Melanie and I arrived at the airstrip near Mala Mala and were met by our own personal ranger who's name was Billy, he was accompanied by a huge black man who was our native tracker. He explained that while we were there, his job was to solely look after us and nobody else. Each couple or group had their own personal ranger which went further to prove the exclusivity of the place. We got into Billy's open top Land Rover for the journey to the camp, on the way I saw antelopes and giraffe grazing and then he slowed down when the tracker started making a clicking sound which was obviously some sort of language. He veered off the track at the same time telling us that his tracker had spotted the spoor of a rhinoceros. We drove for only a short time and on reaching the top of a small rise, we saw it. It was bigger than the bloody Land Rover and just stood there grazing, it totally ignored us. I was clicking away with my Canon Sure-Shot while Melanie cooed away like a contented dove, knowing I was totally enraptured by the whole event. Here I was, a humble steelworker's lad from Sheffield, on safari in this idyllic paradise, I'd come a long way from the back to back house on

Summerfield Street.

On reaching the camp I could see why it was so outrageously expensive. It consisted of a number of circular "Huts" with thatched roofs and their own verandah. The whole complex was laid out like a Zulu kraal with a high wicker fence completely surrounding it. In the centre of the compound was a communal eating area with a barbeque pit or "Brie" as the S Africans call it.

Our accommodation was palatial by anyone's standards. A very large bed dominated the room with heavily built mahogany furniture dotted around. The fridge was fully stocked with beer, white wine and champagne. Billy told us he'd be taking us out into the bush at 4.30 for a short trip to find some lions. The simple but opulent surroundings were making me feel as if I was Stewart Granger in a Hollywood jungle movie so I did what I thought a Hollywood movie star would do; I showered, had a large glass of Chenin Blanc and made love to Melanie. The trip into the bush was disappointing as the lions had gone on a trip of their own so we didn't see any. I saw my first wild elephant that evening, he was a large bull and he was too busy tearing off the top of a tree to be bothered with us. Billy gave me a strip of biltong to chew on, it's a salted cured strip of lean meat which is very popular in S Africa, I can't say as I found it unpleasant, but it's definitely an acquired taste.

We got back to camp to be told the food would be served at 9pm in the kraal. I could smell it already and the aroma was driving me wild. There were about a dozen other guests at the complex and we all met up and introduced ourselves over drinks in the bar area. Melanie was laying it on a bit thick by telling them that I was a big TV star back in England, but as far as she was concerned, *I was.* In all my life I have never tasted meat as delicious or as tender as the meat you get in S Africa, even to this very day. They had a whole antelope on the spit which was slowly rotating over a pit of glowing charcoal. There were accompaniments to the meat which I'd never seen or tasted, sauces and salads to die for. I was in culinary heaven. After the meal and a few drinks, Melanie asked me to bring my guitar and sing a few songs so I reluctantly agreed. I say reluctantly, because in that sort of "Get up and sing 'em one" situation, I've always been rather shy. I know I go on stage for a living, but when I do, I hide behind the façade of being Bobby Knutt and its like jumping off a log. Sitting around a BBQ with these new friends, I was just plain old Robert Wass and it's difficult to muster that bravado needed to just get up and sing. Needless to say, they loved it and I played for about an hour until my fingers started getting sore.

We were warned by Billy that a very early start was the order of the day so we rose at 5am for a delicious breakfast and were back out in the bush for 6am. The animals were out in force and what impressed me most was the fact that they just ignored us. Billy stopped very close to another rhino and my arse cheeks were starting to twitch a bit but the great creature just paid no heed to us whatsoever. Billy was determined to find us some lions to photograph but once again we were unlucky. We still saw lots of game and I was loving every minute of it all. At around mid-day we stopped by a water-hole which was roughly the quarter size of a football pitch. The black feller, who's name I cannot remember, nor could I pronounce it when I was told it, proceeded to make a fire over which he laid a sort of griddle. Billy got out the cold box containing the choice of wine or beers while some strips of marinated antelope were placed over the fire. The antelope was accompanied by a fiery sauce not unlike the ones you'll find in Caribbean cuisine. It was a meal that I will never, ever forget; it was so simple yet unbelievably tasty. That night we had the traditional communal brie again and went to bed feeling a little tipsy after lots of delicious white wine.

We were awakened a couple of hours later by a huge crashing sound and a tremendously loud bellowing noise. Billy came running up to our door carrying a very large bore gun. He told us to stay indoors as an elephant had got into the compound and was re-arranging the place. They carried the guns just in case he became a threat to anyone but fortunately for us, and the elephant, he decided to move on after a bit more rampaging. The next morning's light

Billy the Ranger &me

On Safari

saw the extent of his running amok. The walls of one of the huts were bashed in and the thatched roof was caved in, thank God it was unoccupied. The fence where he made his entrance was completely trashed, as was the section where he exited. It was all extremely exciting but I must admit I was rather afraid and had to pretend not to be so as to calm Melanie down who was on the verge of throwing a girly wobbler.

That day was to turn out to be one of the most memorable of my life. Billy informed us that one of the Land Rovers had gone on the blink and would we mind this other couple joining us for the day. We'd got to know them from the previous two evening's feasts and they were very pleasant. We set off with Billy's promise of a definite sighting of lions. I was thinking to myself
"I hope they're a bit friendlier than the bleedin' elephants".

Not long after another delicious al-fresco lunch out in the bush, we were driving along when the tracker started clicking again. Billy stopped and listened to him then told us he'd spotted lion tracks. We drove off the track at a slow speed and after another signal from the black feller, he stopped. Billy took the rifle off the rack above the windscreen and bade us follow him slowly and silently. About twenty five yards away was a mound roughly four feet high with what looked like lots of garden canes growing out of it. It was an old ant's nest and there, sitting totally still atop the nest, were three lion cubs. They were nestling there and nature plus their own instinct was telling them to remain absolutely quiet and motionless. They were very small and Billy whispered that they only looked to be a few weeks old. We took our pictures and Billy told us to get back in the Land Rover as we didn't want to be around when mother returned from her foraging expedition. He said a lioness with cubs is the most dangerous animal on the planet. Of all the best things I've seen in my life, those three cubs rank in the top five and the "AHHH" factor was unsurpassable.

We drove off and a very short time later I was overcome by an uncontrollable urge to pee. I'd been drinking beer instead of wine for lunch and I was full up. I asked Billy if he'd mind stopping and I was a little self-conscious about it as the South Africans can be a little Victorian in their attitude to that sort of thing. We had been driving along the top of an embankment not unlike you'd find on an English railway, it had a ditch on either side of it which would conceal me as I did my ablutions. Billy and the tracker came with me and when we were about fifty yards from the vehicle he said "You'll be OK down there Mr Knutt". I descended the slope to the bottom of the ditch where I was well out of sight of the ladies. As I was urinating there was a grunting sound followed by the obvious sound of vegetation being broken by something passing through it. Billy spoke as softly as he could and I remember his words as though it was yesterday.

"Mr Knutt, I want you to walk back up the slope very slowly and very quietly. Do not run whatever you do, there is a lion in the bush". I've described in my first chapter how I crash-landed on the battleship on my Falklands trip. I felt no fear at all, I just took it as it happened and thought about my peril afterwards. On this occasion I swear to you, I was shitting myself. The thought of being mauled and eaten by a fuckin' lioness was not in my plans when I'd agreed to the contract. I have never felt sheer terror like it before or since and what made it worse was as I approached Billy and the tracker, I could see the sweat of fear literally rolling down the tracker's face. We'd been out in very high temperatures and the black lad was always dry as a bone, on this occasion he was dripping wet through. This didn't instill any confidence in my chances of survival along with the fact that Billy had left the rifle in the Land Rover. I reached the top and we started to slowly walk back to the vehicle. That walk was the longest of my life, Billy said not to run under any circumstances, all of a sudden there was an almighty crash and a sort of piggy squealing noise, I was very close to shitting myself. We looked down into the ditch as a bloody great wart hog broke free from the bushes and ran along the bottom of it. We all heaved a huge sigh of relief as this ugly looking porker ran away along the ditch. As we approached the vehicle Billy winked at me and said "Don't worry, if it *had* been a lion, she would have eaten the black feller first". It was a typically S African racist thing to say, but I confess that at the time, it definitely broke the ice.

I finished my contract in Jo'Burg and said a fond farewell to a very tearful Melanie at the airport. She'd made so much difference to my trip with her kindness and extreme generosity. I will always think of her with great fondness and for a while I received letters from her after she moved to America to start up her own production company. I "googled" her today and discovered she's back in S Africa doing the same job and probably making millions God bless her.

I returned home with all these wonderfully rich experiences to store in my memory banks. I'm a very lucky bloke.

The Ladie's Bicycle Saddle Sniffing Club

Very shortly after arriving back from Jo'Burg I embarked on another CSE trip to Belize in Central America. I'd done all the Belfast shit-holes and frozen my arse off in the Falklands so I was very grateful to go on a trip to somewhere a bit warmer. I'd never been there and when I rang Derek Aggutter who booked the acts for CSE, he said it was a jungle paradise. I had to immediately start taking the malaria tablets as according to Derek; the mozzies were like (in his own words) "Fackin' Chinooks". The group of thespians consisted of a four-girl Pan's People type of act, a girl called Tammy Sioux who sang country songs and dressed in a buckskin squaw's outfit, a very young girl singer from Liverpool and a hypnotist called Nigel Ellery who was ex army officer material and spoke very posh. We also had a two piece backing group, keyboards and drums which was a luxury by CSE standards. We flew to Washington then changed planes for the flight down the Eastern Seaboard to Belize City which I think has now been re-named Belmopan. I sat with Nigel all the way down and we got on famously, we had lots in common including the fact that we were both Chauvinistic bastards and confirmed fanny rats who loved the ladies. He had a portable backgammon set with him and taught me to play; I've been hooked ever since. We both agreed that the head girl with the dance troupe was by far the most attractive and definitely worth one so we had a little bet as to who would be the first to become her "special friend".

On arriving at our destination we were driven to our hotel which was very Spartan, but by Belize standards, it was four stars. We didn't have to perform that night thank God as we were tired and jet-lagged. We all went down to dine together and the food was wonderful. I've always adored lobster but as it's so bloody expensive I very rarely have it. It was on the menu and cheap as chips, although we were obviously not paying for anything except our drinks. They laid out one large dining table, a bit like the ones you'd find in a monk's refectory and we all sat down for supper. The head girl, who's name was Sharon, parked herself next to me which pleased me no end as Nigel was down the other end with the squaw. Sharon was a smashing kid with no attachments and free as a bird, I was getting really good vibes from her and before long I knew that poor old Nigel was gonna lose his wager. The next morning we had a visit from the chief medical officer who was in overall charge of the health and well-being of all the numerous camps in Belize. He was a very nice chap with a terribly posh Oxford accent and his main concern was the possibility of any or all of us getting the "runs". He gave us a pep-talk about the symptoms which meant that if we were very loose, we'd got the "squitters". Should the squitters develop into vomiting and stomach pains, we'd got the Montezumas, in which case we had to see the MO immediately for a dose of Lomotil or "the Plug" as he called it.

Our first show was out in the jungle, in fact all our shows were out in the jungle. We were taken in by canvas-topped army trucks and once again, as I had been out in the Falklands, I was amazed at the skills of the squaddies who built us a stage and changing facilities. We got there in plenty of time to set up and rehearse and as the darkness fell, we saw that the lads had placed hundreds of fairy lights up in the trees which surrounded the clearing. It was a wonder to behold when they were switched on. The show went an absolute storm and we got our standing ovation followed by the customary thank you speech from the commanding officer whom we discovered was an SAS Colonel seconded from the "Regiment". A BBQ and lots of drinks in the warm night air followed, and the officers were queueing up to dance with our girls. I was more than pleased when a slightly tipsy Sharon came and parked herself on my knee and asked me to rescue her from the constant stream of would-be Fred Astaires who were competing for her company. We were driven back to the hotel where I invited Sharon for a nightcap in my room, she accepted and poor old Nigel lost his bet.

The next night we were due to perform in the nearest camp to our hotel which was only a couple of miles down the track. We'd been invited there for lunch followed by water ski-ing lessons off a nearby jetty. It was there that we were entertained by the group of absolute raving nutters known as "Butcher Radar". They had their own camp within a camp and it was by special invitation only. They had tamed a number of wild parrots which sat on the bar and tables waiting to be fed tit-bits by the drinkers. In the middle of their inner sanctum was a covered area about three yards square with a bicycle saddle stuck firmly into the ground. It had a "Ladies Only" sign next to it. *"LADIE'S BICYCLE SADDLE SNIFFING CLUB"* was emblazoned over the entrance. I pissed myself laughing as all the girls duly obliged by mounting the saddle and having a little squirm on it, much to the delight of the lads from Butcher Radar who then lined up for the sniffing ceremony. As unruly as these guys were, they had a very serious monitoring job to do as Central America was a bubbling cauldron of potential trouble. Belize is bounded to the north by Mexico, to the east by the Caribbean Sea and to the west and south by Guatemala. It's a land of mountains, swamps and tropical jungles. In 1862 British Honduras as it was previously known, became a crown colony, but an unfulfilled provision of an 1859 British-Guatemalan treaty led Guatemala to claim the territory. The situation had not been resolved when Belize was granted its independence in 1981 so a British force was stationed there to ensure the new country's security and here I was entertaining the barmy buggers.

Our next show was way out in the jungle near the Guatemalan border and we were choppered in for an overnight stay which was to turn out very dramatic. We were taken to our quarters as soon as we arrived; the boys were in a pretty large tent with proper beds, as were the girls. There was a sort of central building which was the only substantial construction in the camp. It was a large Nissen hut and I noticed that it was tied down by steel guy ropes; I wondered why and thought maybe they're afraid someone might nick it. The CO apologised in advance for any soldiers who might get up and go during the show. He reassured us that it had no bearing on our talents but that they'd been called out on emergency duty as the

Sharon squirming

Me & Nigel

Belize Brothel

border was very close. The show started to a big cheer from the lads and I noticed a breeze getting up which forced the keyboard player to keep having to re-arrange the sheet music on his stand. I could see he was having difficulty so I went down and volunteered to hold it steady and turn the pages for him. The young girl singer was first up after the dancers and she had all her eight musical arrangements on the keyboard music stand. Suddenly, the wind got really strong and the trees were bending like wheat stalks. The sheet music just took off and blew away as if it was tissue paper. I saw my Ovation guitar start to tilt forward on its stand and I just managed to grab it before it fell over. At that moment the CO came up onto the stage and stopped the show by announcing that a tropical storm was about to hit the camp and that every man-jack of us should go smartly into the Nissen hut. I remembered that I'd left a large bath towel and a pair of underpants draped over a tree to dry and wondered if I'd ever see them again. By now the rain was coming down like stair rods and the thunder and lightning was awesome. The singer was in tears because she'd lost all her music and believe me, it's not cheap to have arrangements written. The CO had some squaddies erect a curtain for the girls to sleep behind thus preserving their modesty. The storm raged on through the night with great ferocity, Nigel and I sat up playing backgammon and drinking a bottle of local rum which we'd cadged from the barman. Every man on the camp slept in the hut that night, the snoring and farting was competing with the thunderstorm but apart from that, they were all on their best behaviour because the CO had to sleep there too. We were lucky that the lads had the foresight to get all the equipment into the hut out of the way of the storm so we didn't suffer any damage whatsoever.

The next morning after the hurricane had passed, the place looked like a herd of elephants had rampaged through it. The tree over which I'd hung my towel and grundies was no longer there, it had been uprooted and blown away. Only two tents remained but they were ripped to shreds and only held in place by their guy ropes. I now understood why the Nissen hut was secured by steel ropes, it had certainly saved us from a very unpleasant and potentially dangerous night.

The trip ended with memories of overdosing on lobster, backgammon, hurricanes and helicopters, lots of rum and even lots more Sharon.

Fairy Glitterclit

I'm so fortunate that thanks to being in my chosen profession, my life has been enriched by so many fabulous and funny experiences and along the way I've met and made some wonderful friends. One of the most memorable pals was the late great Ronnie Hilton. I'd listened to him on the radio when I was a lad and had got to know him in the summer of 1979 when I was on at the Futurist Theatre in Scarborough with Marti Caine and he was doing the holiday camp circuit down the East coast. Ronnie was a massive star in the fifties but the groups and pop stars of the sixties soon eroded his popularity with the record buying public. His career had a miraculous revival when he recorded a daft little song called "A Windmill in Old Amsterdam" and he shot to the top of the charts which gave him a second bite at the cherry.

Ronnie was a true Yorkshire lad from Hull and although he was quite a bit older than me, we got on like brothers. We were also addicted to the comedy sayings of that great old pre-war comedian, Frank Randle. Randle was a rebel with a gigantic comedy talent, but like most geniuses, he had a dodge; Frank was a confirmed piss-artist who could consume a whole crate of Guinness before he went on stage. Whenever Ronnie and I got together we'd go straight into Randle-mode and spend the rest of the night pissing ourselves laughing. All our conversations would be splattered with loud belches and "Randleisms" like "By gum, I'll fettle thee missus. Thy bum's a biggun. I'd love to cut thy watter off missus".

In the summer of 1983 I did a season at Butlins in Skegness. Paula was there every night for the full season doing the girl singer's job along with Ronnie who was topping the bill and I was the guest comic doing three nights, two in the theatre and one in the cabaret bar. It took care of my midweek bookings and JP fixed the weekends in other venues. Also on the bill at Skeggy were two sisters called the Gemini Twins, they were actual twins with dyed blonde hair that had so many split ends they looked like a pair of Worzel Gummidges. They were a pair of broad Geordie lasses and

Me & Ronnie Hilton

My garden gnome

they put their make-up on with a trowel. They were very sexy in a common sort of way and Ronnie and I used to stand in the wings with them as they waited to make their entrance. We'd say the most obscene things to them and it was like water off a duck's back. Backstage was the only time you could get them on their own as they *always* had their mother with them and she was like a mother lion guarding her cubs. They were possibly the worst act I'd ever seen but the dads in the audience loved them. They actually sang in a Geordie accent and I used to stand in the wings with Ronnie and sing along with them in our Geordie accents, absolutely pissing ourselves. One night as we were standing behind them in the wings, I noticed that Ronnie had got his hand down the back of a twin's knickers and before I could try it with the other one, they'd gone on stage. The second half of the show saw us both with our hands down the twins' clouts and it became a regular way of pushing them onto the stage. They always started giggling when we groped them and I'm sure they quite enjoyed it. Thanks to the eternal presence of old Mother Shipton, that's as far as we ever progressed but I know we both fantasized about the two of them together which must be every mans dream of sexual heaven.

One of the dancers in the show was another Geordie lass whom Paula and I really liked and one night we were talking about our upcoming Panto at Christmas. I can't remember her name but she said she'd never been in a panto but would love to do one. I thought what a great fairy she'd make with her Geordie accent and her amazing legs. I rang Slim Ingram to see if he'd cast the fairy yet and fortunately he hadn't. He took my recommendation and she was over the moon when I told her she'd got the part.

The panto season came round like wildfire and I was starring in "Dick Whittington" at the Theatre Royal St Helens for three weeks followed by a three week season at Rotherham Civic. Paula was playing Dick and the dame was a London drag artiste call Dockyard Doris who happened to be the great grandson of that world famous music hall star Marie Lloyd. His real name was Colin Devereaux and he was one of the best dames I ever worked with. He was gay, but you'd never know it. He didn't mince about and lisp like most of the queens in the business, he wore a flat cap and a donkey jacket and he *looked* like a docker. It was a little upsetting for me to go back to the same hotel where, four years previously I'd received the news of my father's sudden death as I sat in my room at 10am on the 17th January 1979. I managed to work the same oracle on this panto as I'd done on the earlier one and get all the cast into the same town-centre hotel on a very reduced rate for the whole of the run.

On the day of the dress rehearsal, I was in my dressing room which I was sharing with Paula and in wandered the Geordie fairy. Paula had just bought some little pots of a brand new make-up product which was a sort of smear-on glitter. She was gently applying it to her eyelids and the fairy's curiosity was aroused.

"Eeh what's that yev got there Paula?"

"It's glitter Darling, look, it comes in different colours in these little pots".

"Eeh could a try a lirrul bit on mi feyace Pet?"

Paula told her to help herself but be sparing as you didn't need a lot. She asked where to buy it and Paula told her which shop in town sold it. After the dress run, the fairy trotted off and bought about a dozen pots of this glitter gel and when she made her entrance on the opening show, she shone like a super trooper spotlight. She'd got it on her legs, her arms and her face and she looked spectacular. After the show we all went back to the hotel where they'd kindly put on a buffet for us starving thespians and we stayed up and partied till quite late. I'd noticed all the various little attractions and pairings which always occur when an acting company gets together. I was obviously out of it because I was with my Paula. I could see that King Rat was sniffing round the principle girl and the Captain's mate was fancying the fairy. The dame was fancying me and I let him down gently because I really liked him as a bloke and respected him as a performer.

The next morning I was up at about nine o'clock for breakfast and shortly after I sat down, in came the captain's mate. He sat down and he had a very satisfied look on his face. I looked at him and said,

"You shagged the fairy last night didn't you". He grinned and said he had, at the same time his hand dived down to his crotch and he started scratching. He was continually scratching his gander parts so I asked him if he was OK.

"You don't think I've caught a dose do you?"

"Of course you haven't you barmpot, it wouldn't show up as quick as this. But then again, if she's got crabs, they would definitely make you itch".

"I'm gonna have a look", he said and with that he shot off to the toilet. He came back about five minutes later with a relieved look on his face. He said,

"You'll never believe it Knutty; I've got all this fuckin' glitter stuff down my foreskin".

I winced at the thought, even though I was circumcised as a baby, I could imagine what the poor bastard was going through. The glitter was a very fine coloured powdered glass in a sort of jelly not unlike Vaseline. I was in stitches laughing and I couldn't wait to tell Paula. From then on, I christened the fairy "Fairy Glitterclit" and she was quite proud of her newly acquired Nom de Plume. I truly wish I could remember her name but I can't, we exchanged names and addresses after the season ended. Not long after the panto, she got a job dancing on the cruise ships and I used to receive postcards from all over the world from "Fairy Glitterclit" much to the amusement of my postman.

Paula

I've described how I first met Paula in my first book but I'll briefly remind you in case you didn't read it. In the summer of 1972 I did my first ever long summer season at the Derbyshire Miners' Holiday Camp. Paula was about fourteen years old at the time and she was part of the junior ensemble provided by the local dancing school. I probably didn't speak more than a dozen words to her in the whole of the season as the juniors always kept themselves to themselves. I remembered her as a pretty blonde well mannered girl whose mother Barbara also sang in the show as a sort of unpaid chorus member. Eight years later I was appearing for a season in the Isle of Man at the Gaiety Theatre and Paula was there also at the Casino as part of a five girl "Pan's People" type of dance act. She'd grown into a stunningly beautiful girl and without elaborating into the whys and wherefores; we fell in love which was the last nail in the coffin of my very rocky marriage to Carol.

I loved Paula very much and the freedom she gave me was such an adult way of having a relationship and was a million miles from the constant sniping and jealousy which endured in my previous relationship. Paula was so gentle in her general demeanor, she reminded me of a fragile butterfly whom I had to protect. I never heard her raise her voice in all the four years we were together. I got on famously with her parents, her Dad, Austin thought the sun shone out of my amplifiers and Barbara was nothing like the traditional mother-in-law. Paula also got on really well with my daughter Cherine who was the apple of my eye. The acrimonious marriage break-up was in the past and my gorgeous daughter had seemed to emerge unscathed by it all. Paula often went off to dance for a short season on a cruise ship and she'd sometimes go and spend a few days with her family Chapel St Leonards near Skeggy.

On one occasion she'd just returned from a visit with her parents and I found her weeping on the sofa. I asked her what was wrong and she blurted it out and I realised we'd got a problem. Paula's sister Mandy had been recently married to a lovely bloke who was

Paula

an accountant. She'd proudly announced to the family that she was pregnant and Austin and Barbara were ecstatic with joy. Now Austin was the most wonderful father that any daughter could wish for and I'd often seen him actually bounce Paula up and down on his knee as if she was still a toddler. On hearing the news of Mandy's baby, he was cuddling Paula on his knee and said "Just wait till you and Bobby get married then we'll have lots more grandkids". We *were* engaged to be married and I knew I could happily spend the rest of my life with this wonderful girl, but there was a problem.

In 1981, I'd had a vasectomy which I'd discussed at great length with Paula who reassured me that she never wanted children. The problem was, she'd not told her parents of my operation and I realised why she was weeping. She suggested that perhaps I could have it reversed so that we might be able to procreate. I sadly explained that the way in which the surgeon had performed my vasectomy had left no road open for a reversal. I then told her that in no way did I want any more children, ever. It was a heartbreaking thing to say to a lady who I'd cut my arm off for rather than hurt her. I started to brood on the subject but I just couldn't see a satisfactory solution for it. I was beginning to imagine Paula reaching later life and resenting the fact that we were childless. I desperately wanted us to stay together because I really loved her in a protective way that I'd not experienced in any other relationship. I was so frustrated by the whole situation but little did I know that a way out was not too far off in the future.

Donna

The summer of 1984 found me doing a three day stint at Butlins Pwhelli and little did I know it was to change my life forever. I was doing Tuesday, Wednesday and Thursday, two in the theatre and one in the notorious "Spanish Bar" which was known for chewing comics up and spitting them back out as broken men. The majority of the campers at that particular venue were mainly from Manchester and Merseyside and you had to be stronger than them to win them as an audience. I worked as clean as a whistle in the theatre but I was very vulgar in the Spanish Bar. Bear in mind that every Tuesday they had Bernard Manning on the midnight matinee fucking and blinding for a solid hour. I couldn't follow that on the Wednesday with Beano jokes so I went in strong and threw in a few bollocks and bastards and they pissed themselves. It was the only time in my whole career that I've resorted to swearing on stage to get a laugh but it worked.

I was given the same chalet every week and I took my cooking stuff with me so as to eat well while I was in North Wales. The chalets were very Spartan and I couldn't imagine *anyone* actually paying to stay in one. I often went over in my E Type which was a pleasure to drive around Snowdonia during the day and admire the magnificent scenery. I remember one Wednesday morning I was walking over to the Spanish Bar to set my gear up when I saw one of the head redcoats walking down the path with this stunning looking blonde girl who was carrying a large kit bag. I stopped to say hello and he introduced her as Donna Hartley the Olympic athlete who was overseeing the Butlins Pentathlete scheme. At that very moment in time, something hit me like a bomb, I was tongue-tied and felt embarrassed at my lack of communicative ability. She was very pleasant and obviously had not the faintest idea of who I was nor had she ever heard of me. I told her I had a health studio in Sheffield and there we found a common denominator. She walked on and I was numb. I had only spoken to her for a couple of minutes and I was utterly besotted. She had an athletic figure to die for and

Not a bad pose, eh?

as she walked away, I saw the most beautifully shaped behind that I'd ever clapped eyes on. I had to know more about her so I wandered casually into the entertainment manager's office to find out what I could. He told me that she came every Tuesday night, stayed over so as to do the Pentathlete activities with the children then drove off to the next camp early on Wednesday tea-time. He also said "If you've got any thoughts on pulling her Knutty, you've no chance, she's a proper lady and she's married to big Bill Hartley the hurdler". I didn't care what he'd said about her marital status or how big her husband was; I *had* to speak to her again and find out more about her.

I went over to the sports area where the kids were doing their various disciplines for the pentathlon and there she was. I could see she was busy but I sauntered over and struck up a conversation. I was admiring her red kit-bag which was provided free by her sponsors "Patrick" the sports wear company. She promised to try and get me one for the following week. She was totally disinterested in me as a man; I could see she was just a very nice polite lady who was unbelievably modest about her status as one of Britain's best loved and most decorated athletes. We parted company and I was a wreck. I'd only had strong feelings about very few women in my life but this was something which was unimaginably painful. My every waking moment was filled with her image in my mind's eye. I couldn't sleep for thinking about her and as the next week drew nearer, I was like a little child waiting for Christmas Eve.

The following week, I drove over to North Wales a day early on the Monday and cooked a spaghetti Bolognese for the Tuesday. I waited casually around the entrance to the camp so as to perhaps catch a glimpse of her arriving. I must have missed her but I soon found out her chalet number after I discovered she was on the camp. I didn't want to seem pushy by knocking on her door but I was in agony, the butterflies in my stomach were driving me mad. I tapped gingerly on her door and she was in. She opened the door and she was wearing just a flimsy pair of running shorts and a singlet, my pulse must have been up near danger levels and I mumbled something about the kit-bag she'd promised me when we'd met the previous week. She'd remembered and she went into the bedroom to get it. I asked her if she'd let me buy her a drink as a thankyou later on if she was going into the Spanish bar. She said that she didn't usually go out but on this occasion she was going out with Susie, the entertainments manager's wife so they'd probably be in there.

I was very fashion conscious in those days and shopped at a very expensive men's boutique called Robert Brady. Rob's prices were astronomical, in fact they were bordering on the obscene but all the big hitters, posers and crumpet crawlers in Sheffield bought their gear from him. A big designer label popular at the time was "Moustache", and I'd bought a white cotton blouson jacket with matching billowy trousers which I wore with a pair of bright red leather winklepickers shoes and a silk flowery shirt. I must have looked a right twat but I thought I looked spectacular. I wandered into the Spanish bar wearing my "Moustache" outfit and not long after, she came in with Susie. I'd only seen her in training gear, now here she was in her finery with the make-up on and her lovely blonde hair coiffured to perfection. I went over and welcomed her, offering to buy them both a drink. I could tell she was really there under sufferance but Susie had wanted a girly night out and a good natter so my ultra sensitive antenna detected that my continued presence would be unwelcome. I ended up by asking if she'd like to have supper with me later on as I'd cooked a spaghetti, she politely declined.

I engineered another "chance" meeting the next day and explained there was nothing at all untoward nor was there any ulterior or sinister motive behind my inviting her to supper the previous evening. I told her it was an open invitation and that my cooking was a serious hobby which I loved to test out on everybody. We had a friendly conversation and I told her I looked forward to seeing her next week. I was totally hooked; I knew that no other woman in my whole life had had this earth-shattering effect on me. I was now beginning to worry about my little Paula whom I also loved. She was everything a man could want in a girl. She knew all my faults and still loved me, she was kind and thoughtful, very beautiful, sexy and her nature was so quiet and gentle that everyone she met adored her. I was already worried about her suggestion of me trying to have my vasectomy reversed, but she'd not mentioned it for quite a while. I loved her just as much as I'd always done, you couldn't help but love her, but now here I was with this devastating quandary, and I could see no way out of it without hurting this tender, sweet lady. My head was in a mess, I'd only ever spoken to Donna, I'd never even touched her hand, let alone kiss her and yet I knew that I couldn't rest until she was mine and I was willing to do *anything* to achieve it. I'm a tenacious bastard when I get my teeth into something and I never let go till I get what I want.

The following week I found her sunbathing outside her chalet so I asked her if she minded me joining her. We lay there for a couple of hours and talked about everything and anything. I knew I looked good in a pair of swimming trunks so I wasn't worried about the hundreds of very fit men she'd seen during her athletics career, she could have compared me physically with any of them and I'd have measured up. I was discovering so much about her, how her career had been tragically cut short by an Achilles tendon injury which wouldn't mend sufficiently to allow her to carry on running. She'd done a cordon bleu cookery course amongst other things and she lived in Liverpool where she and her husband had a very successful market garden business. I was right when I assumed she'd never heard of me as an actor *or* a comedian. She was completely unimpressed by cars and my E-type Jag was just another lump of metal on four wheels as far as she was concerned. I persuaded her to come for a drink that evening but I was determined to take things very slowly as I didn't want to do anything to jeopardize what progress I'd made so far. I desperately wanted to tell her how I felt about her but I was afraid of that driving her away also.

I decided to write her a letter to try and explain my feelings for her as I couldn't bear for her not to know, no matter what the consequences of her knowing might be. She'd never spoken of her

My Donna over the years

husband in a tender or loving way, in fact she hardly ever mentioned him at all. It took me hours and hours to compose the letter; I'd keep ripping it up and starting again. I didn't want it to seem like the ramblings of a lovesick schoolboy, yet it had to explain exactly how deeply my feelings were for her. I was eventually satisfied with the content of the letter and sealed it in an envelope. I saw Donna again the following week and she seemed to be warming to my company and I even thought that I detected she was glad to see me. I was on the verge of telling her verbally of my feelings but I decided to stick with the letter plan. We parted company that night and much later I walked down to her chalet and slipped the letter under her door. I'd crossed the Rubicon, there was no going back now, and I just had to await her reaction.

During that summer, I'd promised to take my Mother over to Pwllheli for a little break and a few glasses of Guinness. She rang me that weekend and asked if she and her cousin, my aunty Mary, could go with me next week so I had to agree. I knew they were going to be a serious intrusion on my visit to Wales because by now Donna would have read my letter and I'd no idea what her reaction was to be. We set off with my old Mam rattling on about everything and anything and it was just going straight in one ear and out of the other. All I could think about was Donna and her response to my letter. As we drew near the camp I was feeling more and more apprehensive and praying that the letter had not buggered up my chances of her ever speaking to me again. I got my Mam and Mary unpacked and settled in the small bedroom and around mid afternoon there was a knock on the door. I opened the door to find Donna standing there smiling at me. I invited her in and introduced her to my Mother, telling Mother that she was a friend who, like me, worked temporarily on the camp. I made an excuse to Mother and we went out for a short walk. Donna said she'd read the letter and then told me she felt the same way. I cannot explain to you in any words how I felt at that moment in time. I felt as light as a feather, every bell in the world was ringing just for me. I couldn't give her a hug as there were people around and she was a married lady. I told her that I loved her with a feeling so intense that I would never be able to explain it. I promised her that no matter what we had to do to achieve it, we would be together.

I took my Mother and Mary out for a drink and a bite to eat and they thankfully wanted to go to bed early. She'd enjoyed her couple of Guinness but was tired so I settled her in bed and went out to meet Donna. We went back to her chalet and we made love until the dawn came up. I knew then that it was neither an infatuation nor a simple lusting after a beautiful woman; I knew that I would spend the rest of my life with this lady and no power on God's earth would stop me.

All washed up

The Gypsy's Prophesy

When I returned home to Sheffield that weekend I found Paula her usual care free self and as I walked in the flat, she gave me her customary massive hug. I felt like I was being ripped apart inside, the thought of hurting Paula was devastating me. We'd planned to go over to Skegness that weekend to see her parents which I knew would further aggravate my inner turmoil because they thought of me as a son. On the way through Skeggy, we decided to stop and have a stroll along the promenade. I don't know *why* we did, but little did I know that fate was going to take another stab at changing my life. As we walked along the prom we passed a small seaside hut which was owned by Gypsy Rose Lee or something like that, I can't exactly remember her name. Paula said "Why don't you go in and have your fortune told"; I replied that I thought fortune telling was in my opinion the biggest load of bollocks along with horoscopes and suchlike. She turned on her little girl face which always made me laugh and persuaded me to go in and cross the lady's palm with silver. There was no silver changed hands, it was a bleedin' fiver which I thought was a right old rip-off. She said she could give me a more accurate reading with her crystal ball so I covered it with my hands for a while then she held my hands for a short time and started her reading. She told me I was going to live a long and healthy life with only a few medical hiccups along the way and then she paused for a while. She then said the following. "You are torn between two women and you love them both in different ways. One of them is married, you will be with her." I was utterly gob-smacked at what she told me. How did she know? I was still a little skeptical so I asked her if she was sure of what she'd said. She calmly repeated that I would end up with the one who was married and we would be together for life. I came outside and Paula started tickling me and asking me what she'd said. I just said I'd been promised a long and healthy life with much success in my career. Inside me I was shocked and mystified but the evidence was there. I couldn't go on deceiving Paula any longer but the thought of telling her we were finished was breaking me apart. I told her that night as we lay together in her bedroom. I knew she was still hoping in her heart of hearts that I would try and have my vasectomy reversed so I took the coward's way out and told her that I couldn't see a future for us while ever she might want a child. I couldn't bear to admit to her that I'd fallen in love with someone else. I told her I still loved her, which I genuinely did, but I'd made my mind up as I didn't want her to resent being childless in later life when it would be too late.

I drove away early the next morning and I swear to God I cried all the way to Lincoln. I was in a mess and I felt like the biggest, rottenest bastard on the planet. I got home and Paula was everywhere, her picture was on the wall, her clothes were in the wardrobe, and she was still in my heart. The love I felt for her was totally different to the love I felt for Donna. It was a gentle and sort of protective feeling that I felt for her whereas it was a fiery passionate and uncontrollable sensation which I had for Donna. When Donna rang me that night, I told her that I'd finished with Paula and that however long I had to wait for her, I would endure it.

We rang each other four or five times a day for the next couple of weeks and finally she plucked up the courage to tell her husband that it was over and she was leaving him. She was consoled by the fact that she knew of *his* infidelity with a lady athlete while he was out in Australia. Donna is the most upright, kindest and most sensitive human being I've ever known so I know what she went through during that traumatic period in her life. She must have agonized at the thought of telling her husband and the build-up to doing so must have been even more distressing. She finally moved over to Sheffield in late October of 1984 and I gradually introduced her to my close friends and family. I was just so desperately sad that she never met my father who had died five years previously, she would have loved him and he her. The day she finally came over to live with me was possibly one of the happiest days of my life. She arrived with her little VW Golf packed to the back tailgate with her few possessions. We started unpacking her stuff and in a cardboard box, I found a roll of parchment with a red ribbon wrapped around it. "What's this" I asked. She casually replied "Oh, that's my MBE". Here in my hand was a document with the Queen's and Duke's signatures on it denoting Donna's decoration and it was thrown casually into an old box. This wasn't an indication of any disrespect by her towards this wonderful achievement, it was just indicative of her total modesty. Shortly afterwards I took it to a picture framer and had it placed in a most beautiful gilded frame and ever since it has held pride of place over the mantelpiece. I think *I'm* more proud of it than she is.

Because of Donna's sensitivity we were trying to keep a low profile but it was impossible due to the fact that she was still *very* famous and had only retired from competing a couple of years before. The press soon sniffed it out and we had to do the obligatory interviews and photo sessions which really embarrassed Donna as she is basically a very shy sort of person. The snidey remarks soon started sifting through from the rumour mongers saying it would never last but we rode the storm with dignity and fortitude. Those arseholes were all wrong as we'll be celebrating our twenty fifth wedding anniversary in the not too distant future.

Sadly, only a couple of weeks after she moved in with me I had to fly off to work in Gambia for nearly three weeks. It was so difficult leaving her all alone in a strange city but she couldn't come with me as she'd not had the compulsory inoculations which were required for Africa. I took my great friend Keith Healey with me and he kept me sane while I was out there missing Donna like you couldn't possibly imagine. Keith was one of my closest mates and was the proverbial "Mr Sheffield". He frequented all the best night clubs and was the most immaculately dressed bloke in the city. He could make a donkey jacket look like it was made in Saville Row. His nickname was "Jason" because he was the double of Jason King, the character played by Peter Wyngarde. He was in the motor trade and drove a really nasty old Rolls Corniche convertible in white. It was held together with filler and fibre glass but from a distance it was the dog's bollocks. He could out-pose anybody in the town and wherever he frequented, be it a posh café or a midnight cocktail bar, that venue would become the place to be seen in. He was six feet tall and amazingly charismatic but he was worse than me when it came to injections. I literally had to drag him down to the clinic for our Cholera/Typhoid jabs for Gambia. It was only the fact that it was a free holiday in Paradise that strengthened his resolve to go through with it.

Sad Pantomime

I'd not been back from Gambia more than a couple of weeks when panto came around again. I was appearing at the New Theatre in Hull, the panto was Dick Whittington and it was the first panto in which I wasn't topping the bill. My old pal Charlie Williams was topping as the Captain's mate and I was second top playing the usual silly bugger part. When JP asked me if I was interested in doing the show I said I'd do it if I could have the kid's spot at the end. He said that would be up to Charlie Williams so I got straight on the phone to him to ask him if he minded me doing the songsheet. He was over the moon at me offering to do it and his words were "Tha can do it wi' pleasure mi owd flower, I'm not that keen on kids". We ended up sharing a flat together in Beverley which cheered me as I did all the cooking, thus we always had a decent supper after the show. Charlie was notoriously "careful" with his money, in fact to be quite honest, he was dead bloody tight. I would do all the shopping and get the stuff which we needed for our every day living requirements. He never offered to chip in and I was getting a bit miffed about it so instead of going round the houses with carefully disguised hints, I just said to him one day, "Eyup ya tight bastard, when are you gonna chip in for some groceries?". He got the hint because the next day he came in with a carrier bag and proudly announced he'd been shopping. It contained a packet of corn flakes, a pint of milk and a loaf of white bread. I gave up.

The thing which was tearing me up about this particular panto was that Paula was playing Dick Whittington. It had all been fixed up way before I'd met Donna and she bravely carried on like the trouper she was. I knew it was breaking her heart to see me and Donna together and it was breaking mine to see her doing the job so well when I knew she was so despondent inside and putting on such a brave face. She'd rented a grotty little flat in the town and was staying on her own. I knew it was ripping her apart to see me and Donna go off every night after the show together while she went home alone. It was one of the saddest times of my entire life because

I still loved her, but I loved Donna a whole lot more.

I worked with one of the best dames ever that year, his name was Frankie Desmond. He was a little Welshman and he played my Mam. I remember one night we were chatting in his dressing room and the subject got round to money. He said he didn't have to work if he didn't want to as he was quite well off. He wasn't boasting or anything like that; he was just stating a fact. I asked him how he became wealthy and he said it was from his royalties. I was now very curious as to what "royalties" he was referring to. He casually told me that many years before, he'd written the lyrics to "We'll keep a Welcome in the Hillside" which was virtually the Welsh national anthem. I was gobsmacked, here was I sitting with this unassuming little man who wrote the words to one of the most famous songs in the world.

Mile High Proposal

Donna settled into life in Sheffield and everyone adored her. She got on really well with my daughter Cherine who was now in her mid-teens and Donna saw a great potential in her as a runner. We'd go down to my boyhood playground Endcliffe Park and Donna would put her through her paces, it was so good to see them becoming friends. Sadly for us all these weekly visits were not to endure for much longer as Cherine had to go through an inquisition from her mother every time she visited us. She quizzed her on what had been said or done and it must have been very traumatic for the young girl. She told Donna about it in a private moment. It's the oldest story in the world when a marriage ends acrimoniously; one of the parents usually tries to poison the children against the other. I adored my beautiful precious girl and the gradual erosion of our relationship broke my heart, thanks to Carol's vitriolic hatred for me and her unceasing efforts to sabotage my kinship with Cherine. It really hurt Donna also to see me so upset by the whole business but there was nothing we could do and Carol eventually got her way. I have not seen my daughter for twenty years now; she lives in America with her husband and their twins. I am a grandfather but I have never met my grandchildren and probably never will.

In the spring of 1985, Donna and I decided to take a two week holiday in Tenerife. I had never been happier in my life and Donna completely possessed me body and soul. I knew I'd met the great love of my life and I never wanted it to end. I conceived a plan to surprise her on the flight over in the form of a marriage proposal. I borrowed her wedding ring which she no longer wore and took it down to my old mate Peter Hayman the jeweller to choose an engagement ring of the correct size. I picked a bloody great diamond solitaire which he'd got on at about three grand and he graciously knocked me a third off it. I then rang the airline and told them that I was planning to propose to my lady friend on the flight to Tenerife and could they tee up some flowers and champagne in the event that she accepts. They said it was a lovely gesture and they would be happy to oblige. The great day came and we boarded the aircraft, the chief trolley dolly winked at me to let me know she was aware of what was to take place. About an hour into the flight I couldn't wait any longer so I went and told the stewardess to be alert. I must say, I felt a bit of a twat bending down in the aisle but I was determined to do it right. I went down on one knee, offered her the ring and asked her to marry me. She was shocked beyond belief but after a very short time which seemed to me like an eternity, she said yes. I nodded at the stewardess and she came down to where we were sitting holding a massive bunch of flowers. Her companion was in her wake carrying a bottle of champers in an ice bucket and the pilot announced our betrothal over the intercom much to the delight of our fellow passengers who applauded loudly. Donna was gobsmacked at the romantic gesture and absolutely loved the ring, I was on cloud nine because she'd agreed to marry me. I knew that nothing on God's Earth would ever part us and I was going to spend the rest of my life with her.

Donna's 30th Birthday

Biffer & Ben

In May of 1985 we decided to buy a golden retriever puppy. Some friends of ours had a lovely dog of the same breed, his name was Barney and he was a cracker; really obedient and gentle natured. We found a breeder who was highly recommended and arranged to go and choose a pup. The pick of the litter was a lively sandy coloured ball of fluff with huge paws and big floppy ears and we fell in love with him. Donna picked him up and he nearly licked her face off. Over in the corner behind the TV set there was a bit of a kerfuffle and suddenly there appeared this cream coloured, almost white little pup with the TV mains lead between his teeth. He was tousing it and trying to shake it, it was hilarious to see and the breeder said that this one was the naughty one out of the litter. You've guessed it, we had him as well. We named them Biffer and Ben, {Biffer being the cream mischievous one}. Donna worshipped them like the children she'd never had and Ben bonded with her almost immediately. He followed her around like a little lost boy and as soon as Biffer went to sleep, he'd come and steal extra cuddles from his new mother. Biffer didn't give a shit about anything except playing and chewing anything that he could pick up. I recall one occasion when Donna borrowed a pair of mega-expensive designer shoes from her wealthy friend Vicky who owned Barney the retriever. She left them by the bed when we retired for the night and Biffer sneaked in and snaffled one. He chewed it to pieces and on discovering his crime, Donna was totally devastated. We couldn't scold him as he'd already done the deed and she couldn't replace the shoe as the pair was a one-off from the most exclusive shoe emporium in Sheffield. Vicky was wonderful about it, and being a dog lover herself, reassured Donna it wasn't the end of the world. The two brothers from the same litter turned out to be as different as chalk and cheese. Ben was clever, attentive and eager to learn, Biffer was a lovable stupid retard whose lift didn't go all the way to the top. I suppose dogs are no different to humans really, some are much sharper than others. They were soon house trained and they loved the daily romp up through the Rivelin Dams. Ben was a confirmed water baby who jumped straight into any stream or dam and swam like a fish. Biffer was a coward where water was concerned, he'd put his front paws in and that was it. He loved running alongside the water's edge barking encouragement at Ben as he did his lengths. There was one particular dam which housed a large family of ducks. They'd usually congregate at one end or the other and it was Ben's main goal in life to catch one. It was hilarious to watch as he took a running leap into the water and started swimming after the ducks. They would always, quite naturally, keep just ahead of him until they reached the other end then they would take flight and alight back at the opposite end. Ben would patiently turn around and swim back to the other end in the unlikely hope of a capture. The ducks would wait until he was nearly upon them and simply take off for the other end again. I could just imagine the ducks saying to each other "Here comes that bleedin' barmy twat of a dog again, let's wind him up and give him some exercise."

What Goes Round Comes Round

My summer season in 1985 was a corker. I was at the Opera House in Scarborough in a three way bill topper with my old pal David Copperfield and the vent from London, Roger De Courcey. I rented a little terraced house in Seamer for the season and Donna, me and the pups settled in beautifully. I took a portable TV into my dressing room so that Donna could watch Coronation St on Mondays and Wednesdays. I had the best spot in the show, closing the first half, I was a Yorkshire lad in a Yorkshire resort working to a predominantly Yorkshire audience and I was storming them every night. On the bill was a brilliant girl impressionist called Hilary O'Neil and we became best of mates and still are to this day. We have the same wicked sense of humour and every Christmas we send each other the most obscene cards. I've got every card she's ever sent me and they go up every year on my panto dressing room wall and I piss myself whenever I read them. They are not for the feeble-hearted.

David Copperfield would close the show as he's pretty hard to follow and he'd storm them every night. He was going through his heavy drinking period in '85 and he actually had draught lager on tap in his dressing room along with copious amounts of port and brandy though I never saw him go on pissed.

After the show we'd often go over to the Wallis's holiday park to see the late night cabarets and meet the other acts who were in the town. The manager was a lovely bloke called Nigel Hudston and he always made us so welcome at his bar. One night just after the finale of our show I saw Nigel backstage looking rather flustered as he went into Roger De Courcey's dressing room. Let me just explain something about the Opera House. It was a very old building and all the dressing rooms had large air vents in the connecting walls and because of this you could hear every word spoken next door. I was by no means eavesdropping but I could hear Nigel explaining to Roger that Duggie Brown had let him down at the last minute and he had a full room but no cabaret. Roger said he'd do it for eight hundred and fifty quid and Nigel said that he only had a maximum budget of two hundred and fifty which is what Duggie was on for the night. Roger sneered at him and said (and I quote his words exactly),

"You can take your two hundred and fifty pound notes and stuff 'em up your fucking arse one by one." As a very dejected Nigel left Roger's inner sanctum I popped my head round my door and beckoned him to my room.

"Why didn't you ask me?" I enquired. "I'll do it for you for two fifty, what time do you want me on?" He said "How soon can you get there?" I hadn't even taken off my monkey suit which I wore for the finale so I said I'd drive straight over and go straight on. I've never seen a man so relieved but the icing on the cake was that I went on and stormed them for him. The word had gone round that Duggie was ill and they were all expecting no cabaret so when they announced that I had volunteered to stand in at the last minute, I was a hero. Nigel never forgot the favour which I did him and he gradually moved up into the very top tier of show-biz bookers. I did him another big favour about seven years later which got him out of the shit for a second time, I'll tell you about it in a later chapter. Over the years, Nigel has given me some great work. He's one of the real gentlemen of our notoriously bent profession and I'm proud to call him a friend. As I entitled this chapter, what goes around, comes around.

Let me dwell for a while on my mate Roger De Courcey. I really like old Roger, I really do, but he can occasionally be a full weight prize twat. He even admits it himself that he can be a really horrible obnoxious bastard when he wants to be. I love his puppet Nookie Bear, he fuckin' hates it. It's a means to an end as far as he's concerned. He started off as an opera singer and he even made it to the chorus in one of the big opera companies but sadly he progressed no further. He achieved stardom by winning the first ever grand final of the New Faces talent show. As I described in my first book, I met him at a big Royal gala show in the mid-seventies which was held at the Wakefield Theatre Club. I thought his act was great but he didn't pull any trees up with the northern audience as he was trying to take the piss out of them and a southerner cannot get away with that under *any* circumstances. The bear got your utmost attention when he spoke which was very good for Roger as you wouldn't be watching his lips moving. Ventriloquism is a fine art mastered by very few performers, the great ones being Ray Alan, John Bouchier and the daddy of 'em all Neville King. Roger is a very average vent, but a very good act so people don't seem to worry about his technical shortcomings as they focus their attention on what Nookie is saying. There's a wonderful story went around the business a few years ago regarding Rogers ability as a vent. His agent rang him to say he'd fixed him a gig at an event where the audience was predominantly deaf. He immediately complained that he couldn't possibly attempt to entertain a deaf audience as they wouldn't hear what Nookie was saying. His agent replied "It's OK Roger, they can all read lips".

Roger had the difficult job of opening the second half and coupled with the fact that he was taking the piss out of the north and it's inhabitants, he was really struggling for laughs. I tried to drop gentle hints to him that he was stirring the cauldron that is the North-South divide and they wouldn't take it from a Southerner. Nearly every night as I sat in my dressing room around 7-40pm, I'd hear two bangs accompanied by loud cursing, the first bang was Roger kicking his dressing room door open and the second one was Nookie hitting the wall.

Twice a week on Mondays and Wednesdays I'd have Donna, three or four dancers and Hilary all firmly glued to the portable telly watching Coronation St. On this particular evening, Roger entered my dressing room by kicking the door and bellowing about what a shower of cunts the audience were. He was disturbing the viewing of all present so I just said to him in a friendly manner, "Roger, either come in and be quiet or fuck off out, the lasses are trying to watch the telly". He glared at me then turned round and left with a mighty slam of my door. We all took it with a pinch of salt as we were used to his occasional rants. Another thing about old Roger that season was his breath. He was having dental problems which he was trying to sort out but they were causing him to have the foulest smelling breath on the planet, he could peel wallpaper with it. That same night we were lined up backstage for the finale and just before I had to climb the four steps to the on-stage set, Roger jabbed me in the chest with his forefinger and snarled "You! My room after the show". Now most red blooded males don't like being poked in the chest, in my book it's possibly the most antagonistic and aggressive gesture which will usually result in a swift broken nose. As soon as he'd done it I had to go on stage to take my bow so I had no time to react. I was fucking seething with anger as I turned to watch him come down the stage to take his bow to practically no applause. The duration of the finale and the final song allowed me the time to calm down and compose myself because I knew there was going to be a reckoning after the show. I walked into his dressing room and quietly closed the door; I didn't slam it or raise my voice. I was ice calm and had already decided that I wasn't going to hit him because I knew that I was angry enough to put him in the hospital if I did.

"What's your problem Roger?" I asked.

"How dare you tell me to fuck off in front of those scum dancers".

"Roger, it was a friendly *fuck off* not a nasty FUCK OFF or an aggressive *fuck off*. and as far as I'm concerned those dancers are lovely polite girls who definitely don't qualify as scum. Oh! and while we're at it, I seem to recall that you married a dancer. Let me just tell you that if ever you poke me in the chest again you'll not be needing that dentist you're seeing, cause you won't have any fuckin' teeth. Oh! Just one more thing Roger, why don't you try eating some cat shit, it'll tone your breath down a bit" I left after that and the next night he was as right as ninepence and he apologised for poking me.

We used to take Biffer and Ben into the theatre on most nights and after the initial fussing round all the dancers for a stroke and a belly-rub they'd settle down in my dressing room and sleep. I had to keep the door closed as Biffer was prone to exploring. He actually wandered casually onto the stage one night during my act and sat next to me. You can imagine the "Ahhs" from the crowd as this gorgeous, gangly creamy coloured retriever pup made his stage debut. He was the company hero one night when he wandered into Roger's dressing room while he was on stage and did a huge shit smack in the middle of the floor.

Pumping Iron & Tony Toms

The first thing I always did when I hit a new town for a season was to find a gym so I could carry on weight training. Donna was training with me every day at my own gym in Sheffield although she only used light weights and high reps to maintain her aerobic fitness. The gym which we found in Scarborough was called "B-Js" and was owned and run by a nice couple called Bill and Julie. Neither of them had ever remotely heard of me but they were secretly very chuffed that the ex golden girl of British athletics was training at their gym. I coached her as a couple of years before I'd taken and passed my NABBA instructor's course. Donna had a wonderfully aesthetic physique due to her athletics background but her best assets were her legs. Due to her being a sprinter as opposed to a distance runner, her thighs were very well developed and well muscled. The quadriceps muscles in the thighs are the most stubborn muscles to develop and grow. They need intense and highly concentrated training which is painful and slow to show results. You may have seen bodybuilders strutting about with sleeveless vests on to show their upper arms and big shoulders but because they've neglected their leg workouts their skinny legs looked way out of proportion. We used to have a nick-name for them at my gym, we'd call them "NFL"s. {No fuckin' legs}.

Julie was training to compete in the Miss North East Britain which was to be held in Bradford later that year in autumn. She persuaded Donna to become her training partner and very soon, Donna was training with a vengeance and growing very quickly. The word soon got around the bodybuilding fraternity that she had taken up the sport and she was soon doing interviews with the various magazines that covered the sport. She was forced to retire from athletics far too early due to a serious Achilles tendon injury which wouldn't heal but now she had a new sport to compete in. The competitive bug bit her in a big way and she applied the same intensity in her gym training as she'd done in her athletics days. Because of her celebrity as a sportswoman, she suddenly gave credibility to a sport which was widely perceived to be only for freaks. Her only drawback was the posing routines which she would have to learn before she could compete successfully. In any bodybuilding show, the competitors must each do around eight or nine mandatory poses which show off certain body parts to their best advantage. The way in which they change from one pose to the next has got to be graceful and artistic and competitions could be won or lost by the pose-downs at the end. Donna didn't do *"graceful"*, she was the clumsiest human being I'd ever met, she dropped everything. When she first moved in with me I had a full set of beautiful and expensive Gansey pottery which I'd bought in the Isle of Man in 1981. Within nine months of her moving in she'd smashed every single plate leaving me with a solitary gravy jug. *Grace* was not in her make-up so I had to find someone who could help her with her posing. My second cousin was a very successful and knowledgeable body builder. His name was Johnnie Stocks and he was BIG. He'd already won the NE Britain and had placed highly in the Mr Britain. John was huge, his arms were around twenty inches his chest was fifty four and his thighs were like railway sleepers. He was a wonderful poser and when we got back to Sheffield after the summer season, he took over as Donna's coach. He ran a spit and sawdust gym called "Fizzical" and he soon had Donna shifting some heavy iron. She was taking loads of vitamin supplements and obeying all John's dietary advice. Bearing in mind that Donna's appetite is gigantic, she can eat three more potatoes than a pig and not put weight on. Thanks to John's help, she did put weight on, but it wasn't fat, it was all muscle. She'd only been training for about five months when she entered the NE Britain and the worst possible thing happened, *she won.*

She'd really got the bug now and bodybuilding took over her life. I knew how much hard work and pain was in front of her but I didn't try to discourage her because I knew she wanted to reach the top of this sport just as she'd reached the top as a sprinter. Sadly, in all sports there are cheats and when Donna was running for Gt Britain in three Olympic Games, 1972, 76 and 1980, she was up against the

Eastern bloc who were all on steroids. When she ran against Marita Koch in Moscow she was virtually competing with a man. I recall Donna saying that when the gun went off, all she saw was the East German's arse. She broke the world record that day in a time of 48.88 seconds and it will never be broken by a clean athlete.

Bodybuilding was and still is utterly rife with steroids and I always detested it. When I first started training as a teenager it was all about physical fitness and strength. My heroes were Reg Park and Steve Reeves; they were big strong men who never took a steroid in their lives. If I found out that any of the members at my health studio Intashape were taking or selling steroids they were immediately barred. I was aware that my Donna was in for some heartache on two fronts, first she would be up against girls who were on drugs. The second problem was that unlike a race, where the first across the line is the winner, body builders were *judged*, sometimes unfairly. It was all in the eye of the beholder and I've seen many a show where the obvious winner was placed second or third. I'd warned her what she was up against but she tackled her new sport with the same total dedication and tenacity as she'd done as a sprinter. The word soon got round that the golden girl of British athletics was a bodybuilder and the sharks came cruising. The press were all over her as were the bodybuilding magazines and it caused a certain amount of bad feeling amongst her fellow competitors who were merely jealous at the exposure she was getting. This was coupled with the fact that Donna was a very beautiful looking woman while a large number of the "lady" body builders took large amounts of ugly pills and could haunt houses.

A few years previously I'd become very friendly with a guy called Tony Toms who was the Sheffield Wednesday trainer when Jack Charlton was managing them. He was an ex SAS man and a more larger than life character you couldn't hope to meet. He was a devoted fanny-rat and would fuck a spider if he knew which set of legs to open. We took the piss out of each other constantly as I am a devoted Sheffield United supporter and Wednesday were doing really badly at the time. He'd never been that much into weight training even though he was built like a brick shithouse. I used to go up to the gym he'd fixed up at Wednesday's ground and help and advise him on specific exercises for individual body parts and he soaked up the knowledge like a sponge. He was also a great practical joker as I was to discover much to my shame. One day I was up at his gym and we were both pumped up from the workout. He came in with a blue and white Wednesday shirt and asked me to put it on.

Let me try and explain for anyone who's not from Sheffield; the rivalry between Wednesday and United is unequalled anywhere in the country. You can have Manchester's United and City or Liverpool and Everton or any of the London and Brummy teams, in Sheffield it's tribal warfare. You're either red or blue and that's it. My grandfather was a rabid Wednesdayite who would not have the colour red in his house. The derby games in the season draw thousands to Hillsbro' and Bramhall Lane. For a Unitedite to put on a Wednesday shirt was the ultimate sacrilege so I politely hinted for him to fuck off.

"Oh come on Knutty, it's only for my office wall" he pleaded.

I reluctantly agreed and we had the Wednesday photographer take the picture right outside the main entrance. Two weeks later I was the laughing stock of the city as the rotten bastard put the picture in the Sheffield Wednesday match programme. It took some living down I can tell you. He was always coming up with bright ideas to improve the fitness of the players and one of these brainstorms involved taking them up onto the Derbyshire moors to yomp across the heather like SAS men. Never one to miss an opportunity to take the piss out of Wednesday, I was telling my audiences that while they were up there they played a game against the sheep - the sheep won four-nil.

My favourite Tony Toms story concerns his wonderful British bulldog, Henry. Henry had a head bigger than a football and was built like a tank. He used to mount bench press machines in the gym and try to fuck them, much to the amusement of the lads. He was as soft as arseholes with humans, but he didn't like other dogs. He loved bitches for obvious reasons, but dogs were a definite no-no and Henry was strong enough to do a lot of damage. When Tony was working down at the ground, he'd keep Henry in his grotty old V12 Jag which he'd park outside the player's entrance. One particular lunchtime he was allowing Henry to do his ablutions in the car park when up drove another one of Sheffield's great characters, a bloke known as Italian Ted. Now Ted was the manager down at Josephine's night club in town and he was a right bleedin' nutter. Don't get me wrong, he was a smashing bloke but he had a dodge, he really fancied himself as a hard man. The funniest thing about Italian Ted was his accent. He spoke fluent English, but with a broad Italian/Sheffield accent and I would piss myself laughing whenever he opened his mouth. He also suffered from a severe case of Tyrette's syndrome, the swearing disease. A typical "Ted" exclamation would be something like: "Ar don't tek no bluddy fuckin' messin' abart frum nobody me pal, am fuckin' tellin' dee nar, ar fuckinwell goo straight in wit' bluddy eead and stick t' nut on de bastards". (I sincerely hope that any reader from south of Nottingham was able to decipher that last phrase").

Ted had a very large German shepherd dog which was wonderfully clever and highly trained, on this occasion he had the dog with him in the car. As soon as Tony saw that he was going to let the animal out he shouted to warn Ted that Henry was out having a sniff and a pee and not to let him out.

"It's OK Tony, he's bluddy friendly, he'll not hurt your dog".

"I know he won't, it's Henry who'll hurt him, he's a little bastard with big dogs".

"What dar bluddy talkin' abart Tony, if he comes near mar bluddy fuckin' dog he'll be in for sum trubble ar can bluddy fuckin' well tell dee dat".

"Please Ted I'm warning you, keep him in the car till Henry's finished".

Ted wouldn't take heed and he let the Alsatian out. In a flash, Henry was on him, he grabbed him by the throat and he was shaking him as though he was an old slipper. Tony managed to pull him off but he'd torn open his upper chest. The poor dog was in a right state and lying on the ground with Ted prodding it with his foot and saying "Gerrup dar bluddy pufter, gerrup and fight". Fortunately, the poor dog survived the attack and Henry carried on shagging bench press machines. Tony told me that story just exactly as it happened, I thought I'd share it with you.

Tony, or Tomsy as everyone called him, left the club and opened a real heavy "Iron Man" type of gym in the Lane Top area of the city. He took over Donna's training and he was a fierce taskmaster. He had her shifting weights which most *men* couldn't lift. I could have coached her myself and although I was technically better qualified than Tomsy, I wouldn't have been able to motivate her as well as he did. *His* motivation had an amazing effect on her progress and she just got bigger and better. She was taking massive amounts of vitamin supplements which were costing her nothing thanks to her new sponsor Tom Tayback. He was an American millionaire who owned a company called Sports Star and he'd seen Donna in a magazine and offered her his sponsorship. Donna entered the 1987 NABBA Miss Britain which was held at the Blackpool Winter Gardens. She was looking amazing as I applied the bloody awful false tan which all the competitors had to wear. She'd had the skimpiest posing bikini made and thanks to a dance choreographer, her posing was spot on. The main business and pre-judging of a bodybuilding show is done in the afternoon and all the contestants have their supporters shouting for them to "Beef it" as they go through their posing routines. That afternoon in Blackpool I was nervous as a kitten as the Miss Britain girls were called out for their first line-up. This was the point in the show when every competitor was on the stage together so that comparisons could easily be made. Donna was the fourth out and as I examined the other girls I was able to assess her chances. NABBA judges were going through a phase where the criteria for a top place seemed to be "Big is Best". There were seventeen entrants and as they emerged from the wings onto the stage and I realised that there were about four other girls who were on a par with Donna, a couple were bigger and more evenly proportioned than she was but this went right out of the window when the last girl made her entrance. She was a fucking monster, she stood a bit short of six feet tall and she had a back as wide as Canada. Her arms were probably seventeen inches and she was ripped to shreds. Being ripped is a bodybuilding term for having the absolute minimum of subcutaneous body fat just beneath the skin layer so that the muscle sinews and vascularity are visible.

When Donna came out from the dressing rooms after the pre-judging she was OK but she knew she wasn't going to win. What did shock me was when she told me of one of the "Lady" contestants who was also very big but wouldn't place as she wasn't ripped enough. She had to wear two pairs of posing briefs because her clitoris had grown so large it looked like a penis. The problem with taking large doses of steroids without any form of medical supervision is the damaging side-effects. With men it can make them moody and violent, they also take on minor feminine traits like growing breasts or "Bitchtits" as they're known in the sport. Women, however, take on male characteristics like growing facial hair, their breasts shrink and their clitoris grows. I had to laugh when Donna, who is naturally quite demure, whispered to me, "Bobby, one of those girls has got a dick".

It was a foregone conclusion, the big lass won it and Donna came fourth. I was proud of her, she posed like a graceful ballet dancer and got a good ovation from a very partisan crowd. It just made her more determined to win next year. I was beginning to have mixed feelings about it all because to stand any chance of winning, she was going to have to spend more time in the gym than she did at home with me.

A time of affluence

The Tale of 33 Coffin Dodgers

The 1985-6 panto found me back in my favourite theatre in the world, The Crucible. It was to be the first of a long collaboration with one of the most talented and sweetest human beings I ever knew, a man called Mike Kay. Mike was the assistant artistic director at the Crucible and we did five consecutive pantomimes together. The first was Dick Whittington and it reunited me with my old mate David Ross who played the dame. You may recall in an earlier chapter, I'd worked with him in Alan Bleasedale's "It's a Madhouse" in 1982. He had never played dame before and he was sheer talent on legs, you'd have thought he'd been doing it for years. I was over the moon to discover that Mike had cast Finetime Fontaine and Rob McCulley as captain and mate. They were both extremely funny men in their own right, but to put them together as a double act was pure genius on Mike's part. During rehearsals, Mike and I changed so much of the original script that we jokingly agreed that we should have writing credits in the programme. The bare bones of the original script is all that was left and the bloody writer got all the credit and all the chuffin' money for our hard work. We decided that if we worked together again, I would write the panto and Mike would put it all together.

The Dick Whittington panto of 85/86 was a record breaker and was to be the benchmark for all the following ones which we did together. The families flocked to see my return and "Eyup Knutty" rang deafeningly once more around that wonderful auditorium. The slosh scene was utterly memorable thanks to the antics of Finetime, Rob, David and I. We looked forward to the slosh (or custard pie) scene every single performance as I would be covered in eggs and flour which usually went down my trousers, they'd fill a welly with jelly and make me put that on my foot. My face and hair would be covered in slosh and the kids in the audience would scream with laughter.

I recall one particular matinee performance when we'd had a

pretty bad snowfall the night before. Sheffield, for some inexplicable reason, cannot deal with snow. OK, I know it's a very hilly city, but when we get a heavy snowfall the whole transport system grinds to a halt and the place is totally gridlocked. I was still living in Broomhill which was walking distance to the theatre so I made it in with no trouble, as did the rest of the cast. We had a dozen or so school parties booked for the matinee as usual, they all gradually rang in saying they couldn't make it due to the snow. We were due to go up at 2-00 and at 1-45pm there wasn't one single person in the auditorium. We'd all got our costumes and make-up on and were all secretly looking forward to an afternoon off when a call came down from front of house that 33 pensioners had arrived in a mini-bus from Wakefield. Mike decided that we'd have to go on and do the show but there were no children in the audience so how was I going to do my kid's spot at the end. I couldn't get three wrinklies up to do Old MacDonald's Farm could I? We ended up sending three usherettes out into the street to round up some volunteers for a free show and a present from Knutty. We were lucky and I managed to do the songsheet with the little kiddies who'd come in for an unexpected freebie. We sat the pensioners all around the front row and gave them free drinks at the bar in the interval, they loved it. It was bloody hard work though, trying to drum up the energy to keep going when there was virtually no reaction from the audience. The comics feed off the laughter and the timing goes right out of the window when it doesn't come. The show came down twenty minutes early but at least we went on and did it. That's Showbiz folks!!!

The Best Day of My Life

The panto finished on the 18th of January 1986 and on Monday the 20th I married my precious Donna. I woke up feeling like a child on Christmas morning; the excitement which I felt was indescribable. To uphold the tradition of not seeing the bride on the morning of the ceremony, Donna had stayed with our friend Vicky. The night before I had held my stag night at Josephine's night club with some good mates but I'd told Donna she could join us if she liked so she turned up with a couple of her pals and a great night was had by all.

John Peller was my best man, after all we'd been pals for nearly twenty years and I couldn't think of anyone better suited to look after me on my big day. I'd had a new suit made for the wedding - in pink. I kid you not as you'll witness from the wedding photographs somewhere in this book. I thought I looked great but I suspect everyone else thought I looked a right twat. JP took me to the register office in his lovely Daimler coupe. The plan was for us to marry officially at the register office then go straight off to Sheffield Cathedral and have it blessed by the Bishop of Sheffield. My good friend David Wosskow who was my solicitor's cousin, offered to chauffeur Donna in his brand new Bentley Mulsanne Turbo. When I arrived with JP at the registry office I was surprised to find both the BBC and ITV waiting for us so they could film it for that night's news programmes. My Princess duly arrived and as soon as she got out of the Bentley the wind blew her hat off. Everyone was chasing it and JP finally caught it while at the same time trying to keep his Bobby Charlton "comb-over" hair in place. She was wearing a gorgeous blue and white suede and leather suit and she looked absolutely wonderful. I'd had a large port and brandy to steady my nerves earlier in the day and the ceremony went like clockwork. We came out and posed for the TV cameras and the photographers then Donna shot off in the Bentley back to Vicky's to get her wedding dress on.

I was gobsmacked when I arrived at the cathedral, there must have been five or six hundred people waiting outside. They were

Gotcha!

cheering me as I got out of JP's Daimler and egging me on with typical northern banter. The TV cameras had set up again so they were definitely going for it in a big way. I didn't have to wait too long before Donna arrived out side the Cathedral and when I saw her in her magnificent cream coloured wedding gown I realised that this was it for me. My life was at a new beginning and I was going to spend the rest of it with my beautiful, gentle lady. Her gown was the same colour as David's Bentley so the colour coordination was spot on and the crowd cheered her as she stepped out onto the pavement.

I walked her down the aisle and I was the proudest man on the planet. It was a lovely ceremony and the Bishop did us proud, bless him. When we got back outside I was in a whirl as the TV people wanted to talk to us, the smudgers wanted to take their photos and there was even a chimney sweep turned up for good luck. We all drove off eventually to the reception which was held at my dear old pal David Baldwin's Omega Banqueting Suite. I'd just invited close friends and family to the actual reception but I'd planned a free for all in the evening with lots more people plus the panto cast whom I'd just finished working with two days previously. Dear reader, I cannot begin to tell you how perfectly my wedding day went, although there is a tag line at the end which very nearly fucked it up completely.

My guests for the reception included my lovely adopted sister Jaquie Toye who I told you about in my first book. My old mate Emlyn Hughes and his wife were there also, I'd worked with Emlyn so many times on the after dinner circuit and he'd worked with Donna when she was a regular guest on "A Question of Sport". I had two big surprises planned for Donna that day, the first of which was her wedding present. She was running round in a bright red VW Golf GTi with fat wheels and spoilers on it. It was a flying machine which went like shit off a shiny shovel; it was also a police magnet. She used to bomb up and down the motorways in this little road rocket and I was worried about her safety and her driving licence. I called in to see my mate Mick Muscroft who was the MD at

TC Harrisons, the main Ford dealers in town. I told him I was looking for a wedding prezzy for Donna and he showed me this brand new limited edition Escort XR3 convertible in all white. It was colour co-ordinated with a white hood, white alloy wheels and white leather seats. It was a drink on a stick and I arranged for it to be parked outside the main entrance of the Omega with a big pink ribbon around it and "I LOVE YOU" for the front number plate. She was over the moon when she saw it as we pulled up outside Baldwin's.

The next surprise took a bit more arranging but it so well worth it. I was at the time, and still am, one of the honourary vice presidents of the Bolsterstone Male Voice Choir. They have in the past won the world championship choir award and a finer bunch of blokes you couldn't wish to meet. Their president in those days was a man called Terry Ardisty and I rang him for a favour. I'd found out from Donna that one of her favourite songs in the world was "Some Enchanted Evening" from the musical South Pacific. I asked Terry if he could scrounge together about half a dozen of the lads to sneak into the Omega during the reception and at a given signal, enter the room and belt forth the aforementioned song. He said it would be a pleasure and that it would be the choir's wedding present. During the meal, big David tipped me the wink that the choir had arrived. He'd actually put us in a small annex to the main banqueting room which he curtained off to make it more intimate. When I gave him the nod, the curtains opened and there stood not six, but twenty of the lads all resplendent in their matching blazers. They sang Some Enchanted Evening in the sweetest harmonies you ever heard and I swear to you there wasn't a single dry eye in the place. It was one of the most moving experiences of my life and even now as I sit here describing it to you, I'm filling up. Terry did me proud that day, he's sadly no longer with us but I'll never forget him and those magnificent voices ringing round the room on that very special day. Big David gave them all as much food and beer as they wanted and wouldn't take a penny from me for it.

The night time bash was wonderful and my great mates Colin

Wedding prezzy

Me & JP

Fingers Henry and Lance Edwards came and did me their hilarious cabarets much to the pleasure of my guests. I'll tell you about Lance in another chapter, he deserves one all to himself. There were over a hundred people there and half way through the evening, big David wheeled out massive joints of sirloin and turkey. He gave everyone magnificent thick-cut sirloin sandwiches with all the trimmings. When I asked him how much extra I owed him for the food he just said "You owe me fuck all Knutty, call it a wedding present". I had arranged for my new bride and me to spend our wedding night at the Nag's Head hotel in the Derbyshire village of Castleton. David Wosskow had kindly offered to take us over in the Bentley but I honestly felt he'd done more than enough as our chauffeur for the day so I allowed our friend Kevan Johnson to fix the transport. Our night at the Nag's Head and a champagne and lobster supper was his and Vicky's wedding present to us so I naturally assumed the transport would be top drawer as Kevan was one of the local big hitters. He and Vicky were probably mine and Donna's best mates at that time and she and Donna were like sisters. Donna must have been very lonely when she first came to Sheffield, the only people she knew were the ones whom I had introduced her to. We all went on dog walks together with Biffer, Ben and Barney and socialised frequently. Kevan owned a night club called the Limit which booked all the up and coming bands and some of the world's top bands appeared there before they were famous. It was dark, dingy and full of the great unwashed but it made him a very rich man.

The transport to Castleton arrived outside so everyone came to the door to see us off, without one exception, every soul was gobsmacked. It was a Pakistani in an old Lada which looked like it hadn't been washed for months. We all thought it was a joke but it wasn't, Kevan had fucked up royally. No one else could take us as they were all using taxis themselves so we had no choice. The vehicle stank of tobacco, stale curry and old age and I was thankful that Donna had been home to change out of her wedding gown. The poor Pakistani lad had no idea of how to get to our destination so I had to direct him and half way there it started to snow. I had visions of us spending our wedding night in a bleedin' clapped out Lada with an Asian cabby who had chronic BO. The first part of the journey to Castleton is a very long climb to a place called Fox House and he skidded and slewed his way to the top but he eventually made it and it's more or less all downhill from there. We arrived around 11-30pm very much relieved when we thought of the alternative.

I had Lobster, champagne and Donna, not necessarily in that order, yes it *was* the best day of my life.

Three days later we left on our honeymoon for a whole month in Lanzarote at a famous sporting resort called La Santa Sport. Donna got us a marvelous deal from Tchaerborg who used to be her sponsors. It was the place where all the international athletes went for winter training and the facilities were second to none. Our room was sheer luxury and although we did spend some time in the gym, the hotel room was preferable; after all we were on our honeymoon.

Angela

Sometime during the summer of 1965 I was appearing at the Cannon Hall Hotel with the Whirlwinds rhythm group. I recall nothing of the circumstances of how I met and quickly had a swift fettle with the young lady in question. It happened in the back of the group's van which was an old converted ambulance. It must have been one of the least memorable sexual experiences of my life as I can still to this day remember absolutely nothing about it. All I remember was that her name was Anne and that it was a swift opportunist fettle which to any red blooded nineteen year old would have been hard to refuse. I completely forgot about it until one night a few months later when we were appearing at the Sheffield Lane Top WMC. Just after our first spot, I was approached by a group of four or five people led by a fat little woman with a foreign accent. My Uncle Harry and Aunt Winnie were with me that night and Harry was a big bugger with huge shoulders like the rest of my clan, but with one exception, he was well over six feet tall. When he saw this little gathering surrounding me in what appeared to be a threatening manner, he was up like a shot and came over to see what was wrong. The little fat woman had a Spanish accent and she was having a right go at me in her broken English.

"You 'a dat Bob a Andrews, you make a my daughter pregnant, what a you a gonna do abart eet"

I was totally confused and I genuinely didn't know what the hell she was on about. She had a ginger haired Neanderthal looking character with her plus a couple more young blokes and a dark haired young lady. I told her I didn't know what she was talking about but she was having none of it and her voice was getting louder. The little fracas was starting to attract the attention of the club members who were looking on with gleeful curiosity. My Uncle Harry was starting to get annoyed with them and I could see they definitely didn't want a Barney with him so they left. The dumpy Spanish woman was shouting "You not a heard the last of a me Bob Andrews".

I was wracking my brain to think of any lasses I'd fettled during the last few months and suddenly it came to me. The girl who had been part of the little group looked very much like the girl from the Cannon Hall, she must have been her sister. I was praying it wasn't true as my future wife Pat was well pregnant and we were due to get married very soon. I thought to myself "Robert, you silly bastard, why can't you keep it in your trousers". I was hoping it would all go away but I knew it wouldn't. All you had to do to find out where I was performing was to look in the papers to see where The Whirlwinds were appearing. Sure enough about a week later, up popped little fatty and her entourage but this time she was armed with a letter from a solicitor stating that according to a Miss Anne Bradshaw, I had sexual intercourse with her on such and such a date and as a result of that union, she was pregnant. I knew I was in deep shit and the last thing I wanted was for Pat and her family to find out that I'd been unfaithful to her, they thought the sun shone out of my arse. The only thing I could do to keep it all quiet was to admit paternity and agree to speak to their solicitor. I agreed that after the child was born I would pay two pounds a week towards the upkeep of it but I refused to sign anything which connected me to these people.

A little girl was born in early April 1966 and I commenced paying them the two pounds which I actually took to their house as I didn't have a bank account. They named her Angela but I never saw her as they wouldn't allow me to. The girl Anne was now courting the ginger haired Neanderthal whom I'd seen on our first meeting at Lane Top club. They eventually married and about eighteen months later they informed me that they wanted a lump sum of two hundred pounds after which I would be released from any further obligation to pay them any more. I had told my Father about it as I had no secrets from him and his wise council was always worthwhile. He'd shown disappointment when I first told him of the situation but he'd not admonished me as he knew I was a buggerlugs where women were concerned. I told him of their proposal and he said I should first get it in writing from their solicitor and that they should pay for the cost of the letter. It was a good deal for if I paid two pounds a week until the child was sixteen, I would be paying a lot more than two hundred quid. My old Dad gave me the money and I paid him back at two pounds a week. I would have liked to have seen my little daughter but they said I was to have nothing to do with her as if I was some sort of criminal who might poison her mind. I gradually forgot all about her except for the odd times when she came into my mind and I wondered what she was like.

Many years later, it was either 1982 or '83, I got a phonecall from an old mate of mine who was now a big booking agent who looked after many of the top bands in the area, his name is Alan Wood. He told me that he'd had a call from a girl called Angela and that she wanted my phone number. He wouldn't give it to her as it was the agent's code never to give out a client's home number. He did, however, take her number and promised to give it to me. I was wondering who this *Angela* might be and couldn't for the life of me think of anyone of that name whom I knew. I rang the number on numerous occasions until at last I got a reply. I asked for Angela and she said "This is Angela speaking".

I said "This is Bobby Knutt speaking".

She said "Oh hello, I'm Angela your daughter".

It all came flooding back, I could have kicked myself for not catching on that it was *that* Angela. She told me that she'd like to meet me if I'd consent to it. *CONSENT TO IT?* I was a bit shocked but also secretly over the moon about her contacting me. I arranged to meet her in the pub around the corner from where I lived. I was desperately curious to see her and see what she looked like, what sort of person she was, whether she looked anything like me. It was a couple of days later when we met and I was so excited at the prospect of discovering all about my long-lost daughter.

The first thing I realised when I first set eyes on her was the positive realization that she was mine. I had obviously wondered in the past whether or not I was just a patsy for someone else, after all there aren't many girls with the lack of morals to just climb into your vehicle and allow you to have full sexual intercourse with them after one drink as her mother had done. The likeness was amazing, she even had my slightly crooked front tooth. She was very politely spoken and didn't have that broad Sheffield accent which prevailed in the area she was brought up in. She told me how she had known about me since she was a little girl but that her mother never spoke fondly of me. This irked me a little, but I didn't dwell upon it as I didn't know her well enough to do so. We sat for a good hour and I discovered she was a very bright girl indeed. I gave her my phone number and told her she could ring me anytime for anything at all. I tried to explain that I had never been allowed to have any part in her upbringing or anything else for that matter. She fully understood and briefly explained that she had been ostracized herself by her mother for being the reason for her mother's imagined stigmatic social downfall. I thought, how tragic to blame a child for being conceived out of wedlock and even worse, how peevish and petulant to do so. We parted very amicably with me feeling elated that I had rekindled a lost relationship which I was hoping would flourish as time went by.

I didn't hear from her again for over twelve years. I wondered why on many an occasion, but I didn't pursue it as I felt that she must have had her reasons.

Sometime during the spring of 1995 I got another phonecall from my agent pal Alan Wood. He reminded me of the call he'd had from an Angela many years before and that she'd rung him again wanting my phone number. Once again he'd taken *her* number promising to give it to me. It was a Barnsley number so I rang it and all I got was an answer-phone message in an American accent saying I was through to Paul and I should leave a message. I wasn't about to leave my number on a stranger's answer phone so I decided to persevere until I got through to a real person. After a few days I eventually got an answer from this Paul chappie but he didn't have an American accent, it was more like Barnsley. I asked him if Angela was there and she came to the phone. She seemed quite pleased to hear from me and I wasn't about to start interrogating her on why she'd left it twelve years to contact me again. She was living with this Paul in his house in Harley, a delightful little village next to the Wentworth estate. I arranged to meet them both the following Sunday lunchtime at the Rockingham Arms in Wentworth village, a fine hostelry that sold Theakston's Old Peculier on draught, my very favourite beer.

The next thing I realised was that I hadn't told Donna about Angela. There was no devious motive for not telling her, I had genuinely forgotten and I didn't think I was ever going to see her again. Donna took it in her stride as she does everything else and said she'd like to meet her. We rolled up to the Rocky Arms to find them both sitting outside in the sunshine. Angela had totally grown up into a very attractive young woman with jet black hair and the Latin features from her Spanish blood. He was a podgy, fair haired bloke with piggy eyes and a lot of front. He was a salesman of some sort and both Donna and I took an instant dislike to him. We couldn't put our fingers on *why* we disliked him. He had an oleaginous manner about him and he reminded me of a reptile. I asked him why the American accent on his answer machine, he said he'd worked in America a lot and sometimes lapsed into their accent. I thought to myself "What a twat". I could also see that Angela was besotted with him; she gazed adoringly into his eyes and hung onto his every word. They invited us back to their house for Sunday lunch but we politely refused as we'd already got the stuff in for a Sunday feast of our own. Sunday lunch with my Donna is sacred, our favourite meal of the week. He kept on insisting that we join them and his persistence was starting to annoy me but he wouldn't take no for an answer. I eventually convinced him that we were going home for lunch but we'd love to join them on some other occasion. I also learned from our conversations that he was in his mid thirties and he'd been married four times. Now I know that I'd had a rather colourful past with the ladies but I had been settled with Donna for over ten years now and I was utterly faithful, every vestige of my past promiscuity had passed from my personality. On the way home we both agreed that he was a dodgy character who

Angela

would only bring heartache to Angela. We were dead right. Donna could see that I was really pleased to have rekindled my relationship with my daughter. I'd not seen my other daughter Cherine for a long time but I had accepted it, as painful as it was. We saw them on occasion and did indeed join them for Sunday lunch, Angela was a wonderful cook but I noticed her drinking seemed rather excessive. Nearly every time we got together, she would end up slurring her words and I soon realised she had a problem apart from Paul.

My fiftieth birthday party on the 25th November 1995 was a magnificent evening with all my best friends and their wives in attendance. Big David Baldwin did me proud with his legendary catering. Meat and potato pie with mushy peas and thick gravy was wolfed down by all and sundry. The only thing which spoilt it was that arsehole Paul who proceeded to get very pissed and try to grope some of the ladies present. Everyone more or less knew each other but they were all curious as to who this gobby little git was who was annoying the ladies. Poor Angela was out of it too so I bunged them in a taxi and sent them home before either me or one of my mates chinned him.

I'll not dwell for long on Angela's relationship with this ugly little control freak, needless to say he nearly ruined her life with his constant philandering. Angela would leave him for a while and go to lodge with a girl friend then he would beg her to go back, promising never to do it again but he always did. Eventually, she came to live with us for a while. Donna was so kind and understanding, after all she was no relation to Angela but she treated her as if she was her own daughter. Angela changed her mobile number so he couldn't pester her any longer but he somehow managed to find out her new one. I rang him on one occasion and told him that if he didn't leave her alone I would go round and sort him out. He said he was going to ring the police and inform them that I was threatening him with violence. I don't think he did but he was the sort of little snidey little snitch who would go running to tell tales as he probably did when he was at school. I learned from Angela a few years later that he had hit her on numerous occasions and was violent when he'd been drinking. Had I known this at the time I would definitely have gone round and given him a fuckin' major good hiding, cops or no cops.

When Angela had been with us for a few months, she told us she was going to stay with her friends in Wakefield for a few days so off she went. When she'd been gone for over a week we'd not heard a word from her so I rang her friend's house. She'd not been there at all and they told me that she'd gone back to Paul. I was so angry that she could be stupid enough to go back to this monster; I washed my hands of her and decided that she deserved all she got. We didn't hear from her for quite a while but he soon did something so utterly callous and cruel that she finished with him for good. His persistent womanizing was always followed by showering her with gifts and begging for forgiveness, which sadly she always did. On this particular occasion, he took her on holiday to the Caribbean island of Antigua. Four days into the holiday he met a Canadian woman and left with her for Canada where he immediately *married* her. He'd left Angela alone on the island to find her own way home and thankfully this was the straw which broke the camel's back. The happy ending is that this Canadian woman goosed him for everything he had including his house proving that in some cases, what goes around comes around.

About a year later, Angela met a guy who worked at her place and as I sit here typing this chapter on the 27th August 2009, today is their second wedding anniversary. They have a lovely house near Doncaster and her husband Neil looks after her and loves her like no other could. She still likes the odd tipple but she's conquered the habit of drinking a lot more than is good for her. I'm convinced that her excessive alcohol consumption was brought on by the pressures of living with that cretin Paul. Neil is a big soft cockney geezer built like a brick shithouse and I love him as if he was my own son. His only fault is that he's a bleedin' West Ham supporter.

Lance Edwards

I said earlier that I'd tell you about one of by dearest pals, Lance Edwards. His father was one of the greatest Sheffield characters, in fact he was a legend. His name was Joe "Pot" Edwards and he had pottery stalls in the local markets. He was an esteemed figure as he shouted his spiel to the crowds which gathered around his stall to watch him juggling his pots with amazing dexterity and never ever dropping one. Lance was a real chip off the old block and his unbelievably cheery presence is guaranteed to light up any room he enters. Lance was a ducker and diver, I don't honestly think that he ever had a proper job. He frequented all the night clubs in the city and became a DJ at the "Penny Farthing" club which was *the* place for young posers and fanny merchants. There can only be one example of an E type Jag with a trailer on the back, yes, it was Lance's. He used it to transport his DJ equipment around to the various venues that used him. Where women were concerned, Lance had one rule, if it has a pulse, it'll fuck. Lance was a card carrying fully paid up fanny rat and women loved him. He had the patter and the looks but his main attraction was the fact that he was a genuinely nice guy, he didn't have a *bad* side.

When Lance decided that he wanted to be a comedian, he came to me for advice which touched me considerably. I remember one night I was doing a club in York so I offered to take him with me and let him do a spot on his own. The audiences in York were always easy and well behaved unlike some of the toss-pots we had to battle in other parts of Yorkshire, so I felt he'd be OK. Not too long before, Lance had been on Coronation St as an extra and was now making semi-regular appearances in the "Rover's" bar as a non speaking customer. I did my first spot at the York club and the chairman had agreed to let me put Lance on just before the main bingo session. I gave him a great build-up, telling the crowd that he was a regular in the Rover's Return and was shortly to be a new character in the Street. I could tell he was nervous, bless him, I'd just been on and torn the bollocks off 'em and he had to follow it. His bottle seemed to go and he died on his arse poor lad. I felt so sorry for him but I could see there was a lot of potential there for him to develop in to a very funny comic. He did exactly that and went out under the name of Shuggy Bush. He was a really funny guy who took to jesting like a duck to water. He went with my agent JP who soon got him well established on the circuit. I remember the early part of the 1984 season which I did at Butlins Pwllheli, I took him with me. It was just before I'd met Donna who was to walk into my life a few weeks later. Lance was a quick learner and he watched me work the theatre show and then the much rougher Spanish Bar. I did two totally different acts, one clean, the other a bit blue. He said he'd love to have a bash at the Butlins circuit, particularly as how one evening we pulled two sisters from Liverpool who volunteered to stay with us for the night. To Lance a Butlins camp was like having his own personal harem.

The main booker for the Butlins circuit was a bloke I'd known for a few years, a guy called Brett Creswell. I rang him and told him about Lance and that he'd be perfect for the camps. He said that he was booked up for the season in all his venues but he'd stick him one in at the end of the year as a sort of paid audition. Sure enough, he fixed him a date at Bognor Regis in October to do two spots, one in the theatre and one in the snakepit. I didn't have to tell him the drill, he knew he had to be crystal clean in the theatre and a bit nearer the knuckle in the late night gig. One vital thing I did warn him about was not to shag any of the staff, when he asked why I told him "Lance, they've had all season to cop for a dose of clap. There's diseases at Butlins that will frighten the shit out of penicillin, so stick to the punters". As I told him, I thought about the weekly bus that went from Pwllheli camp to the local pox clinic carrying redcoats and chalet maids all having contracted something nasty from their clandestine canoodling. When Lance had done his gig at Bognor, I rang him to see how he'd done. He told me that he'd stormed them in both venues and Brett Creswell was there to watch him. He promised him a season the following year. Lance then went on to tell me he'd had a great shag while he was there saying she was one of the chief redcoats. I called him all the silly bastards under the sun and reminded him about my warning. He said "Don't worry Knutty, she seemed a nice lass". I told him that germs don't differentiate between nice lasses or munters, they go for anybody.

One lunchtime about three weeks later I walked into "Henrys" bar in Sheffield centre and there was old Lance sitting alone at a table looking quite gloomy. I was most surprised because he was *never* melancholy, he was *always* cheerful. "What's up pal?" I enquired.
He looked up and said "I've just got the results back from a test at the spotted Dick clinic".
"Oh fuck me Lance" I exclaimed, "What've you got?"
"I've got the same thing that killed Robin Hood". I was baffled by his strange answer until he whacked his fist into his chest in the manner of an arrow striking him and at the same time uttering "SSSSSSSYPH". I was amazed that he could still muster the courage to make a gag of a very serious sexually transmitted disease. His main concern was the fact that while he was taking the antibiotics to clear it up, he couldn't have a drink. He was also devastated that until he got the all clear from the clinic he had to totally abstain from any sexual activity.
I could have cried for him and then I thought "There but for the grace of God". I'd done a fair bit of fettling myself in my time and I'd been very lucky to have kept a clean sheet. He's still one of my best mates and he confesses that these days he'd sooner have a curry than a fuck. He packed in being a comic a few years back but he's still just as funny when we get together for a jar or two. I love him like a brother.

Four Trees for Charity

Over the years, I, like thousands of other members of the entertainment profession have done more charity shows than I could count. We all usually referred to them as "Nowt jobs". I've done grand affairs at the Victoria Palace in London and the Dorchester Hotel, I've also done them in back street pubs and clubs. No matter where you do a charity show, they're always done to raise funds for somebody less fortunate than yourself. I recall last year I was involved in a massive show at Batley Variety Club (now known as the Frontier). I compered the first half of the show and the bill was a who's who of showbiz talent. All the lads turned out for this magnificent extravaganza to help a fellow musician who'd been on kidney dialysis for over fifteen years and was now desperately in need of a transplant. His name is Mike Ryal and a finer bass player would be hard to find. He'd been the MD for Tony Christie, Cannon and Ball and Jane McDonald and done a wonderful job despite having to spend many hours three times a week hooked up to his kidney machine. The show was organised by a guy called Neil Crossland who has a business called Stagewear Unlimited. He makes outfits and costumes for just about the whole of the showbiz fraternity and is one of the kindest blokes you could hope to meet. On the bill were Cannon and Ball, the Bachelors, Bernie Nolan, Jean Ferguson from Last of the Summer Wine, Paul Shane, Billy Pearce, Johnny Casson, Rick Wakeman, The Grumbleweeds and Syd Little. The show was a sellout and it raised twenty four thousand pounds on the night. Mike has had his transplant and now has a new lease of life.

Sometime in the early eighties when I was still living at my flat in Broomhill I received a hand written and hand delivered letter from the lady administrator at the Weston Park cancer hospital which was just at the back of my abode. The hand writing was beautiful and she was asking if I could go to this venue and accept a cheque on behalf of the hospital. I walked round to the hospital and asked if I could possibly see her. She came down to the reception area and invited me to her office for a coffee. Her name was Angela and she was young, free, single, highly intelligent and very good looking. I agreed to accept the cheque and she asked if she could come with me as the official representative of the hospital, well I wasn't gonna say "No" was I.

We had a swift visit to collect the cheque followed by a lingering meal at a nice restaurant and cupid's arrows were flying thick and fast in both directions. She asked me if I'd be willing to become a patron of the hospital's Day Care Unit which was there to house the patients who had just undergone the trauma of chemotherapy. They were allowed to stay in the unit until the effects of the chemo had subsided and then taken home. I agreed immediately and decided to dedicate all my charitable time and effort to that one charity alone. It wasn't too long before Angela and I were enjoying a very highly charged sexual affair. There were no strings attached and we just saw each other occasionally but we were like two wild things when we did get together. I continued for many years to raise money for the day care unit and made many good friends amongst the staff. I used to sell signed photographs to the people who came to see my live shows and as I was working nearly every night, the money rolled in. I still have all the receipts that Cynthia gave me every time I took them a box of cash. She was the lovely lady in charge of the unit and welcomed my visits warmly. I suppose over the years I raised quite a few thousand quid for them and it was a pleasure to do so. Angela eventually moved to another hospital away from Sheffield and got married, I hope she lived happily ever after as I never saw her again.

Because of my very close relationship with my manager JP I got to know all his Jewish friends and got on famously with all of them. I have such admiration for the Jewish people because of their extremely strong family values. The family is everything to them and *nothing* comes before it. JP was an obvious choice to oversee all the many charity shows which were held at the Kingdom Hall which I think also doubled up as a synagogue. The highlight of the Jewish calendar in Sheffield was the annual Maccabi ball. A kosher

LORD MOUNTBATTEN OF BURMA MEMORIAL FOREST

*Anglo-Jewry's tribute in honour of
a Great Man*

Lord Mountbatten of Burma Memorial Forest
Migdal Ha'Emek Israel

This is to record the planting of
FOUR TREES

in the name of

BOBBY KNUTT

with grateful thanks

by
Sheffield Maccabi

13th. March 1983   28th. Adar 5743

Signed Lou Stoltzman, President, JNF for Great Britain and Ireland.

meal was followed by raffles and dancing then a top cabaret. Over the years we had stars like Frankie Vaughan, Marti Caine and Bob Monkhouse, I even did it myself one year but unlike the big stars, I did it for JP and I could hardly ask for a fee could I?. I compered the Maccabi ball nearly every year for quite a few years and also did the charity auction for them. I knew who all the big hitters were so it was easy to blag money from them for the charity. At the end of the evening on the 1983 ball, I was called forward by my dear friend David Wosskow, (the chap who chauffeured Donna and I on our wedding day). Much to my surprise, I was honoured to be presented with one of the highest accolades that Maccabi can bestow. I was to have four trees planted in my name in the Lord Mountbatten Memorial Forest in Israel as a thankyou for the work I'd done over the years for Jewish charities. I was totally gobsmacked and quite overcome with emotion for this wonderful way of saying thankyou.

It's now twenty six years since my trees were planted so I suppose they'll be pretty tall by now. I've never had chance to go to Israel and find them but you never know, maybe one day.

Cottages & Cornwall

By the spring of 1986 I realised that my flat in Broomhill, as much as I loved it, wasn't adequate for Donna, me and two very boisterous golden retrievers. I'd had some amazing sexual adventures there and the memories of them will stay with me forever. I was beginning to realise that a woman's psyche is totally different to a man's. I had lived there with another woman for nearly four years, in fact I'm ashamed to say that there was still a photograph of Paula on the wall in the hallway. I was so insensitive to realise that this must have irritated Donna so much but she never said anything. Her pal Vicky was the one who told me how galling it must have been for Donna see this image of my ex girlfriend staring back at her every day. I realised what an inconsiderate thing it was and how thoughtless it was of me to be impervious to her feelings. I took it down and humbly apologised to my wonderful wife.

I'd got rid of my big Granada estate car and bought a brand new Toyota Landcruiser because I was booked for a full season down in the West Country doing the Haven-Warner holiday camps. This was another form of thanks from my great mate Nigel Hudston whom I'd helped out the year before when Roger De Courcey refused to help him. Donna and I had decided to sell the flat as soon as the season was over and look for something bigger and out of the city. The season was sixteen weeks, six nights a week in twelve different camps with every Friday off. I rented a big caravan on a private park not too far from Torquay which was a pretty good base of operations geographically. Also staying on the park were two great lads who I'm still great pals with, Billy Bean and Gary T Thompson. I'd done a tour of Germany round the bases with Billy a few years before when he'd been the drummer with a group called the Statesmen. He's a really good comic and he looks funny too, he's a big fat guy with a funny turn in one of his eyes like Ben Turpin and he's one of the nicest blokes in the business. Gary was very young and totally fearless; he did impressions and gags in a sort of Freddie

Starr style. Gary was one of the biggest fanny rats I'd ever met and his tales of his nightly conquests kept me and Billy in stitches. Every Friday morning, me and Billy would do the shopping for the Friday BBQ and piss-up, and Oh boy did we get pissed. Billy was a very good cook and he encouraged me with his simple but very effective marinades and rubs which he anointed his chickens with. Donna was still on the Butlins circuit but she drove down to Devon every single Thursday night so she could be with me for the weekend.

The only problem with doing a circuit like I was doing that year was the difference in the venues. Some were wonderful with great facilities and receptive audiences and others were comic's graveyards. The worst night for all the comics on this circuit was Saturday. The punters had all been on the roads all day stuck in the standard Devon-Cornwall traffic jams with their kids wailing and whining and the fat wife whinging. They'd all had a moan at reception because their curtains wouldn't close all the way to the middle and people would be able to see into their caravan plus the can-opener was missing. I had two different Saturday venues and I struggled for laughs at each one every single week of the season. The audiences were invariably lethargic, bad tempered and pissed. The last thing they were going to do was laugh at a comedian.

Some of the camps were down in the south of Cornwall so I'd bung Biffer and Ben in the back of the Land Cruiser and stay the night in the "Artiste's caravan". This bijou accommodation was always a van that was ready for scrapping and usually parked round the back of the cabaret room near the stage door and the bins. All the camps had the same acts every two weeks so I always followed the same acts at every camp. At one particular place which I stayed away at because of its distance from my base camp, I always followed this group who left the caravan like a fucking tip every week. There were cigarette butts every where, unwashed crockery just left on the table and empty food containers strewn on the floor. The bathroom was the worst with the toilet bowl left without having been flushed and skidmarks everywhere. I complained every week but nothing was ever done so I eventually started

135

driving the hundred miles back after the show rather than endure the squalor of that bleedin' filthy pig sty.

You see folks, show-biz isn't all glamour and glitz and sometimes it can be downright bloody dangerous. I remember one night I was at one of the best camps on the circuit. It was a huge place with the best cabaret lounge of the lot of them. It was a massive room with seating for about twelve hundred punters all on one level. It sloped upwards from front to back like a sort of amphitheatre so that everybody could see the stage without any restricted sight-lines. The house band at this gaff was the best of all the camps with three guitars, keyboards and two brass. In those days I always finished the act with Cavatina on the old Fender Strat followed by a medley of sixties pop songs which they all joined in with and it usually brought the house down. I'd never had a bad night at this camp and it was my favourite one of the whole fortnight. The sheer size of the place made it a daunting challenge for a lone stand-up comic and I could see how it would intimidate lesser men with less experience. The only negative thing about the room was the dance floor in front of the stage. You've got to get over that space with your comedy so you have to perform much bigger. On this particular night I'd only been on for about five minutes when this little fat lass about eighteen years old got up from her front row seat to the left of the stage and waddled right across the floor to her mates who were sitting on the front row stage right. She'd got a pint of ale in her chubby little paw and she was definitely a double bagger. (For the uninitiated, a double bagger is a girl who's so ugly that when you shag her, you put *two* bags over her head in case the first one bursts). She parked her fat arse down next to her mates and proceeded to talk very loudly much to the annoyance of the nearby punters who were trying to enjoy the show. I steamed in with a few choice lines and the audience applauded each one. After about five minutes, she got up and paraded back across the dance floor to her original seat so I steamed in again, she just stuck two fingers up at me and shouted "Fuck off ya cunt", in a broad scouse accent. I'd now got a new act which was building around taking the piss out of this foul-mouthed obese little gargoyle who kept on getting up and going to chat to her mates on the other side. The audience were getting annoyed with her, as was I and I'm surprised that the two bouncers who always stood at the back didn't make any effort to get her out as she was by now very drunk. She was sitting with what must have been her boyfriend, a scruffy looking individual who had his Doc Martins up on the table, he appeared to be asleep. He had a cadaverous look about him with a very pale skin like a drug addict. As I was picking up my guitar towards the end of my show, the gorgon returned to her original seat and started to bollock this bloke for not defending her when I took the piss. They were close enough for me to hear him say "I'll fuckin' do him then". He got up, he was well over six feet tall and he staggered over towards the front of the stage. Now I'm a comic, not a gladiator, I'm not a hard man although I've made it hard for one or two who thought they were. I very very quickly assessed the situation, he definitely wanted to punch me and I definitely wasn't going to let him. I was standing there in front of twelve hundred people in my best stage outfit with a very valuable guitar round my neck and this fucking cretin was about to mount the three steps which led onto the stage. As his foot touched the first step I gripped the finger board of my Stratocaster and held the other end of the guitar as if it was a machine gun. I then hit him as hard as I could with the end of the headstock right in the middle of his chin, you know, the bit where the dimple usually goes. I only pushed the guitar a matter of about nine inches but it did the trick, he went down like a sack of spuds. The band were pissing themselves laughing and applauding me, then the audience started clapping and finally the bouncers arrive to hoist him out, not before bleedin' time I thought. The little fat scouse troll was shouting and bawling at them using every expletive in her considerable repertoire so they hoisted her out as well. The audience was loving every minute and I got a standing ovation.

When I arrived there a fortnight later I was summoned by the camp manager for a very slight bollocking. She said she'd had a full report of the events two weeks previously and understood my actions but she'd rather I didn't assault any more of her guests. She also said that the police found a quantity of drugs both on his person and in his caravan. We parted friends.

The season eventually ended and we started the long trek home to Sheffield fully loaded to the back doors with all my stuff. I've never travelled light and I always take as many home comforts as I can carry so as to make life as comfortable as possible. Now began the task of finding somewhere else to live. It was 1986 and property prices were very reasonable. I'd spent a small fortune on the flat so I made a handsome profit when I sold it. We found a beautiful house in the old village of Stannington high up over Sheffield. It was two 18th century cottages which had been knocked into one with very old original sand stone fireplaces and oak beams everywhere. The plot was very large with a huge back garden and a separate garage for the E type. We moved in around mid autumn and I had to do some re-thinking about our furniture and paintings. The ceilings in the cottage were seven foot six high as opposed to fourteen feet at the flat. I had a magnificent antique Welsh dresser in the dining room which was a foot too tall for the cottage. There was a boudoir grand piano which wouldn't have even gone through the door and three beautiful Montague Dawson nautical limited edition signed prints. I'd bought them in a sale at an art dealer's which was closing down and I absolutely pinched them at three hundred quid each. They were very large but fitted perfectly on the spacious walls of the Victorian flat. I've always loved art and although by no means an expert, I just derive much pleasure from gazing at a good picture. There wasn't one single wall in the cottage which would have fitted any of them so I reluctantly sold them for a magnificent profit of three thousand one hundred pounds which quite took the sting out of not owning them any more. The piano went to a dear friend for his daughter's benefit and the dresser was bought by the geezer who bought the flat. The cottage was our little bit of heaven and we were to have twelve very happy years there.

The Strange Tale of the Vanishing Egg

The Crucible panto of 1986-87 was Jack and the Beanstalk, I wrote it and Mike Kay directed once again. We were becoming a formidable force in panto land and my usual cast of regulars just made it that bit more special. My dear old mate Finetime Fontaine played Fleshcreep the villain and he was wonderful. He opened the show on his own by emerging through a trap door onto a green lit stage, he had a very scary green made-up face and a Dickensian Mr Pickwick style out fit with a padded stomach. His entrance would be accompanied by a bright green flash and his opening line was delivered in loud stentorian tones, "MY NAME IS FLESHCREEP AND I *HATE* CHILDREN". He frightened the shit out of the really small kiddies and they always screamed and cried at his antics. I would be listening to the dressing room tannoy speaker enjoying every moment because the more they hated old Fleshcreep, the more they'd love old Knutty. It was a wonderful panto with some amazing special effects; we had an exploding car which gradually fell apart as the scene developed. We had a cottage for dame Trot which had an unending number of ways for the door to open; it was genius in its design and always got a round of applause when the Dame did her bit with it. The slosh scene was one of the best ever when we had to cook the Giant's "Din Din". The ingredients were on the Giant's din-din table which happened to be seven feet high with a ladder which enabled us to reach the table top. You can imagine the fun we had passing down the custard and jellies down to the recipients below. As usual I ended up getting the lot down my trousers and on my head - Paradise!!

Let me dwell on the slosh scene for a while. It's one of the most traditional and if done properly, funniest examples of live theatre that you'll ever witness. Charlie Caroli was the master of the slosh scene and it has to be planned and regimented to perfection. You don't just smash a custard pie into someone's face for no good reason, they have to get it when somebody else ducks or turns around. Most important was the recipe for the actual slosh, it had to be just the right consistency and not too watery. I taught the assistant stage manager at the Crucible exactly how to make up the slosh, her name is Ali Fowler and she's still there, although she's now a top boss. She became known affectionately as the "Slosh Queen". First you grate 3 sticks of Erasmic shaving soap into a large bucket, you then add about two tablespoons of glycerine which stops it stinging your eyes. Next you put a common kitchen whisk into the chuck of an electric drill then proceed to whisk it until it grows into a bucket full of stiff creamy white gunge. The ASM would then ladle it out onto paper plates ready for the delivery into the comic's face. Eggs were another common ingredient for the slosh scene because of their fragility and their utter yukkiness when broken on top of someone's head or poured down the front of their trousers. Rob's favourite trick was to not just pull my elasticated trousers away from my waist, but my underpants as well. This meant that I got this gooey mess right down to my goolies. It's not much fun trying to walk with broken egg shells stuck to your todger and testimonials.

I remember the most amazing thing happening during the slosh that year. Rob and Finetime both happen to be accomplished jugglers and we decided to use their juggling skills in the slosh. It went like this. I would throw them three eggs each and as I threw each egg I'd shout "One egg", Finetime would catch it and shout "One egg". It went on with "Two eggs", "Three eggs" and so on until they'd each got three eggs which they juggled. The audience was obviously dying for them to drop one but they never did, not once in 72 performances. The next bit was them throwing their eggs back to me which I had to catch in a large plastic bowl. They always used to throw them to my left or right in the hope that I'd miss one but I never did. Rob was a little demon when it came to mischief and he used to throw his eggs higher and higher and the crowd loved it when I just managed to catch them. Directly above the Crucible stage area are the walkways and girders which go to make up the roof space. They're all painted matt black so you couldn't really see them. On this particular night, Rob threw his last egg much higher than usual and guess what, it didn't come down. I swear to God we stood there in amazement along with the audience who laughed and applauded, but the bloody egg didn't come down. There could have only been one explanation for how it happened. I'm no scientist but I do know that when you throw an object up into the air, when it reaches its highest point, I think it's called the zenith, for a split second it stops, motionless, before it begins its descent to earth. The egg must have reached its zenith as it drew level with a girder and just stayed there because it did not come back. We all went off for the interval cuppa and the talk of the company was "Where the fuck's that egg?"

The show ended and as I was doing the curtain speech and thanking the orchestra, the egg came down and smashed on the stage right in front of me. Had I been standing a foot further forward it would have landed on my head, which would have been a true showbiz comedy miracle sent from Heaven. It must have rolled off its lofty perch and fallen back down onto the stage. We were in hysterics, the timing of the eggs return was so perfect yet uncanny. I can guarantee that a large percentage of the audience probably thought that it was a well planned gag but I swear to you on my Donna's life that it happened just as I've described it.

I Belt a World Class Superstar

1987 was another very busy year and I was fortunate enough to land a leading role in a YTV long running series called "How we used to live". It was made for schools and each series dealt with a particular period of English history spanning roughly twenty years. It was meticulously researched and all the props and costumes were either genuine period pieces or specially made for the job. I was to play Uncle Albert, the sort of head of the featured family in the series. The programme covered the period from 1952 to 1972 and all the major historical happenings of that period were dealt with as each episode was filmed. I was actually forty one years old in 1987 and I was playing a man who was to age from fifty two to seventy two. We had two directors for obvious reasons, one would never have been able to manage the workload of shooting, planning and editing twenty episodes. The producer was a guy called Ian Fell who also elected himself as one of the directors, the other director was a very talented lady called Carol Wilks, she was brilliant, and Ian wasn't. She'd sail through the scenes like a dose of salts because she knew exactly what she wanted before she arrived on set. Ian would fuck about for hours doing take after take which really annoyed the cast and crew.

I remember one episode where on of our family, a lad I'd watch grow from a boy to a young man, was killed in a smash on the new motorway. I had to cry at his funeral and thank God Carol was directing it as she knew that big emotional scenes don't come off if you have to do a lot of takes. She shot my crying close-up in two takes which was bloody marvelous. My motivation to induce the tears, which had to be genuine, I wasn't going for the glycerine down my cheeks, was my fathers death. I just stood there and thought of my lovely old Dad lying dead in the funeral home and the tears flowed.

We shot ten episodes in the spring and the other ten in the autumn which left me free to do a short summer season on the east coast holiday camps. I'd done them all before and they were OK as long as

Uncle Albert
in
'How We Used To Be'

you got on early enough before the crowd became pissed and noisy. The biggest gig on that circuit was the Primrose Valley holiday park; it was a massive sprawling mass of caravans which stretched as far as the eye could see. The cabaret room was huge with a very high stage that overlooked the fifteen hundred seats in the auditorium. You had to get stuck in straight away and keep batting with strong gags; it wasn't a room for subtlety and clever stuff, you had to go straight for the jugular. I'd always gone very well at Primrose, but this year they'd changed the rules to allow 14 to 17 year olds in without being accompanied by their parents. It was a big mistake as these youngsters were buying booze and sitting in gangs getting ratarsed. One night I had the misfortune to have a pack of these young bloods right on the front row and they were talking and shouting during my act so I steamed in with some lines which made them look like the scrotes that they were and got the usual rounds of applause from the crowd who were trying to listen to my act. I think someone must have complained to the manager because about half way through my show a couple of large bouncers came and hoisted them out. They didn't like that at all and shouted some banal obscenities at me as they left the room. I finished the act and got my stuff together, I had the guitar, the very heavy Fender amp and my suit bag. The carry out at Primrose was a bit of a bastard as it was down three flights of steps and out through a fire door into a sort of courtyard surrounded by very thick well matured rose bushes. I always carried everything down to the fire door first so that I could load up the Land Cruiser all at the same time. As I opened the tailgate, they came out of the darkness whooping and shouting like a bunch of demented Apaches, there was six of them, all in their late teens and a couple who looked a bit older.

"We all got fuckin' chucked out because of you ya fuckin' bastard" said one of these yobs. I was thinking I'm gonna get filled in here no danger. I'd have given my left bollock for a mike stand, they make formidable weapons but I'd left it at home as I always used the one at Primrose. I knew I was in for a pasting unless I did something drastic. I said "Who's the hardest man amongst you lot, eh? Come on who's the fuckin' top lad?" They pointed at the biggest and said "Him". I ran up to him as quick as I could and punched him straight on the nose as hard as I could, he was totally unprepared for the speed and ferocity of my actions and he staggered back and fell into the rose bushes, the thorns must have been agony. I didn't stop, I turned round and snarled at them "Right! Who's fuckin next, come on you cunts who's next?" I was in full "Gone berserk mode" and must have seemed like a fuckin' mental case to them. One of them said "Sorry mate, it weren't us it were 'im what wanted to cause trouble", pointing to the geezer lying in the rose beds "We'll take him away". They slunk off with their wounded champion and I leaned against the car and thanked God. I was sweating like a navvy and my hands were shaking, if it had gone the other way I would have been going home in an ambulance.

One of the nicest venues on the weekly circuit was the Cayton Bay Camp. It used to be Wallis's where I helped out my pal Nigel a couple of years before with the Roger De Courcey business. The compere at Cayton was a great guy and a good pro called Pete Conway. I always got there early and had a cuppa and a natter with him in his caravan. I didn't need my big guitar amp at Cayton as the band had a spare for me to use so I didn't need to go over in the Land Cruiser. If the weather was OK I'd go over in the E type, it was a lovely drive and I could open her up on the York by-pass. One particular week, Pete told me that his twelve year old son was coming over the following week to visit him. He was divorced and didn't see the lad as much as he'd like to so he was really looking forward to seeing him. He asked me that if I came in the Jaguar next week, would I take his lad out for a ride in it as he was mad on cars. I told him of course I would and sure enough the weather was fine the next week so I went over to Cayton in the E type. He was a nice well mannered kid and when it came time for his ride I could see he was really excited. He got into the cockpit of the car and slammed the door with such force it rattled my teeth. It was a sheer reaction but I clipped him round the earhole and said "Don't slam the bloody door, it's a precision made car not a bleedin Lada". Don't get me wrong I didn't belt him hard, it was only a tap and he immediately apologised. We went for our little spin and he loved it.

Many years later I got a phone call from Pete Conway, we'd sort of stayed in touch via the odd phone call but this call was quite interesting. The conversation went something like this.

"Hiya Knutty, it's Pete Conway, can you remember when you took my lad for a ride in your E type jag at Cayton?"

"Course I can, I remember clipping him round the earhole for slamming the bleedin' door".

"Right, well he went into showbiz you know".

"Gerraway! Did he? How's he going on?"

"Well, he joined this boy band after an audition and they're doing pretty well"

"That's great Pete, what's their name?"

"Take That"

"You're fuckin' joking, their record's at number one".

"I know, my lad's Robbie Williams".

Old Pete was so proud bless him, as was I when Pete said that Robbie sent his best regards to me and he remembered his ride in my Jag.

Josh in 'All Creatures Great & Small'

146

The Trouble With Cars is ....

I sold the E type later that year because I'd got the horn for this Bugatti replica that I'd seen at a car show which was designed and built by a company called Teal cars in Altringham. It was a very well built kit-car with an aluminium body and MGB engine and running gear. It was sheer wind in the hair excitement with an open cockpit and half moon aero screens instead of a windscreen. I bought a real world war two flying jacket, leather flying helmet and a pair of goggles. When I'd paid for it I still had plenty of change out of the E type money so I bought myself another guitar for my collection. I've always had a great love of guitars whether they are jazzers, classical or solid body rockers. Being a Shadows fanatic, I've always had a Fender Stratocaster just like Hanks. I was building up a fair collection which hung on the wall of the cottage and I got as much pleasure from just looking at them as I did playing them. I had a Gretsch Country Gentleman just like the one George Harrison played, a gorgeous Gibson Super 400 identical to the one used by Bill Haley but my pride and joy was a 1953 Gibson J200 jumbo which had been previously owned by the world famous country singer Willie Nelson. I met him a couple of years later when he came to the Sheffield Arena with The Highwaymen, a quartet made up of Willie, Johnny Cash, Waylon Jennings and Kris Kristofferson. He signed the guitar and verified the valuation slip with his signature which increased its value tremendously.

Getting back to the Bugatti, I've got to say that over the years that I owned it, I had more fun with it than any car I ever owned. I became very pally with a little guy from Leeds called Ben Trumble who had appointed himself as the secretary of the newly formed Teal Bugatti owners club. He printed a magazine called the Teal Spiel which was circulated among the slowly growing membership of Teal owners. He was only about five foot four but he had a great personality and like all men of diminutive stature, he liked to lead the way. His was one of the first Teals and it had a fibre glass body so we called it the

"Plastic Pig", mine had its name emblazoned down both sides of the very long aluminium bonnet, "Pneumonia Wagon". Whenever we had a club meeting, old Ben would be out there speeding along up front egging the more boring and sedate members to keep up. The Teal members were from all over the country and from all walks of life, some were great guys and some were prize tedious twats whom I kept at arms length at all times.

Some time after I'd bought the "Bug" which it was affectionately known as, Ben and I agreed to go on a trip to France to visit the world famous Schlumpf museum in Mulhouse. It is without doubt the greatest automobile museum on this planet and it houses the largest collection of Bugattis under one roof than anywhere in the world. The story of the Schlumpf brothers, Fritz and Hans, is quite sad and very intriguing. They were Swiss but were educated in Mulhouse just over the French border which was their mother's birth place. They became highly successful in the textile industry and owned mills all over northern France and the departments of the Rhine. Next to his professional activity Fritz devoted an extraordinary amount of energy into collecting old cars. So in addition to his heavy professional obligations as an industrialist, he daily saw to restoring cars to pristine condition and set up his collection in an old factory which he acquired for the purpose of storing and renovation. The brothers amassed a huge collection of every conceivable make of classic and vintage cars that were worth millions. The factory where they were stored was renovated to perfection with row upon row of vintage iron lamp-posts to light all the fabulous cars on display. The odd thing was, the brothers had done all this work over many years and not told anyone about it. The workers who restored the cars were made to swear an oath of secrecy. The profits from their vast textile empire had gone into the car collection and in the mid seventies, a world crisis in the textile industry reached the brothers' business and they reluctantly filed for bankruptcy. The factories closed with the loss of over two thousand workers' jobs and after the collection was discovered in March 1977 the workforce occupied the premises, demanding the cars be sold to refloat the company. They claimed that the vast amount of cars could only have been collected to the detriment of the industrial activity of the Schlumpf companies. When they became threatening towards the brothers they fled over the border to Switzerland, deprived of all their possessions. The local authorities became quickly aware of the immense benefits that a museum of this importance would generate for Mulhouse and the Alsace region. I suspect that in no doubt, owing to a modicum of political chicanery, the French government, after describing the collection as a French Historical Monument, sold the factory and the complete contents of the museum to a newly formed association, the "National Museum of the Motor Car" at a very knock down price. The "Association" just happened to be the state, region and local authorities of the city of Mulhouse and Alsace region. The museum opened for visitors in July 1982 and in its first ten years it received over four million visitors.

The brothers lived just over the border within spitting distance of their beloved car collection never able to return to France. They left a great legacy, the action of gathering, collecting and the passion that inspired them to do so should guarantee them a place in history. Their memory will live on forever in the museum they created.

When I mentioned the French trip to my great friend and doctor, Gerald Benjamin he begged to go with me. He even bought a leather helmet and a flying jacket so as to look the part. We looked like Biggles and Algy in the cockpit of the Bug. Ben had arranged everything as usual and we were to drive down to Dover and catch the ferry to Calais. He didn't book the ferry, which only takes just over an hour, he booked the hovercraft, or the "Vomit Comet" as it's known. I've spent the past thirteen years of my life on cruise ships and I've been through some bloody fantastically rough seas without any ill effect thank God. On the trip over to France I was sick after the first five minutes. That fuckin' hovercraft was bucking and bouncing over the wave tops like a wild bronco. I felt desperately sorry for Gerald, he first went white, then a sort of greeny-grey pallor and then he was violently sick. Thank God the trip was over quickly and we could get off that monster. The main problem with seasickness is that the illness doesn't subside when you get back on dry land. Depending on how susceptible to the illness you are, the longer it takes to diminish. Gerald just lay there in the cockpit of the bug and moaned. He was in a terrible state and it took him about three hours to feel anything like normal. I felt so sorry for him, what with him being a doctor and all, I wished so desperately that I could make him better as he'd done me in the past.

There was something else pretty questionable about Ben's leadership qualities. When he was route planning, he'd look at the map of France and see that Mulhouse was only about six inches from Calais, when in actual fact it's roughly the same distance from Edinburgh to London. He'd booked a hotel about twenty miles from Mulhouse so we could get an early start for the museum visit. This meant that we had about a four hundred mile drive in a totally open car making us overdose on oxygen and feel sleepy. I was still running in the engine so I didn't want to be exceeding 70mph on those long French motorways. What does Ben do? As soon as we hit the motorway he's got his foot down and he's clocking a ton so he's very quickly way out in front. About two hours later and with Gerald thankfully feeling better, I notice steam coming out of the louvres in my bonnet. Oh shit, don't say she's overheating, I know I've forked out for the AA foreign insurance but I do not want to break down. I slowed down, then stopped and upon raising one side of the bonnet I saw the steam puthering out of the engine bay. The temperature gauge was off the scale so I checked the hoses; they were OK so it could only be the water pump or the head gasket and which ever one it was, I was well and truly fucked. While the engine was cooling down, Ben came back along the opposite carriageway looking for us and honked his hooter. He stopped and came across to see what was wrong. After about an hour, the radiator was cool enough to take what bit of water we'd got between us for drinking and off we went. The engine soon got too hot again and then there was an almighty bang, water was everywhere. It *was* the water pump and I was in France and I was feeling very angry and very sorry for myself. I'll say one thing for the efficiency of the AA five star insurance which I'd paid twenty two quid for, it's top drawer. I rang this number from a roadside phone (no mobiles then) got connected to a geezer in England who took all my details and then kindly rang me back ten minutes later to say a truck was on it's way to tow me to a garage and a water pump was on it's way from England to the designated garage which would do the repair. He also told me that a hire car was on its way to the same garage and would be waiting for us when we got there. I thought, now that's not bad for twenty two quid.

Sure enough, when we arrived at the garage in a small town about fifteen miles away, there was a little Renault waiting for us with all the necessary paperwork. We were soon on our way and the whole delay had robbed us of about two hours travelling time. The garage had promised to have the car ready in two days time so I couldn't grumble really. Thanks to Ben's crappy planning, we didn't reach the hotel until early evening after a very tiring trek across North Eastern France. Gerald and I were knackered so we had a well deserved bottle of wine which I drank most of thanks to Gerald's abstemious nature, followed by an early night.

I was hugely disappointed to discover the total lack of decent food at a French breakfast table. I was looking forward to a large plate of Barnsley muesli, which, for the uninitiated is, two eggs, bacon, sausage, mushrooms, tomatoes and lots of buttered toast. I got a fucking croissant with a tiny plastic tub of jam. I was just praying that the hoo-doo which had befallen us the day before wasn't going to roll over to today. Ben told us that the museum didn't open until 10am so we lingered over coffee and set off so as to arrive there in good time. We got there to be greeted by a sign in French which boldly stated "Ferme Mardi" which my schoolboy French told me that it was closed on a Tuesday, today was Tuesday. I've never seen four more dejected people, our disappointment was boundless, we'd come all this way and endured sea sickness, breakdowns and shitty food to be met with closed doors. I am a tenacious sod when I want to be and I thought there must be something I can do. I noticed a small Judas gate in the main doors of the museum so I tried it and it opened. We parked up and all four of us went in. Ben was travelling with his current girlfriend, a pretty little thing who was smaller than him. I spotted a bloke in a uniform and cap with a shiny badge on it; he was in a small office which probably doubled up as the gatehouse and security gate. I asked him politely if he parlez vood the Anglais to which he replied a curt "Non". He didn't look to be the friendliest of fellows so I knew that extreme diplomacy and a keen acting ability was needed. I whispered to Ben's young lady to be prepared to start crying if I gave her the nod. I explained as best I could along with the help of Gerald and Ben's basic French that we'd come all the way from England for this special trip and we couldn't come back tomorrow as we were booked on the ferry home. I then took him to one side and slipped him the equivalent of about twenty quid in francs. This did the trick and he agreed to let us into the museum. The foyer was chock full of Bugatti memorabilia and various scale models which we sadly couldn't purchase because the man explained that the lady in charge of the shop wasn't there.

Upon entering the vast building which housed the car collection, we were all utterly gobsmacked. It was easily as big as a football pitch and there were over four hundred of the most desirable automobiles on this planet. We went straight to the Bugattis; there was row upon row of them. I'll not bore you with all the different types but the cheapest Bugatti today in half decent condition would probably fetch over half a million pounds at auction. There were two Bugatti Royales on display, one being the famous Napoleon coupe which would smash all price records if it were ever to go on sale. Ettore Bugatti built only six Royales between 1929 and 1933, their price then was forty three thousand dollars new. Only three were sold outside the company and Ettore kept one for his own personal use until his death. It was a magnificent machine, 21 ft long with a 300hp engine and the unique engineering which went with the marque. In 1990, a Royale sold for 15 million dollars, the highest price ever paid for a car. Small wonder, as it's the biggest, rarest and most desirable motor car in the world.

Ben, Gerald and I spent a good four hours in the mechanical holy of holies, taking photographs and wondering what sensational stories these cars could have told of their many famous and royal owners, it's what dreams are made of.

It was a bit of an anti-climax when I journeyed back to the French town to pick up my replica Bug. It was all repaired and tested with the new pump working like a ten bob watch. I kept that Bug for twelve years and never had another single thing go wrong with it.

Pumping Iron & Spare Tyres

All through 1987, Donna was working harder and harder to build her physique as she had now become obsessed with winning the Britain contest. Not a month went by when she wasn't featured in one of the bodybuilding magazines and the media were beginning to be really interested in her progress. During the autumn of '87 I was back finishing off the last episodes of "How we used to live" for YTV so I was out on location for very long and tiring days and nights of filming. It was taking up all my time and when I *was* home, Donna was in the gym pushing weights. Her physique was now honed to perfection in my opinion and I truly believed she could win the final. It was held at Wembley and I couldn't go because of work commitments. She placed second. She was obviously disappointed but her strength of character and devotion to her sport just made her more determined to blow 'em all away next year. She had been headhunted by two businessmen from London to open a brand new health studio on West Street in Sheffield town centre. They gave her carte blanche to order the very best in gym equipment and machines. It had a Jacuzzi, saunas and luxurious changing facilities for both sexes. It was called the Fitness Experience and was the last word in training and beauty. Her newly elevated position in the world of fitness and her established reputation as a world class athlete gave the place a status and prestige which money couldn't buy. Despite the best equipment that modern technology could provide, when it came to her own personal workouts, she still trained at Tony Tom's spit and sawdust gym with the permanent smell of sweat, farting and WD40.

As a much needed diversion from my workload of filming and one night stands, I started seeing my two great mates Neil Bridges and Glen Ibbotson for weekly guitar sessions where we were gradually building a considerable repertoire of Shadows numbers. Neil, you may remember was one of my oldest pals from my early days in the Whirlwinds rhythm group but had now retired from showbiz and was running a small garage business in the Darnall area of Sheffield hiring and repairing cars. He wasn't happy as Darnall was and is now a ghetto of Asians and they were very difficult to do business with. He told me they never ever would pay his already cheap prices and always wanted discounts. They always returned the cars in a filthy state with hardly any petrol in them. Neil is the nicest straightest and most honest bloke you could meet, but mention Asians and his hackles go up like a tomcat in a dog's home, he fucking hates 'em. He's the best rhythm guitar player I've ever heard so he augmented our playing sessions beautifully. Glen was also a retired group member who'd evolved into a double act then he ended up buying a shop on London Road just out of the town centre and started selling guitars.

At the time we started practicing, Glen's shop was one of the best guitar emporiums in the city and was always full of lads plonking away on instruments that they couldn't afford. We'd now started going to Glen's house every Tuesday as he had a very large glass roofed out building attached to his garage which was ideal for rehearsals. He also brought all the equipment home from his shop so our gear was the best you could imagine. We needed a drummer so Glen recruited his old showbiz partner Pete Courcey, but the whole world knew him as Pete the Pie because he had a door to door pie round selling pies from his van. Pete was the most easy going bloke you could meet, nothing phased him and he was dead funny. He had a bicycle bell bolted to his drum kit and every time I dropped a bollock when I was playing, he'd ring it. I played lead guitar, Neil was rhythm and Glen played bass. Glen could also sing very high notes so Roy Orbison stuff was well within our scope. As the months went by my playing skills improved tremendously and our Shadows sound was spot on accurate. I say my guitar playing had improved but I was still an average lead guitarist with limited skills. I'm a natural rhythm guitar player and I love chords, I know nearly every chord on the fingerboard but as far as fast fingering is concerned, my abilities are restricted. We cleverly adjusted our repertoire according to my playing skills and soon built up a fine range of Shadows instrumentals and sixties songs. Glen would

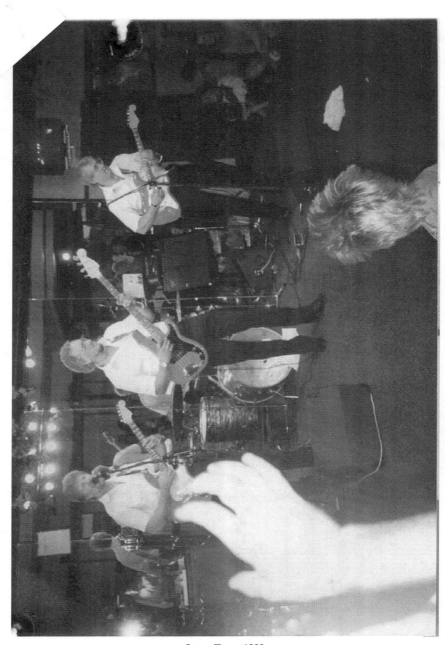

Spare Tyres 1989

borrow a red Fender bass for himself from his shop and a red Strat for Neil.

We soon became aware that we were easily good enough to go out as an act but the problem was the fees. The top paid club bands of the time were getting in the region of four to five hundred quid a night between them and I was getting more than that on my own as a comic. The lads understood this and said that as the "Star" of the band I would get the lion's share and they would get some expenses. I immediately told them to get stuffed as we would be splitting it four ways or not at all. We went out and got four matching fawn coloured jackets with red shirts so now we had our stage outfits.

We hadn't got a name for the band so I suggested "Age Concern", along with a suggestion that we donate a percentage of our fee to that charity. The lads thought it was a grand idea and when I approached the Age Concern charity with our idea they point blank refused to allow us to use their name. I couldn't understand their refusal as they would only gain by our efforts both financially and publicity-wise. I just thought "Fuck 'em, it's their loss".

We were now a band with no name so I rang a mate of mine who's a producer at YTV and told him of my newly formed band and would he like us to appear on "Calendar", the nightly news programme and get the viewers to write in with a name for us. He thought it was a great idea and the following week we were up at YTV in Leeds bashing out Apache and Wonderful Land in front of the cameras. The lovely Christa Ackroyd was still at YTV in those days and she did a great interview with us all and told the viewers of our need for a name. I love old Christa, she's a great looking lass with the best arse on the planet.

On subsequent programmes over the next month, she flashed up about thirty seconds of our original spot to remind them not to forget to write in with suggestions for our name. About ten days after our initial appearance, I received a very unexpected cheque from YTV for two hundred and twenty quid which was our fee for our being on the show. I put it in my bank and drew out the lads' share in cash. I stuck their dosh in three envelopes and presented it to them on the next band practice; they were over the moon, particularly Pete, who didn't earn a fortune from his pies.

Five weeks after our first appearance I received a list of names from Calendar and after much deliberation, the lads and I chose "The Spare Tyres". It was a great name because apart from Glen who had always been slim, the rest of us had put on weight since our early years and were quite rotund. My good mate Alan Wood started booking us out on the odd Saturday when I wasn't working and we were tearing the bollocks off 'em. I was doing gags I wouldn't have dreamed of doing on my own and it was one huge laugh from start to finish. Glen had a van which we travelled in to the gigs and it was just like the old days, farting, belching and telling filthy gags all the way there and back. The actual experience of standing on the stage playing lead guitar with the amazing backing which I got from the lads was like being in a time warp from which I never wanted to escape. Being back on the road with my mates was so bloody different from trailing round the country all on my own with no-one to talk to but myself.

Around two months after our initial showing on Calendar, I received another cheque from YTV, this time for just over two thousand quid. I was utterly gobsmacked; I worked out from the accompanying paperwork that each time our spot had been shown as a short excerpt from our original appearance, we'd been paid again. I drew the cash out and arranged a curry night for the lads at our regular Indian nosh house at Crookes in Sheffield. I wish I could describe to you the look on the lads' faces when I handed out the envelopes each with a few hundred quid in them, it was priceless.

Drinks with H.R.H

Sea Harrier take off

Dad and I, 1965

*Uncle Terry who died
in 2010*

We love guitars

Green Goddess

What about the sign behind me

Freddy Pyne

My alter ego, Ricky Livid

Jack Jones reunion wit a fat bloke

David Lonsdale

Three merry lads, Glen & Neil

The Eiger in fog

Me lobster

Would you buy a chop from this butcher?

Panama

Paul Burrel

On the commode at Ephesus

Some of the cars I've owned

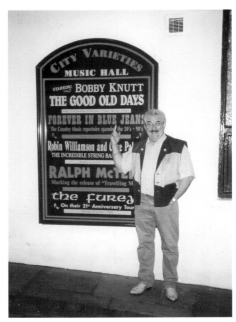

The best theatre in the world

Last of The Summer Wine

The Questors, Then & Now

MONDAY 13TH SEPTEMBER TO SATURDAY 18TH SEPTEMBER 1999

Ian Dickens Productions presents

BOBBY KNUTT   ANNA KAREN

Starring in

AGATHA CHRISTIE'S

'Coronation St. & 'Emmerdale'

'EastEnders' & Olive from 'On The Buses'

THE UNEXPECTED GUEST

DIRECTED BY IAN DICKENS

Ian Dickens Productions

SET & LIGHTING DESIGN BY DAVID NORTH

Designed & Printed by R&B Printers, Eastbourne. 01323 733378

THEATRE ROYAL ~LINCOLN~

Monday to Friday 7.30p.m. Saturday 6.00 & 8.45p.m.
Ticket Prices: £8.50, £11.50, £13.50
(Concessions available for Senior Citizens & Children)

BOX OFFICE: 01522 525555

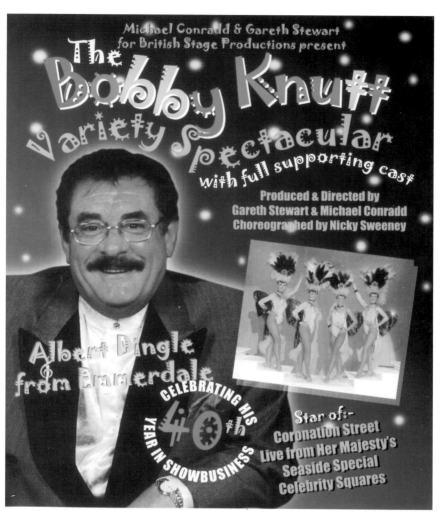

Michael Conradd & Gareth Stewart
for British Stage Productions present

The Bobby Knutt Variety Spectacular

with full supporting cast

Produced & Directed by
Gareth Stewart & Michael Conradd
Choreographed by Nicky Sweeney

Albert Dingle
from Emmerdale

CELEBRATING HIS
40th
YEAR IN SHOWBUSINESS

Star of:-
Coronation Street
Live from Her Majesty's
Seaside Special
Celebrity Squares

The Pavilion Theatre, Whitby
Saturday 7th September at 7.30pm
Admission £7.00 · Concessions £6.00
Box Office: 01947 604855

Cadbury's PANTOMIME SEASON IN ASSOCIATION WITH Save the Children

PAUL ELLIOTT presents

MARTI CAINE   **BOBBY KNUTT**

Sponsored by
TRANSPORT EXECUTIVE

'Marilyn' from 'Home & Away'

EMILY SYMONS

Snow White
AND THE SEVEN DWARFS

KIM ISMAY
SEAN CANNING
TOMMY WRIGHT

ANDREW HALLIDAY

DANNY BLACKNER   KEVIN HUDSON
ANTHONY GEORGHIOU   JULIAN SKELTON
JOHN GHAVAM   JIMMY VEE
DAVID HARRINGTON

Sponsored by
TRANSPORT EXECUTIVE

THE CONSTANCE GRANT BABES

LYCEUM
Theatre
S H E F F I E L D
BOX OFFICE
0742 769 922

DIRECTED BY **DEREK GRIFFITHS**
WRITTEN BY **TUDOR DAVIES**
ASSOCIATE PRODUCERS BRIAN HEWITT-JONES & CHRIS MORENO

CHOREOGRAPHY BY **PAUL MADDEN**
MUSICAL DIRECTOR **RICK COATES**
LIGHTING DESIGNER **MICHAEL CALF**

THUR 22 DEC 1994 - SUN 29 JAN 1995

WE ARE SUPPORTING THE
75th Birthday Appeal
Save the Children
Registered Charity 213890

Cadbury's PANTOMIME SEASON IN ASSOCIATION WITH **Save the Children** Registered Charity 212890

PAUL ELLIOTT presents EVANTE Pantomime

BRIAN GLOVER
as THE SHERIFF OF NOTTINGHAM

BOBBY KNUTT
as THE GOOD ROBBER

FROM THE GLADIATORS **FALCON** as THE COSMIC FAIRY

IN

THE LONDON PALLADIUM PRODUCTION OF

BABES IN THE WOOD

WITH THE CONSTANCE GRANT BABES

FINE TIME FONTAYNE
as THE BAD ROBBER

FREDDIE LEES
as THE NURSE

GARY LOVINI
as ALAN A'DALE

YORKSHIRE GOLD **STEVE FOUNTAIN** as LITTLEJOHN

Sponsored by ✚ TRANSPORT EXECUTIVE

SOPHIE-LOUISE DANN
as MAID MARION

AND

HILARY O'NEIL
as ROBIN HOOD

LYCEUM THEATRE · SHEFFIELD
BOX OFFICE 0114 276 9922
BOX OFFICE (55 Norfolk Street, Sheffield S1 1DA)

DIRECTED BY STEPHEN BARRY
DESIGNED BY HUGH DURRANT
ASSOCIATE PRODUCERS BRIAN HEWITT-JONES & CHRIS NIXZERO

CHOREOGRAPHY BY SAM SPENCER LANE
LIGHTING BY FRANCIS REID

**THURS 21 DEC 1995
· SUN 28 JAN 1996**

Southport Theatre

December 18th 1998 to January 17th 1999   Seats £9   Child/Seniors £6.50
(Group Concessions)

TEL 01704 540404

Duggie Chapman presents   'A Star Studded Circus Pantomime'

It's New It's Different

Goldilocks
and the
Three Amazing Bears

"Brookside's" Max Farnham
STEVEN PINDER
As 'Prince Paul'

From 'Emmerdale' 'Uncle Albert Dingle'
BOBBY KNUTT
As 'The Mayor'

Introducing
KATHRYN TRAVIS
As 'Goldilocks'

Star of the 'Sooty Show'
CONNIE CREIGHTON
As 'Fairy Godmother'

New Comedy Star
STEVE ROYLE
As 'Muddler'

JONATHAN OWEN
As 'Dame Tilly'

PAT & GUY HOLLOWAY
JACKIE QUEST

From 'Russian Circus'
LARRY OSCA
Thrills in The Air

Directed by
Duggie Chapman

Formby School of Dance
Choreography Hayley Bachelor

Musical Director
Lawrence Knight

From T.V.'s Chucklevision
THE PATTON BROTHERS
as Bill & Ben

Full Supporting Circus Specialities

Donna winning Commonwealth Gold

Canberra 1996

Ladder Of Swords

The panto of 1987-88 was my third time playing Buttons in Cinderella. I had my usual Knutty's repertory company of Finetime and Rob McCulley who played hilarious ugly sisters. I had a new addition to the cast, a guy called David Sterne who played Baron Hardup. David was a very proper classical actor with a stentorian voice and a perfect Oxford accent. He is one of the driest, wittiest human beings I've ever met; his nick-name is Stumpy. At the time he was working with me, he had been dry for about six months having been a massive drinker. He was a Shakespearian actor who'd mixed closely with the likes of Peter O'Toole and that sort of clan, hence the heavy drinking. I loved him immediately and we became the closest of pals and still are to this day.

The best fairy godmother I ever worked with was also in the show, a delightful lady called Meg Johnson. Meg has been in Emmerdale now for the past few years playing Pearl. She'd had a great history of musical theatre and her production songs in the panto were a wonder to behold. Meg had some sort of aggressive cancer while she was doing the show and she was visiting Weston Park hospital every day during rehearsals and during the run. She was having radium treatment and some days I must admit she looked absolutely exhausted. I asked her what the treatment was like and she replied, "Imagine a really bad case of sunburn, but inside your body instead of outside". She never missed a performance and stoically went on when she must have been feeling shocking. She's the bravest lady I ever met.

It was during this particular panto that I decided I must stop smoking. It was a very physically demanding show for me with many flights of stairs between upstage and downstage entrances and exits. I was still very fit but the fags were slowing me down and making me breathless. I was smoking between fifty and sixty roll-ups a day. One morning I coughed something up and it looked like all it needed was a shell and legs and it would have walked away. I felt so guilty at my excessive consumption of tobacco that I made the decision to stop on New Year's Day which was about a week away. I had a new year's eve party at the cottage to which all the cast were invited and when I'd had my last fag at about 3am, I gave all my surplus baccy and my roll-up tin to Stumpy and announced that that was it, I'd quit smoking for good. He scoffed and said "Don't worry dear boy, I'll keep them safe for you so that when you're dying for a facking fag you'll know where to come". The good Lord above must have given me strength because I never craved for a ciggy at all after that. Today, nearly twenty three years later, I've still not touched a cigarette.

Donna's dedication to body building was really paying off now and the Mail on Sunday did a full three page spread on her with the professional make-up experts and the top photographers looking after her. She did the Terry Wogan show and was a guest on Jonathan Ross's show. I went with her to the Wogan show as he was an old pal from the days when we did Pop Score for radio two. I'd also done three Blanketty Blanks with him and he made a fuss of me when he saw me. Donna's posing routine was poetry in motion and her physique was honed to utter perfection, I knew that if she didn't win it this year there was no justice. She'd put on some extra pounds of muscle yet her shape was so symmetrical and aesthetic that it couldn't be faulted. She won it with ease and now there was the Miss Universe two weeks later. That two week break in between the two contests was an absolute bastard because she had to stay sharply cut yet not lose any size. Bless her, she managed to keep her magnificent condition intact but was beaten into second place by an Australian girl who was built like a brick shithouse. When it was all over she decided to pack it in, {much to my joy}as she couldn't go any further without turning professional and going to America. As far as she was concerned, she'd got involved in a totally different sport to what she was known for, and reached the top again.

During the spring of 1988 I went for a casting for a cinema film, I'd only ever done TV films so I was really hoping I'd get it. It was called "Ladder of Swords" and the two stars were Martin Shaw and Juliette Stevenson. The director was a guy called Norman Hull and he wanted to see me at his home in Derbyshire so I went down in the Bug as it was a glorious sunny day. He wanted me to play this mega-rich land owner whose stately pile was up on the Yorkshire moors so I had to do my best posh accent. I got the part and got to do some scenes with Miss Stevenson who although very thorough in her approach to the scenes, did step out of character a couple of times so we could chit-chat about life in general. I never got to meet Mr Shaw as he stayed in his caravan all day when he wasn't shooting a scene. I suppose *his* great regret in life is that he finally got to work with Bobby Knutt but never got to meet him.

My Heroes

Most people, upon meeting a professional comedian like me, will invariably eventually ask, "Who's *your* favourite comedian?" To narrow it down to one would be impossible in my estimation but I'll name a few. Tommy Cooper, who I knew well, Eric Morecambe who I met only once very briefly, Doddy whom I also know quite well. I consider Doddy to be our last great living comedian, a total master at his craft. Bob Monkhouse was a great friend and was the comedian's comedian, a comedy guru whose knowledge of comedy stretched beyond belief.

One of my greatest regrets is that I never got to even see, never mind meet, the greatest comedian of the 20th century, Jimmy James. I worked often with his son James Casey who was his father's double in both looks and voice. James was a radio producer with whom I did many comedy broadcasts from the BBC theatre in Manchester. Jimmy James always had a pair of stooges to whom he was usually related by blood, the longest serving was his stammering nephew Jack Casey whom he named Eli Woods. He gave all his stooges ridiculous names; his brother- in-law Jack Derby was called Hutton Conyers after a remote village in Yorkshire, his brother Andy was renamed Bretton Woods. My old mate Roy Castle spent a good length of time with Jimmy James and it was from Roy that I learned so much about my hero.

Jimmy's material was so silly and off the wall and it comprised of lots of sketches. He'd go out with Eli whom he'd introduce as the Singing Skunk Trapper, six foot three, eight stone wet through, in a Davy Crockett hat. He'd ask him, "Have you caught any today?" Told no, he'd sniff the air twice and say, "It's you then". I remember sitting with Roy in his dressing room at the Gaiety Theatre, Isle of Man in the summer of 1980 when we did summer season together, he told me this hilarious anecdote. Jimmy's Brother Peter had lost a leg in childhood and walked with the aid of a single crutch. He was deaf as well so he kept coming into the conversation three conversations back. What with Peter being out of sync with the rest of the people present and Eli being a life long stutterer, a chat between the two of them became what Roy described as a long job. He also told me that Peter's one legged problem had been solved as far as shoes were concerned when he found another bloke in Northampton who'd lost the other leg. They had the same foot size so they used to buy a pair of shoes between them.

Bob Monkhouse wrote his wonderful autobiography "Crying with Laughter" and followed it up in 1998 with the sequel which he called "Over the Limit". They are compulsory reading for any aficionado of comedy and in the second book he actually features, word for word, Jimmy James's most famous and well remembered sketch, The Box. I don't feel the least bit guilty at copying Bob's idea of sharing the Box sketch with you. As Bob says in his book "Nothing James did was more mysteriously wonderful than his Box Sketch. Certain lines occur in this routine that are quoted by lovers of comedy like shibboleths to test mutual acceptability"

Picture Jimmy James in a natty suit and trilby as he concludes eight minutes of insanity with Eli Woods. From the wings comes a stranger in a horrible hat and a coat that covers him from neck to ankle, carrying a box under his arm. Henceforth the stranger SPEAKS IN CAPITAL LETTERS, while Jimmy James speaks in lower case and *Eli's lines are written in italics*.

"HEY! ARE YOU PUTTING ROUND THAT I'M BARMY?"
"No, no, it's not me"
"WELL SOMEONE'S PUTTING IT ROUND THAT I'M BARMY. IS IT HIM?"
"I'll ask him. (TO ELI) Is it you that's putting it around that he's barmy?"
"I don't want any"
"He doesn't want any".
"How much are they?"
"How much are — no --- never mind, it's not him".
"WELL, SOMEONE'S PUTTING IT ROUND THAT I'M BARMY".
"Did you want to keep it a secret? Listen, your face is

familiar — where have I seen you before?"

"OH, I'M OUT OF THERE NOW!"

"Oh, that's where I saw you, in there. I didn't know *I'd* been in. No, I've seen you making a political speech somewhere."

"OH YEAH, I'M THE MEMBER OF PARLIAMENT FOR ROTHERHAM".

"What are you, Conservative, Labour or Liberal?"

"YES".

"Well it's nice to know we've got one. (TO ELI) We've got one"

"Have we?"

"When I look at you I think we've got two".

"I'VE BEEN AWAY Y' KNOW".

"It doesn't show, no one'd guess, no".

"I'VE BEEN TO SOUTH AFRICA. I WAS VERY POPULAR IN SOUTH AFRICA AS WELL. JUST BEFORE I CAME HOME THEY GAVE ME A LOVELY PRESENT".

"What did they give you?"

"TWO MAN-EATING LIONS".

"Real lions? Did you fetch 'em home? Where do you keep 'em?"

"IN THIS BOX".

(TO ELI) "Go and get two coffees, one with strychnine in it".

"ARE YOU TELLING HIM ABOUT THE LIONS?"

"Oh yes, you've got two lions in that box, are they in there now?"

"YES"

"I thought I heard a rustling. (TO ELI) He's got two lions in that box".

"How much are they?"

"He doesn't want to sell them".

"I'VE BEEN TO NYASALAND AS WELL".

"AH, they're nice people, the Nyassas. I bet they gave you a present".

"THEY DID, THEY GAVE ME A GIRAFFE".

"Did you bring the giraffe home?"

"YES".

"I don't like to ask him. Where do you keep the giraffe?"

164

"IN THIS BOX".

(TO ELI) "Get on the phone, 999, I'll keep him here".

"ARE YOU TELLING HIM ABOUT THE GIRAFFE?"

"He's got a giraffe in that box".

"Is it black or white?"

"Our Eli wants to know what colour the giraffe is."

"The coffee I mean".

"You have the one with the strychnine in it".

"HERE, DID I TELL YOU I'VE BEEN TO INDIA AS WELL."

"Oh hell, he's been all over, did they give you a present as well?"

"YES"

"What did they give you?"

"AN ELEPHANT."

"Male or female?"

"NO, AN ELEPHANT."

"I don't suppose it makes any difference to you whether it's male or female."

"It wouldn't make any d-d-difference to anyone, only another elephant."

"I'll have to stop him going to those youth clubs."

"Hey, ask him where he keeps the elephant. Go on."

"Our Eli wants to know where you keep the elephant, is it in the box?"

"DON'T BE DAFT, YOU COULDN'T GET AN ELEPHANT IN THERE."

(TO ELI) "Why don't you mind your own business? You couldn't get an elephant in there. There's no room."

"He could ask the g-g-giraffe to move over a bit."

"HE'S CRACKERS."

"I think it'd be a photo finish between the two of you."

"I KEEP THE ELEPHANT IN A CAGE."

"In a cage, of course. Where do you keep the cage?"

"(SPEAKING TOGETHER) "IN THE BOX!!"

Bob goes on to finish the chapter on Jimmy James by saying:

"One of James Casey's fondest memories of his father encapsulates the man's humour, the mixture of the surreal and the wry. Together they passed a gang of workmen hard at work in the sun, sweating and gasping with effort. Jimmy stopped and drew his son's attention to the exhausted labourers. "Look at those lazy buggers. Too idle to learn a song and a routine of patter." The great man died on the 4th August 1965 but he'll be remembered whenever someone warns "I'll stop you going to those youth clubs."

Mother Goose

1988-9 was the Crucible panto to top all pantos. It was the most spectacular, technically brilliant and funniest show I ever did. It broke all box office records and I honestly don't think that record will ever be broken as it did 98.9% business for the whole run. I never saw an empty seat during any performance. The eponymous role of Mother Goose was played by a superb jobbing actor called Russell Dixon. I'd seen him previously playing Willy Loman in "Death of a Salesman" and he was wonderful. Russell is gay but you'd never guess it in a million years as he doesn't mince about with a limp-wristed manner like many queens do. He was the best Dame I ever worked with and to this day, apart from Damian Williams, no one has even come near him when it came to his magnificent Mother Goose. It's the only panto where the Dame gets to play the title role and the whole story revolves around her and her magic goose. I played her son Knutty and we had the most fun I've ever had in any panto role that I've played. We used to do stuff ad-lib and if it got a laugh we kept it in. I did a bit with the kids so they could get me to come on stage by shouting a certain phrase. It's standard panto practice to do it and the kids in the audience love it as it gives them a chance to shout their little heads off. The idea is to place an object by the far side of the stage and ask the kids to guard it, then if anyone goes near it, they shout like bloody mad and Hey-Presto!! You've got your entrance. I had this bit of business with Mother Goose when she asked me where her knick knacks had gone from off the mantelpiece. I told her I'd took 'em to sell so we could buy some groceries. She then goes barmy and accuses me of nicking her knick knacks saying I'm nothing but a knick knack nicker. My next bit was to put the knick knacks down by the far right stage side and ask the kids to shout "Knick knack nickers Knutty" if anyone went near them. It worked like a charm.

Russell was a drinker, he used to keep a large carboy of rough cider in his dressing room and then go on the large scotches in the bar after the show. He'd be steadily drinking throughout the day yet I swear to God I never saw him even a little bit worse for wear. OK I confess I could always smell alcohol on his breath during our scenes, but it *never* affected his performance. He'd sometimes get a bit maudlin when he been downing the whiskys in the bar. I recall one night when he was drowning his sorrows with me and Stumpy after the show. Stumpy was now firmly established in the Bobby Knutt / Mike Kay repertory company and this year he was playing King Gander. He was still off the booze and was now a councilor for AA. He always had a wicked glint in his eye and you never knew what would roll off his tongue next, he genuinely didn't give a fuck what he said or who heard it. Russell had just split from his long term partner and was feeling very emotional, in fact he was near to tears. Stumpy and I could see it was a whisky induced mood he was in so we were allowing him to amuse us with his drama-queen melancholy. He then said in almost a sob, "Oh why can't I find true love Stumpy?" To which Stumpy replied in his perfect Oxford accent, "Because you're a facking ugly old puff, that's why". I pissed myself laughing and even Russell cheered up a little.

One night during the panto run, I was doing the cabaret at the Omega Banqueting Suite staff party for my old mate Big David Baldwin. The cast had asked me that if I was doing any gigs after the show, could they come and see me. I asked the Biggun if I could bring them and he said no problem, the more the merrier. I mustered about a dozen of the cast and I managed to pile them all into my big Land Cruiser. Baldwin always puts on a magnificent bash for his staff in January as they work their bollocks off for him over the Christmas party period. It was free food and free booze all night and Russell thought he'd died and gone to heaven. He got so pissed that he was totally incoherent and physically incapable of walking. Stumpy agreed to take him home safely but I was now worried about tomorrow's matinee. I had never in my life been as completely out of it as Russell was but I remember the odd occasion when I'd been badly affected by booze, I couldn't function at all the next day thanks to raging headaches and vomiting. I knew Russ would never make the matinee, he would probably be unconscious for the next 24 hours. The next morning, I rang Mike as early as I dare and explained that we probably wouldn't have a Dame as Russ had been out for the count the night before. We didn't have understudies for either me or Russ as to be quite honest, we couldn't be replaced. Mike said he'd have a stab at it so he called in the whole company at 11 AM to rehearse his scenes. I got there at 10-50 and as I walked past Russell's dressing room, there he was, large as life, sorting out his make-up. He looked at me and said "What a bloody marvelous party, I thought your act was fabulous Love".

I said "How do you feel? Don't you feel ill? You were fuckin' dead last night, you couldn't stand up or speak"

"Yes Dear, I'm a bit of a cunt when it comes to free whisky, but don't worry Love, I'm fine".

"Haven't you got a headache?"

"WHAT ME? No Love, I *never* get headaches".

I was flabberghasted, I just couldn't believe that a man could get that pissed and still be OK. My alarm had been unnecessary and he went on and did his usual flawless performance. I think when he dies, someone ought to donate his liver to the British Shoe Company for research into indestructible soles, God bless him.

On hindsight, I should have been keeping a better weather-eye on my friend Mike Kay for unbeknown to me, his drinking was increasing to a degree where it would do him great harm.

There are many reasons why the 1988/9 production of Mother Goose was so memorable for me, here's another. It was the Saturday night of the penultimate week and we were all in the bar after the show having a few sherbets. The lounge was packed and we were tucked away in our usual spot in the far corner of the long bar. I suddenly felt a tug on my jacket and when I turned round I couldn't see anyone, until I looked down. There was this tiny elfin-like boy who looked to be about six years of age but again I stress, very small for his age. He was quite poorly dressed and had a chocolate ring around his mouth. He said to me, "Knutty, tha shudda got me up on dat stage t'neet cus ar wudda been a lot gudderer dan dem uvver kids wot cummup wiv dee". He was an enchanting little mudlark who could charm the monkeys out of the trees. He went on admonishing me by saying, "Awoz shoutin' at dee like mad but dar dint see me when da'woz pickin' kids". I could see straight away that if I'd chosen this little lad to come on the stage with me, he'd have stolen the show. I said I was really sorry for not picking him and then I had a brainwave. I said "Where's your Mam and Dad?"

"Dey're sittin oer deer, cummon, al show dee". With that he grabbed my hand and pulled me over to this young couple who were sitting by the window. He shouted "Dad, I've got Knutty 'eer, ee wants dee".

The father said rather sheepishly, "What's 'e dun nar?"

I told Dad his lad had done nothing except make friends with me and could I buy them a drink which they gratefully accepted. My intention was to invite them back the following Saturday, (the final performance), and get the little lad who's name was Paul, on stage with me. As I was suggesting my plan the mother interrupted and said that they couldn't afford to come back and see it again. I told her not to worry as I would sort all that out myself. I asked for their phone number and she said they weren't on the phone so I took their address and assured them that the tickets would be in the post with instructions who to ask for when they arrived. My dear friend Ali Fowler fixed it all up for me on the following Monday and I had a surefire feeling that little Paul was going to live up to all my expectations.

The last night came and the front of house manager had told me exactly where Paul would be sitting so that I could go and grab him for the song-sheet spot. The house was totally full and my excitement was growing as I felt they were going to see a bit of true magic that night. We'd got lots of toys left as they always over-ordered and I'd had them all placed on the large trap door from which Mother Goose used to appear in the Pool of Beauty scene. When it came to the time for choosing the kids, I confessed to the audience that I'd met Paul the week before and that he'd rollocked me for not picking him which resulted in lots of "Aahs". I got him on the stage after having picked the other two first and he got a round of applause. I was flabberghasted to see that his parents had bought him a proper little suit with long trousers in a sort of shiny maroon mohair material. To complete his ensemble he had on a little white shirt and a red tie and they'd brylcreemed his hair down so that he looked a bit like Alf Alfa out of the little rascals, he looked like a thirty bob salad. I was very careful not to spend too much time with him and ignore the other two so the "interview" part of the spot went very well as usual. I did the Old MacDonald's Farm spot with tiny Paul snorting for Britain as the pig, which brought waves of laughter from the crowd. It was amazing to see this miniature little boy letting forth these enormous snorts which really rattled the speakers in the auditorium. At one point he fetched the place down when he said "I'm sorry Knutty, I've done a snotter on yer microphone". I gave the other two children their presents and got them loud cheers from the audience as they returned to their seats to rejoin their parents. Next comes the bit where I pretend that there's no toys left and the last kid gets a balloon and one toffee. Now he wasn't daft and he'd already seen the show the previous week so he *knew* he was gonna get a good present and he was acting a little blasé. He got the biggest laugh of the whole evening when I told him how much I liked his new suit. He'd kept on scratching his bum the whole time he'd been on stage and when I asked him if he'd got something in his eye, he replied "No these trousers are gooin' reyt up my arse". The place erupted to hear this miniscule little waif saying things way beyond his years.

I went to the wings and came back with his final present, a stick of rock. I told him that as it was the very last show, we really had run out of prezzies and that's all we'd got left. The audience were really giving it some "Aahhs" and his bottom lip started to go so I quickly said to him, "Come and sit next to me on the stage". I sat us both down right behind the trap door and you could hear a pin drop as I quietly said to him, "Priscilla the magic goose gave me this stick of rock and it's got magic powers. If you bash it as hard as you can onto the stage, it'll let all its magic powers out and something special might happen". I got the audience to count to three and he bashed it down so hard that it broke into several pieces. At the same time the lights went out, there was a flash from the front of the stage and when the lights came back up there was this great pile of toys right in front of him. The audience went bloody barmy. They clapped and cheered and whistled at the stage miracle which they'd just witnessed. As for Paul, he was speechless, beaming with delight, but speechless. Four usherettes came down to the edge of the stage with lots of large plastic carrier bags to hold Paul's swag. There were construction kits for ships, cars and aeroplanes, big cuddly toys and even a few dolls which he could donate to any girls that he knew. I was quite close to tears as the moment was so magical to see the look on this little lad's face which was so illuminated with joy. In all my years of doing pantomimes, I have never known a more rewarding instant than that incomparable time that I spent on stage with that memorable little boy. I never saw or heard from him again, he's all grown up now with possibly a family of his own. I hope he gets to read this book, if he does, cheers mate! You're a star.

Clouds On The Horizon

As usual after the Panto finished it was back to the same old routine of clubs and travelling round the country doing one-nighters. I'd been booked back at the Crucible to do what would be my last ever panto there. It was to be Babes in the Wood and my old mate Lesley Ashe was playing principal girl. The Lyceum was in the process of being refurbished at a cost of twelve million quid and I had been promised the first pantomime in there the following year. I couldn't wait.

As far as I can recall, 1989 was an uneventful year but I do remember me gradually getting really pissed off with the few remaining WMCs that JP was still booking me into. Whenever I had any bother or problems within the sphere of my employment, it was nearly always in a club. The audiences were getting rowdier and the comics were getting bluer. I must have seemed like Noddy with my clean topical comedy and I gradually felt an erosion in my popularity at those types of places. The TV work was dropping off as the "New Wave" comics were filling up all the slots on the few shows that still had a comedian. The big cabaret venues were closing down due to lack of attendances and the exorbitant fees demanded by the big name acts.

Donna was surviving at her health club on West Street but unknown to her she was being undermined and stabbed in the back by a woman who worked for her. The club was having financial problems due to constant problems with the plumbing and electrical systems, the repairs for which were eating into the profit margins quite considerably. The two seedy businessmen who'd employed my lovely Donna were now giving her a hard time in every way possible. The woman whom she trusted completely, her name was Bernie, falsely accused her of allowing steroids to be taken and sold on the premises. She also told them that I was helping myself to drinks from behind the bar which was also totally untrue as for most of 1989-90 I was teetotal. Donna eventually became so stressed out by these outrageous lies which this vitriolic bitch had concocted that she handed in her notice and left. The bitch was made manager and her total incompetence caused the place to close shortly afterwards. We often wondered why she'd done it as she always came across as all sweetness and light in both her manner and her work ethic. She'd been to our home for meals and even had two of our cat's kittens. She certainly fooled me, and believe me folks, you've got to get up early in the morning to con me. I was so devastated for my Donna as I know her to be the sweetest, trusting most honest and upright person I've ever known. She couldn't cheat if her life depended on it and steroids have always been her pet hate above all things. I just did my best to comfort her and assure her that she'd come out of it with her head held high.

The Spare Tyres were becoming very popular and although it cost me money to go out and gig with them, I enjoyed it more than anything I'd done for many a year. My guitar collection was steadily growing and I really felt that they would be an appreciating investment for the future.

The panto came around all too quickly and for me it was an anticlimax to the magnificent Mother Goose the year before. It still sold out and we even did an extra week making it the longest panto run ever done at the Crucible. During the second week of the run, something happened to me which was to affect me for the rest of my life. On the Thursday night of the second week, I went for a curry with Donna and an old pal whom I'd done Panto with twice before, Colin Devereaux, or Dockyard Doris as he was known in the business. He'd come to see the show as he knew both me and Jonathan Owen who was playing the Sheriff of Nottingham. I drove home and as I pulled round the sharp hairpin bend which led into School Lane where I lived, I found the road to be blocked by a BMW which was parked right across the roadway. Donna noticed two thuggish looking characters having what looked like an altercation with a small bloke who lived round the corner. They were pushing and shoving him and looked like they were going to set about him. On hind sight I should have ignored it and squeezed around the

BMW on the pavement, but I didn't. I got out of the Land Cruiser and said something like "Come on lads, leave it out, move your car and leave him alone". One of the youths came straight towards me with his fists raised shouting for me to fuck off and mind my own business. I knew he was about to hit me so I thought I'd better get the first one in, I hit him as hard as I could and he went down. I then went over to try and reason with the other one who was still having a go at the neighbour. Unfortunately for me, I didn't hit the first one hard enough and the next thing he was on my back with his hands round my neck, that's when the other one hit me in the throat. Donna jumped down from the car and tried to assist me but one of them hit her too and the blow broke one of her back teeth. I now went berserk and picked up a piece of wood which was lying at the bottom of my driveway. I went for them with the plank and Donna took the keys out of their ignition and threw them over some bushes into someone's garden. By now a neighbour had come out and said he'd called the police at which the two thugs legged it. By now my throat was really hurting me and I could hardly speak. I drove my car up my drive to clear the roadway and went back to my neighbour's house where he poured me a brandy. The police arrived shortly after and said they'd arrested the two hooligans who'd said I started the fight. To top it all, the twat of a neighbour whose aid I'd gone to also said that I'd struck the first blow. OK that was true, but I was defending myself against a surefire attack from a drunken man who was about to hit me. The policeman who seemed to be in charge said he sympathized with me but it was debatable as to who was to blame and it was best forgotten. I couldn't believe what I was hearing, my wife had been assaulted and I had been grievously damaged in my throat. The copper took me to one side and gave me the names and addresses of the two assailants, he sort of winked then said "Bide your time Knutty".

The next day my throat was on fire and my voice was virtually gone. I rang the throat specialist at his home and he agreed to see me right away that very morning. He put a camera down my throat and there was a blood blister the size of a cherry on my larynx. My vocal chords were unable to function and I had two shows to do that day. He said to me "I'm going to tell you to do something which I know you cannot do thanks to your commitments at the Crucible. You must not speak above a whisper for at least six weeks or you'll do irreparable damage to your voice". He might as well have told me to go and stick pins in my eyes. I *had* to do the panto, I had no understudy and the place was sold out. I went to the theatre for the matinee and immediately had a meeting with the head of sound, my dear friend Trevor Dunford. I explained what had happened and that he must mike me up as high as he possibly could. The show was agony for me, both physically and mentally. My injury prevented me from projecting any volume whatsoever so I couldn't give the audience what they were used to no matter how much Trevor turned me up. I only know one way to do panto, and that's at full blast one hundred miles per hour. The more I tried to put some volume into my voice, the more damage I did and the more it hurt. I got through the matinee, they were a schools audience who didn't really give a shit about my throat, and they enjoyed it without probably realizing anything was wrong with me. The night show would be the tester and my voice was worse due to the hammering it had taken during the matinee. I was also beginning to feel feverish as my throat was beginning to become infected. I did the night show like a zombie, but Dr Theatre took over and did his best to help me through. By the end of the night my voice had just about given out and I apologised to the audience during the finale, I got a round of applause and I could feel the waves of sympathy washing down over the footlights.

The next day I was very ill, my voice was totally gone and I had a high temperature. I had never missed a panto performance in my life except for the night my father died and there had been times when I was ill but I'd always gone on and done it. This time I knew that no amount of stoicism or determination would allow me to perform, I was going to let my kids down and I knew that the theatre would have to cancel two fully sold out Saturday performances. Oh how I hated those two mindless thugs who'd caused all this to happen. I wanted to kill them, they'd started a chain of events which was by no means over for me. I spent the whole weekend in bed with antibiotics to help me over the infection and never uttered a sound. I went back on Monday and just struggled through the rest of the run. The damage I did to my vocal chords by choosing to continue working was to get worse as the years progressed. The first and for me, the most tragic thing was the total loss of my bass register. I had a beautiful bass-baritone singing voice and I could rattle the speakers with the bottom note in "Old Man River". The damage to my vocal chords had destroyed my ability to hit the bass notes in any song which I tried to sing. Over the years, my voice has got steadily worse and decreased in strength and power which affects my ability to project like any normal actor. I've had operations and exploratory cameras down my throat, much to my extreme discomfort but nothing can be done. I have a permanent hoarseness which will never improve. I just pray that as time goes by, I don't lose my voice completely, should that happen my ability to earn a living will be curtailed. All this because I went to the aid of an ungrateful neighbour who was being attacked by two mindless morons. He never even came round to thank me for trying to help him. It's a lesson I've learned, but sadly too late, never interfere in someone else's problems because you may live to regret it, as I did.

I know who they are, I've followed their progress through life over the years, but I've still not decided yet whether or not to let it lie. Who knows, maybe I will, and maybe I won't.

Courts & Committee Men

Sometime in March of 1990 I was booked to appear at the Arundel WMC in Sheffield for a Saturday night double with another club in the city. The clubs had cottoned on to the agents' suggestions that to book a comic for one spot for about two thirds of his normal fee would obviously save them some money. He then went to another club for the same fee and he ended up getting one and a half his normal fee for the slight inconvenience of going to two separate venues. I was booked to double up at the Burngreave WMC which was only ten minute's drive from the Arundel. There is a very long thoroughfare in Sheffield called City road which houses the vast General Cemetery half way up and three WMCs right next door to each other further up. They were the Arundel, the Manor Social and the Park and Arbourthorne WMC. Arguably, for most comics, there were four cemeterys on City Road, as the reception for most comedians was pretty frosty in those three clubs. I'd been appearing at the Arundel Club for years and was reasonably popular there although I was wise enough never to rest on my laurels and take them for granted. I was due on at 8-45pm for a 45 minute spot which gave me plenty of time to get to the other club for my 10-15 show.

The club was packed with the usual Saturday night crowd of bingo addicts and piss-artists who'd also been considerate enough to bring their unruly, snotty nosed offspring with them so they could run amok around the club to their heart's desire. The first act on was a guitar vocalist who kindly offered to let me use his mike. This was a boon to me as the house system was fuckin' useless and just about adequate enough for calling out the bingo numbers. I was also still suffering from a very weak voice owing to the incident to which I related in the previous chapter. The vocalist went on and he'd done what a lot of guitarists used to do, he'd wrapped his guitar lead through the carrying handle of the amplifier before he plugged it in to the input socket so as to prevent him pulling it out should he walk too far from his gear. Unfortunately for him, he'd walked too far and the guitar lead pulled over his complete rig with a resounding crash onto the floor of the stage. His PA amp was damaged to the extent that it wouldn't work at all so after much pissing around and fumbling with wires, he had to use the house mike. I felt really sorry for him as there was no echo for his voice and it sounded as if he was singing into a tin can. The audience didn't give a flying fuck about his predicament and thought it was a jolly good jape.

I went on at 8-50, five minutes late, and they gave me their attention. I had a line of small children aged from about six to eleven all gathered round the front of the stage, all chattering and trying to clamber up the five foot distance from floor to stage. They all had mucky hands and matching candlesticks running down their noses onto their top lips. One enterprising young urchin had scrounged himself a stool onto which he climbed so that his head and shoulders were level with the stage floor. He then went about his task of pulling out the mike cable which was plugged into a socket exactly in the centre of the stage apron. I was already having problems with the mike, it kept going on and off so I did a few ad-libs about it but after a while it became very annoying as the fuckin' thing would go off just as I was hitting the tag line of a gag. The plug wasn't very securely fixed onto the cable and as the kid fiddled about with the connection it caused an intermittent failure of the circuit so that I sounded like Norman Collier. I tried to gently prise him away with my foot but the little bastard was having none of it as he continued to tug at the plug socket. Nobody, including the bleedin' stupid club chairman made any effort to stop this little twat from his mischief until he finally succeeded in pulling the wire out of the plug which completely disabled the microphone. I now had a mike in my hand which wouldn't work, I couldn't use the other act's mike as that was knackered and the club didn't have a spare. My voice was totally unable, in its weakened state, to work a six hundred seater concert room without amplification so my only recourse was to walk off after first apologizing to the audience as loudly as my voice would allow. I had got changed in the dressing room and went in search of the chairman so he could pay me and let me get off to the next club. I eventually found him at the bar and when I asked him for my money he said he wasn't going to pay me as I'd not done my time as contracted. I knew it was useless trying to argue with this intellectual dwarf so I went off to the committee room to hopefully find the club secretary who I'd known for years and had always been a reasonable and intelligent man. He was holding court with his minions in the inner sanctum and when I told him what the chairman had said. He just replied casually, "Ar, I told 'im not t' pay thee cus tha cut thy act short". I tried to explain that I couldn't carry on with no microphone and that the clubs responsibility was to furnish me with a serviceable sound system which they had failed to do. He repeated that I wasn't getting paid and that was the end of it. I told him that he wouldn't have a leg to stand on when my union Equity took him to court. He just laughed at me, so I left.

The very next night, I was working with a very well known lady club act who did a bit of everything and played a few musical instruments. She had with her, her brother who happened to be a lawyer. When I told him of my run-in with the Arundel club the night before, he was fuming, he said that his sister had been in similar situations in the past and he'd gleefully sued every club in question and won. He begged me to let him handle the case and for me not to go to Equity as they would take years to settle it. He said he wouldn't charge me as he'd get his fees from the costs and that he would delight in fucking them up royally. Here was a man who hated the club committees and their bombastic attitude towards the artistes, he was on a mission and I was going to delight in watching his devout enthusiasm in solving my case.

He was good as his word and he vigorously pursued them with the tenacity of a dog tousing a slipper. He sent the club numerous letters which they predictably ignored. He graciously kept me informed of his progress and assured me of his anticipated success. He added that the club was doing exactly as he knew they would in ignoring him and that each letter he sent was upping the eventual costs. I must confess, I was really enjoying the process as it evolved and was looking forward to seeing them get their cum-uppance. He eventually secured a court date but as an added inconvenience to the committee men concerned, he summoned them to a court in Leeds instead of Sheffield. Not too long afterwards, I received a cheque from the lawyer for my full fee plus the vat along with a gleeful letter stating that the club had to pay his costs plus the court costs. I was so chuffed that the club secretary's arrogance had been easily overcome by the rightful decision of the court.

Bob's Your Uncle and Fanny's Your Aunt

By the early summer of 1990 I had still not heard from the Crucible people regards the panto at the Lyceum. JP eventually discovered that they were opening the newly refurbished theatre with a lavish production of the Pirates of Penzance starring Paul Nicholas and the full Broadway cast. This completely fucked me up for finding a panto that year as all the main shows had been cast much earlier in the year. The Crucible/ Lyceum complex had taken on a new head of operations and poor old Knutty definitely didn't figure in his plans. Mike Kay had been relieved of his duties so I no longer had an ally in the camp. I couldn't believe that I wouldn't be appearing in a Sheffield panto, I felt that I belonged there after so many triumphant box-office winners, but I was wrong. I didn't realise at the time but I was being foolish in thinking that I had a God given right to perform in a Sheffield panto every single year. Things have to change but I found it difficult to accept. Instead, it looked as if I would have to do the rounds of the December Christmas cabarets, trying to entertain drunken revelers who didn't give a shit about the entertainment.

One thing which *did* turn up however was series two of a situation comedy which I'd had to turn down the year before for the first series. It was entitled "All Change" and it starred Frankie Howerd and Peggy Mount. The basic plot was set around two branches of one family, mine, from the north and the southern branch headed by that fine actress Maggie Steed. We hated each other but we had inherited a million pounds from Uncle Bob, (Frankie Howerd), and the terms of the inheritance stated that we had to work together amicably for a full year in order to collect the money. Aunt Fanny, (Peggy Mount) was the comedy villain who ran an old folk's home; it was called "The Dunramblin Home for the Comfortably Bewildered". She had her brother Bob locked away there, refusing to let him out until he changed his will in her favour. Playing my wife was Pam Ferris who had just finished filming her role as Ma Larkin in The Darling Buds of May. She was not yet nationally known as it had not been transmitted yet. It's funny how you meet people in my profession, I met Pam at about 8am on the first day of the shoot and twenty minutes later we were in bed together for the next five hours while we shot the first scenes of episode one. She was a very nice lady but I found her to be a little on the "Grand" side if you know what I mean; having said that, it was a pleasure to work with her as she's a bloody wonderful actress. The shoot took nine weeks and I stayed down in London for the duration at Joyce Taylor's fabulous pro-digs for poor thespians in fabled Wanstead. She was a fantastic personality who did the Times crossword in about thirty minutes but sadly she had ceased to do an evening meal owing to her work commitments as a dental nurse. I had no choice but to have a take-away Ruby Murray every night which increased my already expanding girth.

Peggy Mount was an absolute treasure and I did a lot of scenes with her. She was a real lady of the first order and I had so much respect for her long years in the business playing so many different roles. We spent a lot of time in between scenes chatting and chewing the fat about all aspects of our profession. She was particularly impressed at me being a stand up comic and she couldn't for the life of her understand how I could go out alone onto a stage for over an hour without a script. We told each other many stories, mine mainly being about my adventures in the clubs and hers about all the many films she'd done. I was always very mindful about not swearing in her presence as I had never heard her utter one single expletive during any of our many conversations. She was so different from the scary gruff voiced characters she'd made her fortune playing on the big and small screens. She was a quietly spoken gentle lady with a smile that lit up the room and the most beautiful magnetic eyes you ever saw. I remember one day, I asked her what was it like shooting that legendary movie, "Oliver" in which she played the role of Mrs Bumble, the Beagle's wife. It's my all time favourite musical and the songs by Lionel Bart stick in my memory so vividly that I know the words to nearly all of them. She related a story about the filming of the song "Food, Glorious Food" which had me on the floor laughing. As far as I can recall, this is how she told it to me.

"It took us a week to shoot it Darling because there were so many shots and angles and scenes within a scene. The many boys who were involved playing the workhouse lads were all taken from local schools and stage academies and some of them were tough little characters. The boy playing Oliver would sometimes try his luck with them by nipping or hitting them. He got away with it because they'd all been warned not to touch him under any circumstances as he was the star of the show. He could be a right little barstard and when the scene was finally over the director Carol Reed shouted "That's a wrap"; they grabbed him and knocked the shit out of him". To hear Peggy suddenly swear in such a bold and uninhibited fashion made me piss myself laughing.

Frankie Howerd was a different kettle of fish altogether. We only had him on set with us for three days as they crammed all his scenes in to one specific shoot for his own convenience. I was really excited at the prospect of meeting him as I'd admired him greatly for many years and considered him to be one of Britain's comedy legends. I was equally excited at the fact that we had quite a few scenes together and had learned my lines till I knew them backwards. He was in the make-up wagon when I met him. My very first impression on setting eyes on him was to think to myself, "How come a bloke with as much money as this one probably has, spends tuppence halfpenny on the worst fuckin' rug I'd ever seen". Wigs can be almost undetectable but the one he wore looked like someone had plonked a piece of coconut matting on his bonce. I went up and introduced myself and held out my hand to shake his. He looked at me, he didn't smile, he just said "You're a comedian aren't you?" I replied "Yes I am".

He just sort of murmured, "Hmm, I see". When I shook hands with him it was like holding a dead herring, there was no attempt on his part to even slightly squeeze my hand, it was as if I had been given the honour of squeezing his. I wandered over to my make-up lady and sat down and she gently grasped my shoulder and rolled her eyes to the ceiling. When he'd gone she quietly said, "He can be a

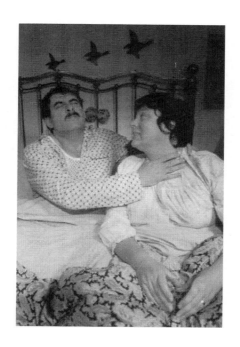

All Change with Pam Ferris

Knutty in drag   *Lovely Peggy*

Maggie Steed

funny bugger when he wants to be and he probably feels insecure because you're another comedian".

Once we got onto the set and started shooting the scenes, he seemed to settle down but I was amazed to see him keep halting a scene and telling the director that he ought to be doing it this way or that way. I couldn't believe he had the temerity to insult a fine director by trying to tell him how to do his job. He then got right up my fucking nose when he stopped a scene and told me if I changed my delivery of a certain line to the way he suggested, it would go better. The director, Garth Tucker could see I was getting ready to blow so he called a quick tea break and took me to one side. He told me not to worry about it and that I should play it the way Frankie suggested, it would then end up on the cutting room floor and my original effort would be the one that went out on the screen. He went on to say that Mr Howerd had behaved like this during the first series and we thankfully only had two more days of his charming company after which we could go back to being the happy cast that we were before. I suffered Frankie's insufferable temperament for the next couple of days and all I can say is how desperately disappointed I was at working with him. I was hoping it was going to be one of the highlights of my career but it turned out to eminently forgettable. I still considered him to be a comedy icon and that would never change, but instead of meeting one of my comedy heroes, I met a sad, insecure old Queen, a flawed genius who I'm sure would have been a much merrier man if only he'd have chilled out a little. He died about a year or so after the series and I felt a twinge of sadness for him because he seemed such a melancholy man with possibly quite a few hidden demons.

Unhappy New Year

Ever since the early days of my career I have always hated working on New Years Eve. The reasons must be obvious even to a layman; the poor comic has to endure a roomful of over-intoxicated revelers who don't give a fuck about anything else except hokey cokeys, congas and Auld Lang Syne. I've had numerous bad experiences on the fateful 31st of December, so much so that I vowed never to do another unless I could have a written guarantee that I would be on stage for 9pm at the latest. I remember one particular year in the mid seventies when I was doing Christmas/New Years week at Jollees Night Club in Stoke. I finished on the Saturday night which was the 31st at about 11pm and I got out of the place at 11-30. I spent midnight in a snow storm on the Derbyshire hills approaching Buxton. Everybody else in the country was dancing and boozing with their loved ones and I was trying to tune in to a fading Radio Luxembourg in a bleedin' blizzard.

As I wasn't doing panto for the first time in many years I had to put myself about for the festive parties and I was offered a New Years booking at a cricket club in Warrington. The money was reasonable and after getting them to agree to my going on no later than 9pm, I took the job. 9pm my fuckin' arse, I ended up going on at 10-30 and they were getting rowdy. I cut my act short to around thirty minutes and came off while I was in front. I copped for my dosh and swerved out as quickly as I could. I'd not had a single drop of alcohol and I was dying to get home and have a large port and brandy. At around 11-15pm I was driving through Glossop on my approach to the Snake Pass when a copper just jumped out into my path with his torch shining on my windscreen. He must have been lurking in a shop doorway out of the rain and decided to give me a pull. As it happens there were two of them, the other one sauntered out as I hastily came to a halt. I was taxed and insured, the car was in perfect order and I hadn't touched a drop so I thought there's no need to be too nice to these two fucking bounty hunters. I said to the young copper, "You'll get yourself killed jumping out into the road like that". He was obviously a jobsworth who was mightily pissed off at having to work on New Years Eve so he went straight into his script. "I have reason to believe Sir that owing to the speed you were travelling at in a built up area, you have consumed alcohol and I require you to take a breath test. If this test proves positive you will be required to accompany us to the station where you will be required to give a blood or urine sample". I said to him, "How do you know what speed I was doing, do you have a portable device which assesses my velocity?" He looked a bit miffed at the fact that I was obviously unafraid of his assumption at my alleged speed. I then said "I was doing thirty miles an hour and I will gladly take your breathalyzer test as I am a committed teetotaler". (Lying Bastard) He called my bluff and said I'd have to accompany them down the road to the station to take the test. He said that as I was suspected of drink-driving I couldn't drive down to the station. I hadn't got a coat and I wasn't about to walk down to the station in the freezing cold rain so I refused politely and suggested they send out a car with a breath test kit on board. I couldn't believe it when he agreed and radioed for a car. I had been waiting for this to happen for years. I was once breathalysed a few years before and it had been borderline but the copper gave me the benefit of the doubt. I swore I'd never drink and drive again because the thought of being banned plus the stigma of the offence made me shudder as I blew into that bag. The car arrived with a sergeant and a constable in it and they produced their breathalyzer for me to inflate.

I blew as hard as I could into his little tube and it was wonderfully negative. I asked if there would be anything else and they reluctantly said I could get on my way. As I pulled away in my lovely warm Land Cruiser I felt not the least bit sorry for those two arseholes who I knew would be spending a cold wet night patrolling the dark streets of a Derbyshire town while the rest of the place celebrated the advent of 1991.

Donna had arranged a party for some of the people who worked at her club. She'd set up a new operation further down the road from the place that had goosed her and she was doing OK. I was a bit reluctant at having this little bash as I'm very particular who comes to my house. I can't help it; I've always been that way. My home is my castle and my own inner sanctum, I don't like strangers coming in and seeing how I live. I arrived back home to the cottage just before 1am and they were really going at it full blast. Donna was a wee bit worse for wear, bless her but some of the "Guests" were fuckin' smashed. Complete strangers, boy friends and girlfriends of Donna's staff who were treating my house like a drinking den. Some of *my* personal friends were there and I was so glad to see them but the rest of them were getting right on my nerves. It's a strange thing to be totally stone cold sober and to walk into a room full of drunks. I thought I'd better go about catching them up so I downed a couple of large port and brandys. Not too long after, a couple of the people who I didn't know started getting a bit lairy and began arguing quite loudly. That was it for me; I put them both outside and told the rest of them to fuck off home as the party was over for them. They could see I was serious as well as angry so they left with no argument. I sat down with my remaining close mates and told them about the two coppers in Glossop and we pissed ourselves laughing. It had been an eventful evening for me to have to go back to what I did years before, God how I missed the Pantomime.

Death In Germany

A comedian's life isn't all laughs and high wages and the nineties were going to prove this to me. My first book was full of hilarious anecdotes about my experiences as I grew up and matured into a professional entertainer with many strings to my bow. My earnings gradually increased as my TV appearances became more regular and I had some wonderful adventures involving lots of laughs and even lots more women. It was a great part of my life which I thoroughly enjoyed remembering and writing about. I've not heard a bad word about the book and I received some extremely complimentary revues from both public and press.

I've now reached a stage in my story when my life takes a turn for the worse owing to many reasons but as I relate it to you, I'll try and keep it as entertaining as I can. 1991 began quite dismally for me as I'd not done a panto for the first time in fourteen years so my bank balance wasn't as healthy as it usually was at that time of year. The wages from panto had always been a big boost to the funds and generally paid big bills like the January half yearly tax demand and any other large debts which may have cropped up. I'd done the December Christmas cabarets but January had always been notoriously slack for one nighters and the only thing left was the WMCs. JP was still booking hundreds of clubs but a lot of them were steadily going downhill and the audiences were getting harder every year. I used to dread doing them and I even suffered a sort of hypertension on the days that I was doing a club. The Crucible panto always went on to the end of January but instead of just nipping down to Sheffield town centre to do two shows, I was tear-arseing all over the country in bad weather doing the loneliness of the long distance comedian.

I remember getting a call from an agent whom I rarely worked for asking if I'd go to Germany in April for a Friday and Saturday entertaining the troops. You already know that I'd done many shows over the years for Combined Services Entertainment and loved every one. There was also another firm which did troop shows and it was the NAAFI, these shows were cruelty to comics and an absolute fuckin' nightmare. I'd done just the one sometime in 1977 with my old mate Billy Bean and his group The Statesmen. It was a three week tour round the bases in Germany and I travelled with the lads in the group van. Also on the bill was my old lead guitarist from the Whirlwinds, Dave Friskney. Dave was and still is one of the best guitarists I've ever heard but he'd got about as much brains as a rocking horse. We took the piss out of him unmercifully on that trip and most of the time he didn't know. Most of our gigs were entertaining the lower ranks in their huge canteens and they were noisy bastards who didn't give a shit about the show. They were just there to get as drunk as possible and hopefully pull a girl soldier or a German waitress. Having said that, the officers could be just as bad, sometimes worse. I remember we did a show in the officer's mess at RAF Vildenrath; it was bad enough to be memorable. Their mess was like a large lounge in a private house with numerous arm chairs and a bar. There was nowhere really suitable for us to set up the gear so we crammed it all into the only suitable corner. They were pretty well pissed before we started and the horsey laughs and guffaws echoed round the room in abundance. I used to open the show with a five minute patter spot and put Dave on. My opening spot was embarrassing as I might as well have been talking to the furniture; they just carried on talking amongst themselves and totally ignored me. Dave's act was very good thanks to his amazing guitar talents plus his voice was well suited to the Roy Orbison type of songs. They totally ignored him and carried on talking and bellowing like naughty schoolboys as if he wasn't there. I was on next and Billy said it would be pointless carrying on with the show unless someone explained to this drunken bunch of "Hoorah Henrys" that it was a cabaret show and not background music. We approached the chap who seemed to be running the affair and explained our problem at which point this officer's wife, who had been eavesdropping, rudely interrupted. She had the same speech impediment as Jonathan Ross which made her sound more of a twat than she already was. Her rebuke went as follows. "I say young man, these cheps are under a lot of pwessure, they fwy Hawwiers you know". I really had to bite my tongue but I was determined not to be rude to this puffy faced over- made up rhino-arsed harpy. I said "Madam! I fully appreciate that flying Harriers is a high pressure occupation requiring highly skilled chappies like the ones we have here tonight. Whatever their expertise and dexterity may embody, it doesn't give them, or you, the right to be rude, obnoxious and loud while we are trying to carry out *our* particular skills. May I suggest you enquire who amongst your pilots can sing, play guitar and tell jokes for an hour because if there is one he's got the job tonight. *We* Madam are going to pack away our gear and return to our hotel where we will partake of a large libation". We packed our stuff in record time much to their amazement and buggered off. They tried to persuade us to stay but we were having none of it, they could stick their fucking "Hawwiers" up their arses. The accommodations we were given on that trip were usually the cheapest they could find and very basic. One particular place was more like a YMCA hostel and the manageress was a right miserable old cow. In the foyer of this bijou little establishment was a couple of photographs of the hotel during the war with the entire front blown in and the roof missing. As I was looking at it she came up to me and hissed, "You English did zat". I smiled and replied, "Yeh, we didn't do a bad job of it did we".

I recall the worst gig of the trip was at the Marlborough Club at Reindalen. Reindalen was the GHQ of the whole forces network in Germany and the biggest base of them all. The Marlborough Club was the licensed shit-hole where the squaddies used to unwind and get horribly pissed. On the night we were there I witnessed a fight between a big lesbian truck driver and a beefy corporal. Apparently, he'd tried to chat up her girlfriend and the dyke had taken offence, she knocked the living shit out of him. He was only saved from further punishment when two burly MPs dragged her out kicking and bellowing like a wounded bull. That same night we had a serious problem with Dave Friskney. When he'd finished his spot he'd gone to the bar to down as many cheap drinks as he could and had befriended a squaddie who was also bent on alcoholic oblivion. This squaddie was, so the story goes, thoroughly pissed off at the fact that he and his drunken mates had been kicked out of a bar the previous night in the local town. He was bent on revenge and he ended up stealing an APC (armoured personnel carrier) with the intent of ramming it through the front window of the aforementioned establishment. Sadly, he roped easily led Friskney in as his accomplice and they ended up getting arrested as they tried to leave the base. They threw poor old Dave in the chokey for a very uncomfortable night's confinement until he sobered up. We had to go and see the Provost Marshall the next morning who in turn took us to see the CO. We explained that Dave was really quite harmless and very pissed at the time. We humbly asked the CO if he could see his way to releasing him into our custody and that we would make his life even more miserable by taking the piss out of him for the rest of his natural life. The CO was a proper gent who, after explaining that purloining MOD vehicles for the purpose of joyriding around the Reich was a very serious offence, allowed a very sheepish and hung-over Friskney back into our care.

Getting back to the beginning of my tale, when the agent rang about my going to Germany, you'll understand I wasn't that keen but the money was pretty good and I wasn't in a position to turn it down. He told me that the first night was a cabaret sponsored by Marlborough cigarettes and the Saturday was a CO's retirement dinner in a camp near Dusseldorf. He was a fuckin' lying bastard who conned me beautifully. I was picked up at the airport in Germany by a Geordie sergeant who'd seen me in the Falklands nearly ten years before. He was all over me with compliments saying that I was the best comic he'd ever seen and all the lads were looking forward to seeing me the following night. When I said that I understood it to be a CO's retirement do, he said "No bonny lad, it's a celebration night for two thousand squaddies just back from the Gulf war. We haven't got a room big enough on the camp so we're havin' it in the toon hall". My arse cheeks immediately clenched with fear at the knowledge of what I could expect the following night.

The first night was in the dreaded Marlborough club and it was indeed sponsored by the cigarette company but it was a big bash for all the staff who worked there and they were mostly young German girls with squaddies for boyfriends. I managed to get on early before they got too pissed but I didn't pull any trees up, I just survived. I could have bleedin' strangled that lying twat of an agent. I went back to my no stars hotel and felt unbelievably miserable, the bar was closed and I'd forgotten to pack a book to read.

The Geordie picked me up the next night and continued to regale me with tales of how much the lads were looking forward to seeing me. We arrived at the venue and I was gobsmacked at the size of it. It was a huge hall about half the size of a football pitch. It was architecturally beautiful and looked to be about 18th century period and in pristine original condition, how the bleedin' hell our lads in their Lancasters had missed it I'll never know. Lining the side and back walls were trestle tables laden to breaking point with food of every description. The army catering boys are legendary when it comes to putting on a spread and they'd pulled out all the stops on this occasion. There were rows and rows of long tables, a bit like the dining room in the Harry Potter films. At the front of this gigantic hall was a six foot high temporary stage on which were stacked speakers and amplifiers and a Disc Jockey's equipment. As I walked into this noise filled bedlam, there was already a group of scantily clad go-go dancers gyrating their ample tits and arses much to the delight of the randy squaddies who were all whooping and screaming at the girls to "Gerrem off". There wasn't exactly much to "Gerroff" as all they'd got on were the tiniest bras and a thong, you know , a sort of dental floss for their arses.The lads weren't buying drinks by the glass, the tables were chock full of full spirit bottles and cases of beer which they were downing as if it was their last day on Earth. The worst thing about the room from a comic's point of view was the vast space between the front row of revelers and the actual stage. It was a huge dance area which is impossible to get over with comedy. The dilemma was that if I worked on the stage I was much too far away from them and if I worked the front of the dance floor They'd never see me as it wasn't lit by any spot lights. I knew it was the kiss of death for me, every single thing that a comedian needs for a good reception was missing. I just told the Geordie lad that I couldn't go on and he didn't have to pay me. He kept on insisting that they were all waiting for me to which I replied that all they were waiting for was the go-go dancers and getting totally pissed. I eventually succumbed to his pleas but insisted that if I went on, I wanted paying in full. He then went straight to the money-man and got my cash which he eagerly thrust into my hand. I asked to see the DJ who sauntered down from his perch on the stage. I asked him to clear the dance floor as much as he could before he introduced me so I could work on the front of it as close as possible to the audience. I gave him the patter for my introduction which I'd written down on a piece of paper and he said I'd be straight on after the next spot from the girls.

Can you possibly imagine what I was up against? The girls went on topless and now the squaddies were in a frenzy, they all ran to the front of the stage to get a closer view. There must have been four or five hundred of 'em howling like wolves at the provocative motions of the dancers. As they left the stage down the steep steps they were mobbed by the soldiers and had to be escorted back to the changing area by the security lads. At that very moment, the fuckin' brain-dead DJ introduced me. He ignored the patter I'd given him and just shouted down his mike, "It's comedy time now, and here he is, Bobby Knutt". The dance floor was full of baying squaddies who wouldn't go back to their seats; he'd not even put the house lights up so they would be able to see me. I didn't move, I just gestured to the DJ to come down the steps so I could speak to him. He eventually got the message at the same time as the audience started gradually going back to their places. When he came down I was honestly ready for chinning him, I went fuckin' mental with him, "Didn't you hear one fuckin' word I said to you, you fuckin stupid moron. How do you expect me to perform on that floor when it's chock full of fuckin' bodies you fuckin' idiot. Now get back up there and give me a proper introduction or I'll shove that fuckin' mike of yours so far up your arse you'll need fuckin' surgery, you cunt!!". I think he got the hint and the Geordie sergeant was pissing himself laughing, he said "Ya dooant mince ya fuck'n words do ya bonny lad". The twat of a DJ must have known he'd really fucked me up so he tried to get them settled down and when he'd managed to clear the floor he introduced me again. As he shouted my name I ran out to the front of the floor which was a bloody good twenty yards and as I got there I shouted "Good evening lads". They all shouted back in perfect unison "FUCK OFF". I replied "Well lads, I don't usually do requests but in your case I will, GOODNIGHT". I walked off to a few cheers as they could now get back to ogling the strippers. The Geordie was disappointed but said he didn't blame me for cutting it short. I just told him that I was a comic, not a bleedin' gladiator. In all my long career as a comic, they were the worst audience I've ever experienced, but I came away with the brass in my pocket. I didn't feel resentful towards the lads as they had every right to let their hair down a bit after risking their lives out there in the gulf, bless 'em.

A Summer of Woe

The summer season of 1991 was the most eventful, and the most gruelling I've ever done. It was for the Haven-Warner company who became and still is the biggest holiday park outfit in the UK. At the time, my old pal Nigel Hudston was the big boss of the firm, he'd certainly come a long way since being the camp manager at Wallis's in Scarborough. I was booked to do alternate weeks in Great Yarmouth and the Devon-Cornwall area. I needed the work and I couldn't turn it down but I didn't realise what I was letting myself in for with all the travelling that was involved. You can't get two areas of England which are harder to travel between than Cornwall and Yarmouth. I worked Saturday to Thursday in both areas with Friday being my day off to do the journey between them. I was given a chalet on the biggest camp in the Yarmouth area which I stayed in all week. This gave me the opportunity to settle in with all my belongings for a week so that shopping and cooking weren't such an inconvenience. All the camps were within a twenty minute drive of my base so I was always back in time for a bit of supper and a video. It was totally different on the Cornwall run as I had a different caravan or chalet every night. Every single morning I had to pack away all my stuff, drive to the next camp and then carry it all into the van and unpack it again. There was all my cooking stuff, my video recorder, boxes of spices and ingredients plus all my clothes. For the first six weeks of the season I was driving home after the Thursday night show so that I could have the one day with Donna. I could do the trip from Yarmouth in about three and a half hours but the Cornwall trip was a right bastard of a journey. At the time I was driving a Toyota Supra Turbo which was an absolute flying machine. It would flash up to a hundred MPH before you knew it so I had to be very careful on the motorways where Mr Plod was always lurking in the wee small hours. I usually got back home from Cornwall around 5-30am completely knackered. I would try and creep into bed so as not to arouse Donna but she usually woke up and made me a cuppa. I missed her so very much; it was an emotion I'd never had to endure before, missing someone. Once the main summer season started in mid-June I realised that travelling back home every week would be impossible. What made me realise this was the Saturday when I set off for Cornwall at my normal sort of time of 9am and didn't get to my Devon camp until 8pm. Eleven hours on the road with every fuckhead who ever drove a car in front of me. It's funny you know, people like me drive terrifically long journeys maybe three or four times a week and think nothing of it. Your average Joe Public does it once a year and he's a fuckin' menace. They pile their little Nissans up with their bad tempered nagging wife and three or four impatient little rugrats. There's a roof rack full of shit they don't need and the back parcel shelf is packed with stuff which obstructs the driver's rear view mirror. They are the sort of drivers who wait at junctions or roundabouts for a huge gap in the oncoming traffic before they'll dare pull out. They drive at 35 mph on an "A" road and nobody can get round them and they *always* wear a flat cap. They are totally oblivious to the queue of traffic behind them nor are they aware of what a danger they are as other drivers risk their lives to overtake them.

The thing I hated most about that particular season was Saturday nights. It was a repeat of the summer of 1986 when due to the fact of a long tiring journey; the punters were hostile and unresponsive. My Saturday night in Yarmouth was the worst; it was a massive twelve hundred seater venue with a high stage and a very big dance floor. The place was full of young kids who ran around incessantly screaming and shouting and their parents didn't give a fuck that a comic was up there trying to die in peace. The Devon Saturday venue was just a bad with just the same amount of apathy from the pissed off punters. I think that particular camp was my least favourite as the accommodation which they always gave me was on the top floor of a three storey block of apartments. This meant I had to hump all my stuff up three flights of stairs and back down again when I left very early the next morning.

It was in this apartment on the Sunday morning of the 28th July 1991 that I received a phone call from my sister Helen. Helen was a quiet spoken gentle girl who was just like my father and had been looking after my mother whenever she could. My mother was suffering from Alzheimer's and had been for quite a while. It's a curse from God which I pray I never get because the person you knew gradually disappears from the body which they live in until finally there is an empty shell. My old Mam never got that far advanced thank God, but she often used to get the bus to town and forget which bus to catch for home. She used to wander into West Bar Police station and tell them that she was Bobby Knutt's mother and she was lost. They usually made sure she got back home OK.

I picked up my mobile phone and Helen just said "Hello Rob, Mam died this morning Love, she had a stroke". We chatted a bit longer and I said I'd be home as quick as I could. I was now an orphan, my Dad had died in 1979 and it tore me apart, I loved him above all others. My Mam and I were very much alike and sometimes we'd disagree on the odd thing or two. I didn't visit her as often as I should have as I was always busy working. When I did visit her, she'd tell me the same story over again as she didn't realise she was repeating herself. She'd write me letters because it was a way for her to talk to me and I'd noticed her once beautiful handwriting deteriorating as time passed. When I got the phone call from Helen, I realised that I'd not seen my Mam for nearly three months and I felt so desperately guilty, now I could never see her again. I couldn't make it up to her for not being there when she needed me just to talk to her. OK, I used to ring her up a lot, but it wasn't the same as a visit. I suppose I'm being a little hard on myself but I only went to see her a couple of times on those Saturdays that I'd been at home during the early season. I should have gone more and to this day I still feel guilty about it.

That night I was supposed to be appearing at Perran Sands Holiday Village in Perranporth which was way down in south Cornwall. I knew the company would never be able to get a comic to drive all that way at such short notice so unless I went down there they wouldn't have a cabaret. I happened to have Nigel Hudston's home number in my book so I rang him. When I told him my mother had just passed away he was really sympathetic and said I should get off home straight away. I told him that I didn't want to let him down at Perran Sands so I would go and do the gig. I asked him for the rest of the week off so I could sort out the funeral. He was so bloody grateful that I'd volunteered to go down and do the show for him. It was a favour which was to be repaid handsomely many years later when I was desperately in need. The journey back from Perran was a killer; I set off straight after the show and only stopped for fuel. I hammered the Supra all the way and did it in less than six hours. I don't remember much about that week but I do remember getting in the funeral car with my two sisters Helen and Tina and completely breaking down. I was sobbing like a baby and they held and comforted me all the way to the cemetery. It was the first time I'd cried since getting the news a week before.

At the start of that fateful season, I'd got three penalty points on my driving licence, by the end of it I'd managed to acquire another nine. I kept getting stopped on that stretch of the M5 down near Exeter. I was being as careful as I could but that bloody Supra turbo was a flying machine and it was so difficult to keep it down to seventy. The last time I got a tug from the plods in the jam sandwiches was near the end of the season and I was on my way back from Cornwall to see Donna at home. I was excited at the thought of seeing her and I wasn't concentrating on my speed. Suddenly I got the instant laxative, the blue flashing light in my rear view mirror. I remember thinking "Where the fuck did he come from". He was a bounty hunter who went straight into the patter, filled in his notebook and booked me. He was a really officious twat who I knew would have been immune to any begging and pleading so I just kept my mouth shut and let him get on with it. I was summoned to go to court in Exeter during the first week in November so I drove down with my mate Glen who owned the music shop. I went in my best freemason's suit with my Masonic tie-pin and Masonic ring on my finger just in case the magistrate might be on the square. He was a She and a right ugly old fucker with a tweed skirt and brown brogues on her feet. I explained that I desperately needed my licence for my job and that I could never hope to get a regular chauffeur to keep my ungodly hours. I laid it on thick with the charity shows I did but she didn't budge. She fined me a couple of hundred quid and banned me for the full six months under the totting up laws. I was right in the shit now but I must admit, my mates rallied round and I never missed a gig. The worst bit was not being able to nip to town or do the shopping. It was the longest six months of my life and I sold the Supra with the intention of buying a more sensible car when my ban was finished.

I Miss an Entrance

The panto of 1991-2 was probably the worst I ever did but I took it because I'd not been offered anything else. It was Babes in the Wood which is one of the least popular panto stories and it was being put on at the Doncaster Dome. The Dome isn't a theatre; it's a bleedin' great sports hall with no stage. The seats were installed in tiers and a stage was built on the long side wall with huge black drapes on either side to mask the wings. The sound just echoed round the room and the director was shite, he couldn't direct traffic, oh how I missed Mike Kay. There were two big rooms on either side of the hall which had to act as dressing rooms, one male and one female. I had a large caravan outside the stage door which I shared with Freddie Pyne who was playing the Sheriff of Nottingham. You may remember Freddie played Matt Skilbeck in Emmerdale; he was a lovely guy and a pleasure to work with. The problem with being out side in the caravan was that we couldn't hear what was happening on the stage so there was the great danger of missing an entrance. They couldn't fix up an intercom for us so we were snookered; we had to hang around in the wings till we were due on stage. Freddie and I would take it in turns to do the shopping for our in-between show meals and we became quite the little Darby and Joan. I recall one visit to the supermarket which was just near the Dome. The checkout lady recognized me and asked what I was doing there so I told her I was doing panto at the Dome. She said she didn't even know there *was* a panto at the Dome, it was then that I realised there were no posters up anywhere to advertise our show. I rang the producer who said the publicity was down to the Dome's own in-house publicity department or "Apathy Incorporated" as I called them. Our show was the best kept secret in Doncaster and I had a reputation for putting arses on seats which was about to be sorely tarnished. The business turned out to be pretty good but nothing like my achievements in previous years at the Crucible.

We did a slosh scene in the panto after which there was a little spot from the dame and then I was back on with the Sheriff for the scene where we kidnap the babes. I used to run off after the slosh and the principal girl would be in the wings with a towel to clean up my face and a clean shirt for me to put on. I just about had enough time to do this before I was back on for the kidnapping. On the day in question, I'd been and got some green lipped mussels from the market to have for my mid show meal, they are one of my favourite delicacies and I'll eat you a bucketful. Sadly, these mussels were off and they gave me a massive dose of the trots. I felt OK until about half way through the slosh scene when I had this uncontrollable urge to go big poos. I managed to get through the slosh but I knew I was on the verge of a serious accident unless I got to the loo in double quick time. I ran off and there was Lizzie waiting in the wings to wipe me down, I just shot straight past her. I now had a serious case of the turtle's head and was struggling to get my shirt over my bonce as I was wearing braces underneath it so I couldn't get my keks down until it was off. Freddie was coming in the opposite direction and as I flew past him I said "You might have to kidnap the Babes on your own Fred, I'm shitting myself". I made it with no seconds to spare, my guts had turned to water and I sat there knowing I'd never make it in time for my scene. Poor old Freddie ad-libbed his way through it on his own like the trooper he was and nobody in the audience was any wiser. It was the only time in my whole panto career that I missed an entrance.

Buckingham Palace

On the 1st of June 1992 the postman dropped a letter through our door which contained an invitation for us both to attend a garden party at Buckingham Palace. Apparently it was 40 years since the Queen's accession to the throne and the garden party was for all the sports stars whom she'd decorated during her reign. Donna had received her MBE in 1979 so was eligible to go, as her consort, I was invited too. I'd previously met Prince Andrew, Princess Anne and Princess Margaret so I was hopeful at adding the Queen and Prince Philip to the list.

I started making plans for the big day by booking us into a swish hotel the night before and for the night of the party so we could relax and enjoy it. I also booked a table for two at Veeraswami's world famous Indian restaurant. It is one of the oldest Indian restaurants in Gt Britain and I, as a curry fanatic was overjoyed at the thought of dining there. I bought a new suit and Donna splashed out on a gorgeous day dress befitting of the occasion.

We got settled into the Holiday Inn on the Wednesday afternoon and got a taxi down to Veeraswami's around 7pm. We were welcomed on the door by a large Indian gentleman swathed in a white turban and a red tunic with shiny brass buttons. He guided us to the lounge where the diners may enjoy a cocktail while they peruse the menu. After staring at the exorbitant, nay, obscene prices for the food and wines, Donna said "We're not staying here, it'll cost you a bloody fortune, these prices are ridiculous". I was taken aback myself by the extortionate prices but I was reluctant to leave as I'd looked forward to it so much. I talked Donna into staying saying that it was a once in a lifetime experience to eat at this famous venue.

We ordered our meal and a bottle of Frascati which was priced at twenty one quid, the same wine was five pounds fifty in our normal curry place back in Sheffield. They brought the pickle tray and poppadums which we didn't order and charged us a tenner for them. The food arrived and sad to say it was very ordinary and the

The Executive Committee of the Central Council of Physical Recreation
requests the pleasure of the company of

Mr and Mrs Robert Wass

at a Garden Party at Buckingham Palace
by gracious permission and in the presence of
The Queen and The Duke of Edinburgh
on Thursday, 9th July, 1992 from 4 to 6 p.m.

Lounge Suit

Princess Anne

206

sauces were quite bland. What made it worse for us was they'd seated us right next to a table of half a dozen yanks who were very very loud and their stereotyped conversation revolved purely about how much money they'd got.

After the disappointing meal, Donna said she'd left her cigarettes in the hotel room and she fancied a fag so could I get her a packet. She smoked about three or four Silk Cut per day so I called the waiter who said they only stocked Benson and Hedges, I asked him to bring a pack. He eventually arrived with the opened packet on a little silver tray; one cigarette had been teased out from the rest so as to make it easily accessible. The bill arrived and I was glad to be seated, it was well over a hundred pounds and then the cheeky twats had bunged a 15% service charge on top. What really made me seethe was what they'd charged me for the ciggys. In those days a packet of Bensons was about two pounds thirty and they'd charged me a fiver for them, PLUS 15% on top. Much to Donna's embarrassment, I called the manager and politely told him that I was reluctantly prepared to pay for his vastly over priced food and wine but I wasn't going to be ripped off by paying over double the price for a pack of cigarettes. He quietly relented and we left, Donna could see I was both upset and angry at my long awaited visit to a curry emporium which couldn't hold a candle to half the Indian restaurants in Sheffield.

I'd forgotten about it the next day and was really excited at the thought of our visit to the Palace. All the invited guests had been allocated a parking spot on the Mall and as we arrived there were police to guide us to our places. I must confess that I felt an amazing tingle as I walked across the palace yard to the entrance, me, a steelworker's lad form Sheffield was about to enter the Queen's house, my old Dad would have been so proud. I was amazed when I entered the main building to discover that it was quite narrow and pretty soon we'd passed through some doors into the massive garden. I realised that the palace is "U" shaped and what you imagine to be a huge square building is really three sides surrounding a huge lawn. The lawn was the best kept example of greenery I've ever seen. It's not grass, it's chamomile and you seem to spring along when you walk on it. Donna was so excited to see so many old friends and I left her alone to catch up on their news. I was chuffed myself to see so many of these sporting legends all in one place, Frank Bruno, Henry Cooper, Stirling Moss and Fatima Whitbread. I got chatting to this Beefeater who was on duty and he told me to stay close to him if I wanted to meet the Queen. When she made her entrance, she was accompanied by the Duke and Prince Edward. The beefeater was straight there as a sort of minder to clear a path through the crowd and I stuck to him like glue. The Queen was right next to me and she gave me a smile, then the Duke spoke to me, he said "You're a weightlifter aren't you?" I replied "Yes Sir I am", well I wasn't lying was I, I lifted weights four times a week at my gym.

I found Donna and we made our way to the refreshment tent but there was no ale to be had, just tea and cucumber sandwiches with the crusts cut off. I was so proud of her that day; she was the best looking lass on that green. It had been a wonderful day and we rounded it off with a fantastic aromatic crispy duck in a Chinese near the hotel, it made up for the shite we'd had the night before.

The Life of a Struggling Actor

1993 saw the start of a massive worldwide financial depression and as usual, the entertainment industry suffered terribly as a result. What a lot of people think, is that all self-employed are well off. The simple fact of the matter is, if you don't work, you don't get any money. I sold my Toyota Supra but had to let my private plate go with it so as to obtain a better price. I bought a second hand Honda which was comfortable and reliable. I'd got my licence back in early May and was thank God mobile again. The one night stands were getting more difficult to fix as the trends in comedy were leaning more towards the blue comics. I didn't get a summer season that year so there was no light at the end of the tunnel which would act as a financial buffer. At the time I had a very bent casting agent who ended up being black listed by Equity and still is to this day. He owed me money from TV work which I had done and he had been paid for. I was overdrawn at the bank and what he owed me would have put me back in the black.

The three biggest lies in the world are "I love you", "Your cheque is in the post" and "I promise I won't come in your mouth". The second on that list was my casting agent's swan song. I had to trail all the way over to Manchester where he had his office so that I could persuade him to pay me. I didn't tell him that I was going because I knew he'd do a runner, I just turned up and told him that he'd be picking his teeth up with a broken arm unless he paid me right there and then. He gave me a cheque for the required amount which he assured me wouldn't bounce. I calmly told him that as his bank was just around the corner from his office, we could go there immediately and cash it. He wasn't expecting that strategy but agreed to come with me and make sure I was paid. I got my money and sacked him as my agent. I later learned that he'd been sued by a number of actors who'd been goosed by him and sadly, few of them got any money. This shyster had fixed me a series at Granada TV called 3-7-11. It was a comedy drama about a junior and infant's school which went out at 4-15pm in the afternoon. The character I played was Councillor Len Bamber; head of the school governors and ex England footballer. Playing one of the teachers was a great pal of mine, a Sheffield born actor called Ray Ashcroft. When I told Ray about my crooked agent he said I ought to ask *his* agent if he'd be interested in looking after me. He was a London based agent called Tim Scott who insisted on studying my already healthy CV before he made a decision. He eventually accepted me into his stable of actors and I've been with him ever since.

The biggest problem with acting is that you have to audition for *every* part. No director will cast an actor unless he's seen him read for the part in question. My problem was that 90% of the castings were down in London so it meant a whole day going there and back to the capital plus the cost of the rail fare, and then being one of a dozen actors auditioning for the part. On average, you'd get one in ten castings and the more parts you failed to get, the more it eroded your confidence. I'd get really depressed sometimes when I'd not get a part which I knew I was perfect for, and then see the actor who *did* get it fuck it up on the TV. Another thing about the acting side of the job is that the wages are bloody rubbish and they take ages to pay you. Thanks to Tim, I was suggested for many roles, some of which I successfully auditioned for. I did a decent role in four parter called "Body and Soul" which starred Kristin Scott-Thomas and Anthony Valentine. I had most of my scenes with Anthony and he was a lovely bloke. Sadly, all the parts I was getting were small ones and while it was good for my CV, they weren't doing my career much good. I did a couple of Heartbeats, Hetty Wainthrop Investigates, Stay Lucky, Rich Tea and Sympathy and many more. They were all average sort of money but I was grateful for the work. I got a part as one of the bin men in a series called "Common as Muck" which starred Edward Woodward, he was one of my acting heroes and he turned out to be a proper gentleman. He had his own mobile home as a dressing room and rest area while the rest of us shared a caravan in the car park of the base. It rained an awful lot during that shoot so we spent a lot of time in our shelters. We felt a bit sorry for old Edward all on his own in his luxury Winnebago so we often invited him to join us and he loved our very ribald and sometimes disgusting conversations.

Donna started doing a mobile step class so as to keep busy. She bought a little Nissan Vanette, forty steps and a tape recorder. I still had my sound system so I gave her that to save her buying one. She managed to keep her head above water financially but the amount of work and time she put in made me feel even more frustrated that I couldn't be the solo breadwinner any more.

I'd slowly gathered a beautiful collection of guitars which were worth a lot of money but I gradually sold them to try and get my overdraft down. All my mates in both the acting side of the business and the comedy side were each saying how bad the business was, they were all struggling to make ends meet. I was accepting work in places that a couple of years previously I wouldn't have shouted "Bollocks" through the door of the club. I was on the crest of a slump and felt so helpless because there just wasn't the work available to sustain me. The bills kept coming in though and my overdraft was creeping up to its limit. I was beginning to feel like the eternal Mr Micawber who was always waiting for something to turn up and luckily, it did. I'd had some building work done on the cottage and the builder was a nice bloke called Dave Lambert. I had a massive back garden and he asked me if I'd be interested in selling him a piece of it so he could build himself a house. It seemed like a way out of my financial problems subject of course to us getting planning permission. I had the land valued as a potential building plot and was delighted to discover it was worth about thirty thousand pounds. This would easily wipe out my overdraft and leave me with a financial cushion to lean on if things didn't improve. It all went through but sadly I never got the money in a lump sum as Dave was struggling too. He wasn't trying to avoid paying me but he didn't have the whole amount. He paid me in dribs and drabs and eventually built me a new stone garage at his own expense which enhanced the value of my property.

During my "Knutty recession" period, I secured a part in a TV mini-series called Love and Reason. It was written by an old school chum of mine called Ron Rose. He'd done a lot of stuff which had been televised and politically he was a bit left of Lenin. The subject of the series was a miner's strike in Yorkshire and the director was Carol Wilkes, I'd worked with her in 1987 for nine months on "How We Used to Live". I went up for a very big part and was extremely confident that I'd get it, I knew that if I did get it, it would put me back up there. I didn't get it and it was offered to a Scottish actor whose Yorkshire accent was abysmal. Don't misunderstand me, it's not sour grapes but I know for an absolute fact that the only people who can do an authentic Yorkshire accent are Yorkshiremen. He was a nice guy, but every time he murdered our lovely Yorkshire twang I felt like screaming. The part I was offered had me in nearly every scene but with very little dialogue. I felt like a glorified extra, it was so frustrating to have to get up at five in the morning and spend a whole day on set with fuck all to say. The only consolation for me was working with Jack Watson. By then he was 72 years old but he, like Peggy Mount, had a million stories to tell. You may remember Jack Watson; he was in nearly every war film that was ever made. Probably his best remembered role was as the sergeant major in "The Wild Geese", his name was Sandy and he whipped Richard Burton's soldiers into shape then got shot at the end. I also discovered from our conversations that he was the son of that famous old music hall comedian Nosmo King. He related to me his times in Hollywood where he was taught to ride a horse by non other than John Wayne, he was a truly engaging old man.

Panto With Mother

In the spring of 1994 I received a phone call from my casting agent Tim Scott asking if I fancied doing panto at the Lyceum Sheffield with Marti Caine. I was over the moon, not only was I going to be back in a Sheffield panto but I was to be working with one of my best friends in the world. There was a new regime down at the Crucible/Lyceum complex and the new broom had swept very cleanly indeed. He was a man called Stephen Barry and I realised after a short meeting that he was a very cold fish who I kept at arm's length at all times. Marti, or Mother as I always called her, had been playing the wicked Queen in Snow White for a number of years and had made it her own. The producer was a grand gentleman of showbiz called Paul Elliott and was at that time the country's panto king. He was a very important entrepreneur and didn't take any shit from anyone, including the big name stars that appeared in his shows. Being a true Yorkshireman, I wouldn't doff my cap to him but I gave him the utmost respect and found him to be a very straight and honourable man.

We rehearsed the panto down in London which was a pain in the arse but I was lucky enough to stay with my good mate Freddie Pyne whom I'd worked with two years before in the Doncaster panto. He had a beautiful house in Wimbledon very close to the tennis ground. Mother had a flat in London which she shared with her second husband Kenneth Ives, a rather grand well spoken fellow who had ceased acting to become a director. They were as different as chalk and cheese and she confided to me that she'd gone off him not long after they'd married. He was always polite and friendly towards me so I can't knock him, but then again, I didn't live with him. One night during rehearsals, Mother invited me back to her flat for stew and dumplings which was her speciality dish. We feasted and reminisced about the old days and she did her faultless impression of our manager JP; we never stopped laughing for three hours.

I was disappointed to discover that the panto wasn't a panto in the true sense of the word. There was no shouting and joining in and no kids on stage at the end which had always been my party piece. It followed the true Disney story in a very honest and truthful way so it was in fact a Christmas story instead of a Christmas panto. I played three different roles which was an excellent way of testing my acting ability. First I was the narrator, dressed in the style of the mediaeval minstrel who kept coming on in a pin spotlight to relate the story. Then I was the magic wise owl who caused all sorts of nice things to happen. The owl was a very expensively made puppet which I manipulated on my arm in the manner of a ventriloquist's dummy. I made no effort at ventriloquism; I just turned my head away from the audience and worked the owl's beak and spoke his dialogue. The final role was Bungo Beanie, King of the gypsies, a benevolent soul who shelters Snow White from the Red Queen's assassin. The music in the show was wonderful and I must confess it was one of the very best productions I was ever involved in. Snow White was beautifully played by the gorgeous Australian soap star Emily Symons who had the grandest pair of Walters I'd ever seen and I got to feel one every performance. During the gypsy scene in the forest, the villain would appear which was my cue to guide Snow White upstage to hide in the gypsy caravan. We both had our backs to the audience and as soon as we turned round I'd grab her right tit and we'd giggle our way to the caravan with the audience totally oblivious to our antics. It might seem silly and childish but it relieved the boredom of two shows a day six days a week.

I was really enjoying doing this show as it was sheer class and I wanted a record of it for my library so I asked Paul Elliott if he minded me filming it one night and was pleasantly surprised when he agreed. This of course was subject to all the cast and orchestra agreeing also. I thought I might get a few objections from the band but they were dead sweet about it, as were the rest of the cast. I got just one very firm objection from one of the dwarfs; he said that if he was going to be filmed, he wanted paying full Equity rates. He then persuaded a couple more of his vertically challenged mates to insist on payment and I wasn't going to be blackmailed by this Bolshie little twat so I reluctantly decided against it.

One day, about ten days before the end of the run, during the interval, Mother came into my room with a slightly serious look on her face and said "Wanker! I want a word with you". As I explained in book one, Wanker was her pet name for me.

"What's up Mother?" I asked.

"As you know it's my 50th birthday on the 28th of January and I don't want any surprise parties or celebrations or cards or presents or anything. I don't want to be fifty and I don't want anything to remind me of it. Now I'm serious Wanker so take notice of what I've said".

"OK Mother, no problem" I lied, I'd already started a collection and I knew what I was going to get her. Mother had been smoking the waccy baccy for quite a few years now and I remember her telling me that while she was having her various painful and intrusive cancer treatments, she was sure that it relieved the pain and trauma of it all. Mother also had a very serene nature and I'm positive it was down to her smoking the weed. Don't get me wrong good reader, I don't condone it as I know what it can lead to but I must confess that all the people in my game who do use it have the same sort of placid untroubled manner about them. I knew that her current supplier was one of the dwarfs, a pleasant little bloke with a really squeaky voice so I asked him if he could get some for her birthday. I eventually collected just over a hundred quid for her so I made it up to one fifty and asked him if that was enough. He said that he could get me some really top class shit for that amount so I told him to get cracking.

During the show in my role as the narrator, I used a jewelled box as a prop. When I opened it up the orchestra would play quietly so it became a music box. The actual box had been bought in the Crucible gift shop and the lads in the prop department had tarted it up with large artificial jewels, it looked magnificent when the lights hit it. I went over and bought a duplicate box and had the prop dept make it identical to the original. On the day of her birthday I arrived normally and didn't wish her many happy returns, nor did any of the other cast as I'd already warned them about it. During the break between the matinee and the night show, we all gathered quietly outside her dressing room door. It was just before the half hour call so we knew she'd be in there. The four "Star" dressing rooms at the Lyceum all lead off a large lobby with seating for actor's guests so it was easy to assemble the whole cast and crew in that area. I knocked on her door and she opened it to find us all gathered there. Before she could say anything I held up the jeweled box and said "I have here a box".

That was what I said during my opening scene in the show, I would hold up the box in one hand and say "I have here a box, but this is no ordinary box" and as I slowly opened it I would say "This is...... a music box".

I said to Mother, "This is no ordinary box; it is a box of Mother's favourite smoking mixture". I gave it to her and when she looked inside the box her face lit up with delight. She said "You must be psychic, I'm down to my last pinch, oh what a lovely present, thankyou everyone". We finished the panto the next night and as I gave her a goodbye hug, I didn't realise that it would be the last time I'd ever see her. It's funny how you accumulate regrets in your life and they stick to you like old bruises. One of my biggest regrets is that I didn't ring Mother very often during the following year for our customary chats about life in general. She died on November 4th at home in Buckinghamshire with her best pal Pam Rigby by her side. She'd discharged herself from the hospital because she wanted to die at home and she knew that she was very close to death. Pam told me much later that as she sat with Mother, she had a bad twinge of pain and she asked Pam to pass her medicine over. The doctor had told her to expect some severe pain but the medicine would hopefully calm it down. She took a bloody great swig of it and Kenneth said "You know Darling; you're only supposed to have a five millilitre teaspoonful". Mother replied, still sharp as a tack, "I haven't got bloody time to get addicted have I". Pam also told me that as they were chatting during that final few hours, Mother said "Have you been watching that new drama on ITV on Sunday nights?" Pam said she had, to which Mother replied "Bugger, it's a three parter".

Her funeral was a grand affair at Sheffield Cathedral and thousands turned up to see her off. I was standing outside with Colin Fingers Henry after the service, we were sobbing our hearts out when a fuckin' insensitive BBC reporter came and shoved a microphone under my nose for a comment. I was very nearly very rude to her but I realised she was only doing her job so I just told her I was too upset to speak. The final service was held at the crematorium so Colin and I went up together. As we were waiting for mother to arrive in the hearse, I was surprised to see about four of the dwarfs who'd been in the recent panto waiting outside. The little bolshie one who'd put the mockers on me filming the show was among them. He came up to talk to me and I said to him "But for you, I would have had a lasting memory of my final work with Mother to cherish forever, but because you blocked it, I have nothing. Now I know you're a dwarf but if you don't fuck off out of my sight in the next three seconds I'll roll you down that fuckin' grass slope like a snowball".

The whole of showbiz mourned Mother's passing for she was dearly loved by all who knew her. She was hugely courageous and bore her pain with great fortitude at the same time never losing her warmth and wit. She was a wise, special woman who I loved like a sister.

Knutty on the Square

In 1989 I became a freemason, I can't tell you about it, it's a secret.

Heartbeat

In the spring of 1995 I got a call from my casting agent telling me to go to YTV and see top director Graham Wetherell about a part in an episode of Heartbeat. I'd known Graham for many years and I'd worked with him on numerous occasions on programmes like 3-2-1 and Cryer's Crackers. He was directing a few Heartbeats and this one involved a bent wrestling promoter which he thought I'd be perfect for. He'd already rung me to describe the character and I suggested that I play him as a cowboy with the boots and Stetson. I related to Graham my experiences with the wrestlers in my early days as a comic and told him about "Cowboy Jack Cassidy" who I described in my first book. The producer has the last word so when I went to meet him and Graham I got myself all togged up in my best snakeskin boots and a cowboy hat. They were my own clothes as I'd been an amateur cowboy for many years and it was my standard mode of dress. The producer loved the idea and gave me the part that day. It was a leading role in the episode and the fee reflected it. I'd done two previous episodes a few years before but they were only small parts so I think I got in the region of about seven hundred quid for them. This one was two and a half grand and very welcome. I received a call from the head of costume regarding my outfit and he was over the moon when I told him I'd be providing my own boots for the show, one best pair for in the ring and the others for everyday wear. He was very camp as most wardrobe guys are, and he said I had to go down to London to be measured for a suede "Kit Carson" jacket with all the tassels and buffalo horn buttons. They also measured my head for a genuine Stetson Rancher hat; it was identical to the one which "JR" wore in Dallas and cost a hundred and fifty pounds. I was hoping to be able to buy the jacket and hat for half price at the end of the shoot which was a common custom if an actor liked an outfit. The guy who was to play my "Masked Marvel" was none other than big Pat Roache, the ex wrestler who'd turned to acting and had a fantastic career doing Bond films Indiana Jones and a couple of films with Schwarzenegger plus his unforgettable role in Auf Wiedersehen Pet. Old Pat was an absolute sweetheart, mild mannered and quietly spoken and we got on like a house on fire reminiscing about the old days in the wrestling halls and talking about weight training. He was about six foot six and probably weighed over twenty stone. In the storyline, he was bitten by Alfred, Greengrass's dog and his leg gets infected which prevents him from fighting. So as not to be out of pocket, Greengrass and I recruit a local giant to take his place. He was played by Adam Fogerty, a huge rugby player from Castleford who also went on to do many films.

I had so much fun filming the episode and one day Graham suggested we all go up the road to Whitby and see Ted Rogers who was doing a season at the Pavillion. Graham had directed every single episode of 3-2-1 and was a close pal of Teds. The Whitby Pavillion is not the entertainment Mecca of the northern hemisphere and I felt sorry for old Ted being reduced to working in the number threes after having been a big TV star. The producer of the show was probably paying the bulk of his budget to Ted because he was only spending five bob a week on the supports. They were absolute shite and reduced the show to a cheap affair which I knew Ted must have been ashamed to be involved in. Ted made us so welcome and did the whole second half just for us. There were no more than thirty or forty people in the audience and they were mostly coffin dodgers. He didn't do his normal act, he did his Jackie Mason routine which was hilarious but went right over the punters heads. The four of us all sat pissing ourselves laughing and the wrinklies just stared at him.

A couple of days before the end of the shoot I approached the camp costume designer and asked him if I could buy the two cowboy hats and he said with his normal effeminate flourish "Buy

Heartbeat 1997

Big Pat Roach

220

Good Old Bill

them! Buy them! You can have them my darling, you've saved me a fortune in boot hire and you've been a treasure to work with so you have them with my love". I would have had the Kit Carson jacket too but as usual they'd not given me enough in the shoulders and it was too tight. My tailor once told me that because I'm relatively short at five foot eight, my shoulders are far too wide for my height and it's apt to confuse some tailors who only receive my measurements by phone or post so they adjust accordingly.

The last day of the shoot was spent in a field filming the Masked Marvel trying to teach his substitute some falls. It was far too remote for the makeup vans and butty wagon to reach so YTV rented a local farm house to act as a base of operations. We had the magic words "That's a wrap", and we all went up to the farm to get changed. Pat, Adam and I had been given a small upstairs bedroom as a dressing room and I took off my beautiful new Stetson hat and put it on the bed. Big Pat came in and promptly sat on it. I shouted "Ya big daft dozy twat, you've sat on me Stetson". He jumped up and was so full of apologies, "I'm so sorry Bob, I didn't see it". It was flattened, I could have cried, I picked it up and put my hand inside it and it popped back into shape as good as new. I suppose that's why they're so bloody expensive. Old Pat was so chuffed when he saw there was no damage to my hat. I only ever worked with him that once but it was an experience I'll never forget. I was so sad to hear of his passing in July 2004, another victim to that bastard cancer, to me he was indestructible but cancer doesn't pick and choose or take any prisoners, it just zaps you and leaves you with only hope and a prayer.

Brian Glover's T Shirt

The 95-96 panto season saw me back at the Lyceum in Babes in the Wood playing the good robber. The bad robber was played at my request by the inimitable Finetime Fontaine. If there was any man on this planet who I would allow myself to do a double act with, it would be Finetime. He's dead funny both on and off stage and we get on like blood brothers. Brian Glover was to be playing the evil Sheriff of Nottingham and my dear old pal Hilary O'Neil was Robin Hood. Brian was doing his first ever panto and was really nervous about it but I told him it was like falling off a log and he'd love it. One of the problems of doing Babes in the Wood was that you always had to have two sets of babes and you could always guarantee that one set would be better than the other. This was the third time I'd done Babes and it happened again, one set were a right little Spencer Tracy and Katharine Hepburn and the other pair were Dumb and Dumber. Still, they were only kids, bless 'em and they were trying their very best but when we had the good pair performing, it seemed to lift the whole show.

Once again as in most Paul Elliott productions, we had to rehearse in London so FT and I rented a flat for the two weeks and did a nice Indian or Chinese most evenings. One night we went as Brian's guests to dine at the Chelsea Arts Club where he was a member. It's a very Bohemian atmosphere and memberships are rarely granted. There are rooms upstairs for anyone a little worse for wear and they are very cheap. The dining room was set out like a monastic refectory and everyone sat down together, the ambience was relaxed and happy and the two most important things seemed to be drinking and laughing. Brian had a lady friend with him, a very classy and wealthy Iranian woman called Rana who owned an exclusive shoe shop in Chelsea. Brian, completely off his own bat, asked her if I could go down and pick a pair for my Donna and she agreed immediately. She told me she'd be in the shop around lunchtime the next day if I cared to call in and browse. When she went to the ladies room, Brian told me that she'd probably not even charge me and if she did it would be a fraction of the price. She, like every other Middle Eastern person that I've encountered, was utterly charming with impeccable manners and a flawlessly kind nature. It's difficult to believe that the same ethnic races provide us with the unspeakably evil wankers that blow up innocent men, women and children without pity or regret.

The next lunchtime, I gingerly approached her shop and perused her wares which were immaculately displayed in the window. I also noticed that there were no prices on any of the shoes, a bad sign for a parsimonious Yorkshire lad. She spotted me looking in her window and immediately came out and beckoned me inside. She introduced me to her daughter who obviously looked after her business; she was just like her mother, polite and extremely beautiful. I was invited to take coffee with them and look at the shoes on display. She went on to tell me that Princess Diana was a regular customer as were many highly placed actresses. As she told me this my arse cheeks started twitching like buggery at the thought of what her prices would be. I couldn't back down now; I'd crossed the Rubicon by just walking into her emporium and I now felt committed to make a purchase. Besides that, it would be really good to surprise Donna with an exclusive pair of designer shoes; I just prayed I'd be able to afford them. I picked up a pair of gorgeous black patent semi-high heels with a strip of creamy coloured snakeskin down each side, they were so beautiful and I knew Donna would adore them. Rana cooed at my choice saying they had only just arrived from Paris and that I had excellent taste. I asked her how much they were and she asked her daughter to go and find out. She returned from the small office and said "They are seven hundred and fifty pounds Mummy". I tried to act as calmly as possible, seven hundred and fifty quid; you could buy a fuckin' house in Barnsley for that amount. Rana then said, "I'll make it ten per cent my darling". I thought, "Christ she's gonna knock off ten per cent, I'll still have to fork out six hundred and seventy five quid". I'd got about a hundred in cash on me and my credit cards. Rana then said to her daughter "Darling, charge Mr Knutt ten per cent of the purchase price, that's seventy five pounds". My arse cheeks stopped twitching and I thought "There is a God". I'd got it wrong and I paid up immediately, in cash. Donna was overwhelmed when I gave her the shoes which were in a real suede bag in a very posh shoe box. When I told her what they should have cost, she nearly fainted.

I remember one day during rehearsals, Brian came in wearing a bright banana yellow T shirt, it had the Beano comic logo emblazoned on the front in royal blue and I immediately fell in love with it. I asked him where he'd bought it and he said he couldn't remember. I wouldn't let it go and kept on pestering him all day to try and remember where he'd got it. I asked him the next day if he'd remembered and he went into his bag and brought out the shirt, all washed and pressed and as he passed it to me he said "Here, bloody have it, now can I get a bit of peace". I was over the moon; he'd actually given it to me. It became my favourite T shirt and still is to this day although I now rarely wear it as it's a bit well worn with a couple of holes in it. Remember that shirt, for it'll pop up later on in my story.

Brian was wonderful in the panto for he was after all a very talented and perceptive actor. I think his part as the PE master in "Kes" is a part of British film history and will live on forever as his finest hour. He did many memorable parts and my second favourite to "Kes" was a TV film called "The Fishing Party". It's about three Yorkshire lads who go away to Bridlington for a few days fishing and they stay in a boarding house run by a monstrous fat landlady who has a thousand rules to abide by. It's a bit of film magic and if you ever see it billed or perhaps see it on DVD, do *not* miss it. In the panto we did a comedy front cloth together called the Parcel gag. It's a very funny and well worn panto gag which never fails to get a big laugh. We rehearsed it in London till Brian was word perfect but because it was an unscripted comedy piece which I'd taught him privately, he insisted we run through it every day just before the show. I used to say to him "Brian, you *know* it" and he'd always reply "Yes but I don't want to get it wrong so lets just

Outside the Lyceum 2008, wearing the T shirt

run it again", bless him.

We spent a lot of time relating our stories to each other. I told him about my early experiences in the clubs and all the shitholes I'd worked. He, like nearly every other actor I've met, couldn't believe that I could go on a stage and waffle to an audience without a script for over an hour and I was equally amazed at the number of big film stars that he'd worked with. He told me a wonderful story about when he worked with John Wayne in the film "Brannigan". As you probably know, Brian was a pro wrestler in the days of Mick McManus and Jackie Pallo. He was billed as Leon Arras from Paris, France. He was built like a little bulldog with a deeply barreled chest and he actually was a very hard man. In the film with Wayne, he played a shifty little character called Jimmy the Bet who ended up trying to pick a fight with the Duke and getting a good hiding for his troubles. He told me that John Wayne was the biggest man he'd ever seen, he wasn't the tallest or the widest, he was just the biggest. He had massive hands and his fingers were as thick as two Cumberland pork sausages. Brian was strangely against bad language and I very rarely heard him swear. I have a foul mouth when I'm with the lads but even I was conscious of curbing my language in Brian's presence. What upset Brian with John Wayne was that he kept calling him a little motherfucker. The scene wasn't going as quickly as the big man would have liked and he kept on saying things like "OK ya little motherfucker lets do it again". After a while Brian took Wayne to one side and said to him "Mr Wayne, I've got every respect for you as an actor and a big name film star, but I have to warn you that if you call me a little motherfucker once more I shall knock you down, and believe me, I'm very capable of doing so". He said Wayne looked at him for a second then burst out laughing and gave him a huge slap on the back as well as an apology.

Delia Knutt & The Missing Postman

In the spring of 1996 I was cast in a smashing role in a comedy drama called "The Missing Postman". It starred James Bolam as a postman who had been made redundant much against his will so he decided to deliver every letter in his last sack by hand. It took him on an adventure all over the country meeting all sorts of interesting people and the cops were after him as he'd been accused by the Royal Mail of stealing the letters. The cast was huge as each little escapade which he had involved him with a different set of characters. I was playing a barman in a northern pub which the postman had been spotted in and when I read the script, I perceived from the way it was written that the barman was a gay guy. I discussed it with Alan Dossor, the director and he told me to go for it. I had so much fun camping it up like a raving queen and the cast were in stitches at my effeminate posturing. James Bolam was sitting quietly out of shot watching the scene and when I finally got to meet him and have a natter with him he looked quite surprised and said "Oh, you're not gay then"

"Not bloody likely" I replied, "but I've worked with enough of 'em to know how to act like one".

I was having a drink with Alan the director one lunchtime and the conversation got round to cooking. I told him it was my chief hobby and that I was quite proud of some of my recipes. He then told me that a close friend of his was a producer at Central TV and was looking for someone to fill in a weekly cookery slot in a magazine programme which he was doing. I said I'd love to have a bash at it and he said he'd pass on my details to his mate. It was only about a week later when I got a call from his friend inviting me down to Nottingham for a chat. The day before I went to meet him I cooked my special Thai red chicken curry and took a portion down in a Tupperware box for him to taste. He loved the idea that I'd taken one of my dishes for him to taste and he loved the curry even more and I got the job. I did six inserts for him over a period of three weeks and cooked some delicious meals for the show. I only had a fifteen minute slot so there was a lot of "Here's one I prepared earlier" involved. I didn't have a computer in those days so I used to fax him the title of the meal and all the ingredients and he got a sort of comi-chef to do all the preparation for me before we started filming. The camera crew and sound lads were like bleedin' gannets; they'd swoop down to demolish the food as soon as we wrapped each show. I did some of my speciality dishes which I intend to put in this book as the final chapter. I did it in my first book and I've received some very kind comments about the dishes. Sadly, nothing came of my one expedition into the world of TV cookery so I never became an Ainsley or a hairy biker.

Knutty's Soap Box

We all have things which annoy us and some things which make our blood boil. Just in case you might be interested, here are a few of my pet hates.

Quite a few years ago I was coming back from London on the train after having been to a casting. I always try and sit in one of those seats with a table so I can selfishly spread my stuff out in front of me, you know what I mean, sandwiches, thermos flask and newspaper. I always pray that nobody is going to sit opposite me and start spreading *their* stuff in front of them. I know that if no-one joins me by the time the train pulls out of St Pancras I'm safe and my privacy is secure until Leicester. When I do have company, I usually get two women who've been to town shopping and never stop gossiping loudly about nothing in particular all the way back to Sheffield. It's either that or some twat of a business man with a fully charged mobile phone. They always start their clichéd conversations with "I'm on the train" then go on to talk complete bollocks until the train thankfully enters a tunnel and cuts off their banal chatter.

On the journey to which I'm referring, a rather smart looking lady asked if I minded her sitting opposite me and of course I couldn't say no. About ten minutes after leaving London she said to me "Excuse me; you're Bobby Knutt aren't you". I said yes and she said she was very pleased to meet me and she'd seen me many times in panto. She was middle aged, well spoken and still quite attractive looking, her name was Beryl. We chatted for a while and then she told me she was a magistrate. I was tempted to ask her about some of the cases she'd overseen but thought better of it. She then surprised me by saying "I think you'd make a very good magistrate". I almost laughed and told her I couldn't possibly consider it so she asked me why. I said "Can you imagine me sending a couple of scrotes down for six months who know exactly who I am because they might have seen me on the telly. They'd be straight round to smash my windows or worse when they got out".

I also told her I'd make a rotten magistrate because I'd send them all away for as long as I could. I told her that I thought the sentencing of yobs, hooligans and thieves was far too light and that in my opinion they should all be punished much more severely. She seemed mildly surprised by my stern opinion and tried to mitigate the behaviour of these delinquents by saying "Yes, but you've got to understand that a lot of them come from broken homes". I was shocked at her attitude, even though it was kindly and benevolent. I came back with "I've got a son who comes from a broken home, I know because I broke it, but *he* doesn't go round mugging old ladies or hanging around in gangs causing mayhem". We were never going to agree so we changed the subject.

I get so fucking angry when I read of these mindless animals and families from hell being mollycoddled by the courts while their decent living innocent victims continue to be harassed by the incessant mental torture inflicted upon them by these cretins.

You may remember a recent case where an Asian chap called Munir Hussein was imprisoned for attacking a burglar who had tied up and terrorized his family. The gang had threatened to kill them and after Mr Hussein was fortunate enough to escape his bonds he chased and attacked the burglar with a cricket bat and knocked fuck out of him, fracturing his skull. For the "crime" of protecting his family, this upstanding pillar of society was given a thirty month prison sentence. The burglar, a man with 50 past criminal convictions, walked free. The sheer stupidity of our self defence laws was blatantly exposed by the sad case. Hussein was released eventually after an appeal but was left to pick up the pieces of his shattered life.

If a burglar broke into *my* house and threatened to harm my loved ones I would do whatever it took to stop him. Knives, baseball bat or a hammer, I wouldn't care what. If my Donna's life was at stake I'd turn into a fuckin' homicidal nutter and the one thing I wouldn't do is stop to consider the law. As the law stands today, if I went to harm an intruder and injured him in the process, I could be sent to prison. The punishment should fit the crime instead of a slap on the wrist.

These cretins proudly wear an ASBO as a badge of honour.

Here's what I would do. I'd build very Spartan accommodation up on Kinder Scout or perhaps Dartmoor. It would consist of Nissen type buildings with wooden beds and minimal heating. There would be absolutely no attempt or effort at any form of rehabilitation, just punishment. It would be a regime so harsh and cruel that after a short sharp dose of it, they would *never* re-offend in case they were sent back. I feel sure there are enough retired policemen and army drill sergeants around who would be more than happy to staff a camp like this. There would be no radio or TV, no newspapers or games permitted. They would spend all day digging holes in the ground and all the next day filling them in. Any type of infringement would be met with physical punishment and solitary confinement. There will be many who disagree with my draconian views but I think you might reconsider if it was *your* mother who was robbed or *your* father or son who was beaten to a pulp by a feral gang of drug and booze fuelled yobs for no more reason than he asked them to stop swearing. Another solution would be to form a special regiment of yobs in the army with similar training conditions to what I've just described but when they've been tamed and trained up, send 'em to Helmand Province in Afghanistan and let them vent their pent up anger on the Taliban.

Another thing which gets right on my tits is the absence of the letter "T" in our language. All the kids speak like that these days, there are two Ts in "butter" and "bitter" but all you hear is bu — er and bi — er. They use a compu-er, it's very difficult to try and write it phonetically but I think you'll understand what I'm moaning about. They never "think", they "fink", thirty becomes firty, and weather becomes wevver.

Oh and while I'm at it, here's the thing which gets me madder than anything on the planet....., TONY BLAIR.

Oooh I do feel better getting that lot off my chest.

Shortly after writing the last chapter, I received an E mail from a pal of mine. He's always sending me funny stuff down the line but this last one had me rolling with laughter and I feel I must share it with you. This is an actual genuine letter which an Australian sent to the then DFAT (the Department of Foreign Affairs and Trade) minister, the Hon Alexander Downer and the then Immigration Minister, the Hon Amanda Vanstone. The government tried desperately to censure the author, but got nowhere because every legal person who read it nearly wet themselves laughing! Here goes.... see if it makes *you* laugh.

Dear Mr Minister,

I'm in the process of renewing my passport and still cannot believe this. How is it that K-Mart has my address and telephone number, and knows that I bought a TV set and a set of golf clubs from them back in 1997, and yet the Federal Government is still asking me where I was born and on what date. For Christ sakes, do you guys do this by hand?

My birth date you have in my Medicare information and it's on all the income tax forms I've filed for the last forty years. It is also on my driver's licence, on the last eight passports I've ever had, on all those stupid customs declaration forms I've had to fill in before being allowed off the planes over the last thirty years, and all those insufferable census forms that I've filled out every five years since 1966.

Also.... Would somebody please take note, once and for all, that my mother's name is Audrey, my father's name is Jack, and I'd be absolutely fucking astounded if that ever changed between now and when I drop dead. I apologise Mr Minister but I'm really pissed off this morning and between you and me, I've had enough of this bullshit.

You send the application to my house, and then you ask me for my fucking address!! What the hell is going on with your mob? Have you got a gang of mindless Neanderthal arseholes working there?

And another thing, look at my damn picture, do I look like Bin Laden? I can't even grow a beard for God's sakes. I just want to go to New Zealand to see my new grand daughter. (Yes, my son interbred with a Kiwi girl). And would someone tell me, why would you give a shit whether I plan on visiting a farm in the next fifteen days? If I ever got the urge to do something weird to a sheep or a horse, believe you me, I'd sure as hell not want to tell anyone. Well I have to go now, 'cause I have to go to the other end of the city and get another fucking copy of my birth certificate, and to part with another $80 for the privilege of accessing MY OWN INFORMATION.

Would it be so complicated to have all the services in the same spot, to assist in the issuance of a new passport on the same day?? Nooooo.. that'd be too fucking easy and makes far too much sense. You would much prefer to have us running all over the place like chickens with our fucking heads cut off, and then having to find some high society wanker to confirm that it's really me in the goddam photo! You know the photo... the one where we're not allowed to smile?.... you fucking morons.

Signed, An Irate Australian Citizen.

P.S.
Remember what I said above about the picture, and getting someone in high society to confirm that it's me? Well, my family has been in the country since before 1850! In 1856, one of my forefathers took up arms with Peter Lalor. (Do you remember the Eureka Stockade!!)

I have also served in both the CMF and the regular army for something over thirty years (I went to Vietnam in 1967), and I still have high security clearances. I'm also a personal friend of the RSL, and Lt General Peter Cosgrove sends me a Christmas card every year.

However, your rules require that I have to get someone "important" to verify who I am; You know, someone like my doctor.... WHO WAS BORN AND RAISED IN FUCKING PAKISTAN !!!.... a country where they either assassinate or hang their prime ministers, and are suspended from the commonwealth for not having the "right sort of government".

You are all fucking idiots!

Dingling in Emmerdale

I was always aware that regular TV appearances are the life blood of any entertainer or actor if he wants to keep his profile high. I had long since ceased to be required by the TV companies as a comedian as the trends had totally changed and there were no more variety shows being made. The new wave comedians were coming to the fore; they were the guys who made their living in the comedy clubs doing a twenty minute spot. The odd main stream comics like Jim Bowen and Roy Walker had made it as game show hosts and were very good at it. This sort of opportunity always seemed to elude me so I'd hoped that a really good acting role would turn up to bounce me higher up the showbiz pecking order. In 1996, it came like a gift from heaven.

I got a call from my dear pal Graham Wetherell telling me that he was now working on Emmerdale as a regular house director and they were shortly to cast a new member of the Dingle family. He went on to tell me that he'd already strongly suggested me for the part to Mervyn Watson, the producer but Mervyn had insisted on having a casting session for it. Graham said the casting was in six days time and the character was Albert Dingle, Zak's brother who'd just escaped from prison. He'd been on the run living wild for a week so Graham told me not to shave for the next six days and come as scruffy as I could. It was a great tip and I turned up at YTV looking a right bedraggled scruffy bastard. There was the same old bunch of actors waiting in the foyer to see the director but for once I had a really good feeling about this one. I went in to see them and I was a bit wary about Mervyn as he was the producer who wrote me out of Coronation Street in 1983. It went very well and later that afternoon I got a call at home from Graham telling me I'd got it. He also told me that he had an apology from Mervyn saying that I was dead right for it and he should have trusted Graham's judgement.

Emmerdale changed my life when my character was finally introduced. He was brought in on a wave of publicity and I did all the big newspaper interviews. I was made so welcome by the rest of the cast, some of whom I already knew like Stan Richards and Johnnie Leeze. The thing which amazed me most was the way the other Dingles welcomed me like a real family member. Steve Halliwell who plays Zak reminded me of how we'd met before at Granada TV when he was playing a small role in an episode of 3-7-11. He's one of the nicest blokes you could ever hope to meet, quietly spoken and gentle natured, totally different to his alter ego Zak Dingle. In our very first meeting he had to hit me full in the face and knock me out which was a laugh to film. I had advice from the stuntman on how to fall and Steve was so dreadfully worried that he might catch me with his fist.

I had lots of scenes with Jackie Pirie who played Tina Dingle. She was sheltering Albert in a derelict house in the woods and bringing him food and drink. It was heavily hinted in the story line that she was actually my daughter and not Zaks. She was a treasure to work with and considering she was a broad Scots lassie she did an excellent Yorkshire accent. I remember one afternoon when we shot some scenes of Albert hiding in a thickly wooded area and it was bloody freezing cold. It was January and the winter had been a very cold one. I really suffered for my art that day; I hadn't felt as cold since the Falklands and my teeth were actually chattering for the first time since I was a small boy.

My introduction into Emmerdale lasted six episodes and once it was transmitted my profile went sky high. My fees for cabarets and dinners shot up and I was in big demand. The power of television has always amazed me, I was just the same bloke, my act was just the same, but just because I'd been on Emmerdale I was being treated like a star like in the old days of Coronation Street. I was back on the show about two months later so the audience feedback must have been OK. I had more fun doing Emmerdale than anything I'd ever done, my story lines were wonderfully written and my workmates were twenty four carat. They eventually brought in my son Marlon Dingle played by Mark Charnock and it wasn't long before I was thinking of him as my real kin.

What people probably don't realise is how hard a soap opera is for

The Family

YORKSHIRE
TELEVISION

Bobby Knutt
as
Albert Dingle

Emmerdale

237

an actor. It's a constant learning process and you're continually learning up to six episodes at a time. You film scenes totally out of order which really keeps you on your toes. Because I chose to travel back home every day I had to spend all my spare time learning lines with Donna playing all the other characters. During the whole of my time in Emmerdale, the M1 motorway at Leeds was being altered to join the new A1 link road and the delays were fuckin' horrendous. If I had an eight 'O clock call in Leeds I'd leave home at five thirty to avoid the rush hour traffic and arrive at the studio for six thirty. I'd have a couple of bacon butties and go over my lines in the canteen.

One of my most memorable scenes was when Zak and I were out turkey rustling for a couple of Christmas birds. There were all sorts of animal and bird providers who worked for YTV and for this scene we had two very large turkeys about 25lb each. Zak and Albert had to run into shot chasing the birds in a manic scene reminiscent of Laurel and Hardy. To achieve this, I had to stand behind the camera tripod with the turkey under my arm and on "Action", I had to throw it in front of the camera which made it look as if it was trying to fly then I would run into shot to chase it round the yard. Now after we'd done about three or four takes of this scene, the turkey was getting quite pissed off. He knew that every time I picked him up and held him under my arm he was going to get himself thrown on the floor and chased around the yard. He started clawing at my right thigh with his very sharp claws and it was beginning to hurt. Eventually, the turkey man saw what was happening and exchanged him for the other turkey at the same time assuring me that he was more docile than the other one.

We eventually finished the scene so Steve and I started to make our way back to the caravan for a warm. In those days, the new Emmerdale village hadn't been built and the Dingle's farm was way out in the wilds of Lord Harewood's estate. It was a rat infested shell with no facilities; it just had the Dingle furniture in it and was used purely for outside and inside filming. As we made our way back to the shelter of the base I put my hands in my pockets. Albert wore an old navy blue donkey jacket with a badly torn right pocket. As my hand went into the right pocket, I felt something sticky and a bit slimy; I withdrew my hand immediately to find it smeared with turkey shit. That fuckin' turkey had got even with me for chucking him on the floor by shitting in my pocket. I was bellowing with disgust and Steve was absolutely honking with laughter. The worst about it was that I couldn't wash my hands as there were no taps in the vans and the butty wagon, which *did* have a sink, was somewhere else on a bigger base camp. The make-up lady gave me some tissues but let's face it, when you're unlucky enough to get shit on your hands, you want to scrub 'em with soap, hot water and Dettol.

I recall one very sad day for me while I was filming some outside scenes. It was July 27th and I was in the caravan with Mark Charnock waiting to shoot the next scene when my mobile phone rang. It was a reporter from the Sheffield Star newspaper and he asked me what my reaction was about Brian. I'd no idea what he was talking about so I asked him "Brian who?" He told me Brian Glover so I asked him what about Brian. He then told me that Brian had died that day from a brain tumour. I was totally devastated, I knew old Brian had been ill but the last I'd heard from him he was OK and on the mend. I was too upset to talk to the reporter so I apologised and hung up. I couldn't believe it, my mate was gone, we'd only worked together just six months before in panto and he was fit as a fiddle. I had a spooky feeling come over me, I'd done panto with Marti the year before and she'd died the same year and now exactly the same thing had happened to Brian. That unspeakable monster called cancer had taken them both and I began to wonder if I was some sort of jinx.

I felt that I was now well established as an Emmerdale character and I had conditioned myself to the strenuous work schedules plus I'd learned one hard and fast rule, *never make plans because Emmerdale will bollocks them up*. The times I had to cancel pre-made arrangements like dinner parties or even a live gig were countless. You'd get your schedule for the next two weeks and immediately look for the periods when you weren't needed for filming. I'd perhaps arrange a curry with the lads or a cosy night in with Donna and it would all be cocked up because I'd be called in at the last minute for reshoots or rearranged shooting plans. I was beginning to feel like a genuine part of the Emmerdale family and got on so well with the rest of the cast. Chris Chittel who plays Pollard is probably the sweetest most generous guy you'll ever meet. I'd known him for much longer than my time in Emmerdale as we'd done lots of charity events together and we were both pals of Frazer Hines who had played Joe Sugden for many years. He'd married a mate of Donnas called Liz Hobbs who had been an Olympic water skier and we'd met up again at the wedding.

In June of 1997 I got the shock of my life. I was called into the producer's office and I'd no idea what for. Mervyn calmly told me that YTV were not renewing my contract and I was going to be written out of the series. I was numb, I'd gone into work that morning full of the joys of spring and enjoying being part of a very strong storyline and now here I was being binned. He told me that there were too many strong male Dingles and I was becoming difficult to write for. It had been Mervyn who'd canned me from Coronation Street so I was wondering if there was something about me which he didn't like, but I couldn't ask him could I? I just had to take it on the chin and act unruffled while inside I was wrecked.

The other Dingles were just as shocked as me and gathered round me to try and comfort me for they could see I was genuinely devastated by it. Emmerdale had nearly got me out of the financial mire that I'd fallen into during the last few years and six more months would have seen me totally free and clear of any debt. I'd bought us a brand new Land Rover Defender on the strength of my YTV earnings and that still had to be paid for. My last appearance was going to be in the September of that year, I'd be shooting it in late July so I set about letting all the agents know I was free for one night stands.

My One and Only Screen Kiss

The story line for my exit from the soap was a strong one which saw me being exiled from the Dingle clan for trying to seduce a member of the family who was spoken for. It involved me having to kiss the actress whom I was trying to have it off with. I'll not mention her name, she's a very sweet lady but unfortunately for me she had severe halitosis. It wasn't the occasional case of bad breath we all suffer with from time to time, it was full blown death-breath and I'd smelled it every time I was in close proximity to her. My mate Graham Wetherell was the director for the episode and I took him to one side and quietly asked him "Graham, have I *got* to kiss her?" He looked at me with pity and said "I know exactly what you mean mate, I've smelt it as well, but it's the big moment at the end of the episode. As your lips meet I run the credits and play the theme tune but I promise I'll try and do it in one take".

The big scene arrived and I offered her an extra strong mint. She said to me "I'm sorry darling, I'm on homeopathic medicine and I'm not allowed to have mints". Then she raised the back of her hand to her mouth and said in the most coquettish manner "Oh, my breath's not bad is it?" I sort of mumbled back "No no, it's fine, I er just wondered if you fancied a mint that's all". Graham had changed our scene for the last of the day so everyone else had gone, leaving us to concentrate more fully and not rush it. It actually was a very well written and moving scene. The action saw us on the tatty settee together with me sidling closer to her so as to enact the kiss. There was quite a bit of dialogue and as I got closer to her I was trying to hold my breath so as not to inhale her foul smelling exhalations. Sadly for me I couldn't hold my breath and speak at the same time and I was beginning to feel a bit sick. We eventually kissed and Graham shouted "Cut, that's a wrap". We'd done it in one, thank God. I honestly don't think I could have endured having to do it again. I thought to myself afterwards, just my fuckin' luck, other actors get to kiss Jennifer Lopez and Kelly Brooke, I get a fat lass with badger breath. I sometimes think if it was raining fannys I'd get my grandmothers.

I Become The Gaffer

The work situation had picked up tremendously thanks to Emmerdale but something was about to happen which would help the bank balance back to black. I got a call from Tim saying I was up for the Tetley Tea voice over. Brian Glover had been the voice of the gaffer for just over twenty years and had earned a small fortune from it. My pal Finetime Fontayne was also up for it but I felt that if they were looking for something similar to Brian's voice, Finetime's was far too highly pitched. I went down to London to meet the lady producer who'd been doing the commercial for years with Brian. I wore the yellow Beano T shirt which Brian had given me the year before, not just for good luck, but to honour Brian.

When I met the producer, I asked her if she wanted me to do an impression of Brian, which I could do quite easily, or did she want something different. She told me that she didn't want me to sound too much like him, but at the same time she didn't want me to sound totally different to him. I'd memorized all Brian's little intonations and the little underlying laughs which he put into his Gaffer voice so I suggested we put some down for her to listen to. It was a brand new script for a wholly new set of commercials involving the Tetley Tea Folk. I breezed through them and after a couple of takes I'd got the Gaffer off to a tee. I knew she was very pleased with what I'd done and as we were chatting in the studio she suddenly said, "Haven't I seen that T shirt before?"

I told her that it used to be Brian's and that he'd given it to me when I worked with him in his first and last panto. I told her that I was wearing it for luck, and also to honour Brian. She rang me at home three days later and said "Congratulations Bobby, the T shirt worked, you've got the job". I was over the moon, the Tetley voice over was pinnacle of *all* the voice overs and I had secured it. I did it for the next two years before they decided to kill off the Tetley Tea Folk in favour of a brand new set of commercials. Every time I went to London to do one, I *always* wore Brian's T shirt in the studio and never wore it at any other time. I know for a fact that old Brian would have been chuffed to bits knowing that I'd got the job which he'd always referred to as "A nice little earner".

Knutty The Panto Baddie

Emmerdale had been a life saver for me and opened many doors but most importantly it raised my profile so that once again I was a saleable commodity out of Yorkshire. My dear old pal Duggie Chapman rang to ask if I'd be interested in playing the evil Mayor in his panto Goldilocks and the Three Bears at Billingham Forum. We had a chat about the logistics of me playing a villain when I had always been a goodie. He wanted to call me Mayor Dingle as I was so soon out of Emmerdale. We talked about the plot and eventually decided on a solution. At the beginning of the show, I would come on as the kindly benevolent Mayor of Pottytown and do a little opening spot and a song. At the end of the song the lights changed to green and there were claps of thunder and lightning along with an evil voice from beyond. I'd recorded the voice myself and we'd tweeked it with the magic of sound effects so that it was really distorted and scary. It was the evil spirit of the Black Forest and he turns me into an evil money grabbing monster. I've never had as much fun in a panto as I did playing the baddie, I could insult the audience as much as I liked and the more they booed me the happier I was. I had two comedy henchmen played by the Patton brothers Jimmy and Brian. They are actually the two real elder brothers of the Chuckle brothers and they were a gift from God as stupid foils.

The story was set around two rival circuses, mine and Dame Tilly Tart's, the opening of the second half was the most spectacular scene you ever saw. It was a real circus with performing dogs, magical illusions and a real live trapeze act from the Russian State Circus called Larry Osca. Larry and his lovely wife were smashing people with sawdust in their veins. They lived for the circus and their permanent home was a magnificent caravan as long as a bus which they towed with a covered lorry. The lorry housed all their rigs and equipment and they spent their lives on the road. The girl dog act shared a small touring caravan with her dogs; it had basic facilities and no running water. I don't think she had a bath for the

Duggie Chapman & The Patton Bros

Panto Baddie

whole of the run and I always kept upwind of her as her body odour was staggering. I rented a farmhouse near Sedgefield and shared it with the girl who was playing Goldilocks and Mervyn Francis who was Daddy Bear, the Innkeeper and the company manager. It was strange being away from home for panto and I remember driving home on Christmas Eve after the 2-30 matinee feeling like an exited schoolboy at the thought of seeing Donna. Christmas day flew by and on Boxing Day morning I had to set off back to Billingham for the last three weeks of the show. I realised how fortunate I'd been in the past to have done all my previous pantos near to home, there's an awful lot to be said for sleeping in your own bed.

I did three consecutive years for Duggie as Mayor Dingle in Goldilocks. The second year we went to Southport New Theatre which is a bloody great barn of a place. It's more a concert hall than a theatre and it totally lacks intimacy which makes it hard work to perform panto. I shared top billing with a guy called Steven Pinder who'd played a character called Max Farnham in Brookside. He was a smashin' lad and we shared a dressing room with no problems whatsoever.

The last time I did it we went to the Charter Theatre in Preston where I shared the bill with that gentle giant David Lonsdale who was famous for playing Greengrass's nephew David in Heartbeat. He played dame and he was very good indeed. I hated that theatre because the dressing rooms were four floors below the stage and the lift travelled at one foot per hour. It meant four flights of stairs for every entrance so I ended up spending the whole bleedin' show hanging around in the wings. The best two things about doing three years with the same show was not having to learn my lines and working with the Patton Brothers every time. They're like a good wine that just gets better with age. They were in their seventies then so now they'll be in their eighties and they're *still* performing.

The Tragedy of Mike Kay

My collaboration with Mike Kay began with the Crucible production of Dick Whittington in 1985/6. We did five unbelievably spectacular shows together and they just got better every year. I'd have usually got the bare bones of the script finished by June then Mike would polish it up and we'd discuss what we were going to do for the slosh and all the gags. We always had three and a half weeks rehearsals to get things absolutely bang on for opening night. Mike was so good at planning stuff. I recall the Jack and the Beanstalk we did in 86/7, we had the tallest beanstalk in the country which sprang from the stage through a large trap door and grew before the amazed audience, right into the roof of the auditorium. It was a giant telescopic hoist which had been festooned with greenery and artificial vines. It had a small platform on its top onto which Jack would step and he would slowly rise out of sight accompanied by the dramatic music for the first half finale. Mike also acquired an exploding comedy car for that particular show which cost a fortune to hire, but it didn't matter because the show sold out every year and made money.

I became very close to Mike and his lovely family, he was married to Veronica who I think was a teacher, they had a teenage son Dominic and a gorgeous little girl called Gemma. He used to bring Gemma into the theatre and she'd sit for hours in his office with her crayons and colouring books. I knew that like most people in our business, Mike loved a drink, but I was starting to notice that he seemed to drinking very heavily. We *always* bought each other a bottle on opening night, he bought me brandy and I bought him scotch whisky. On the opening matinee of Mother Goose in 1988, I remember giving him a litre bottle of Teachers for his customary gift. In the interval of the evening show I went in his office looking for him but he wasn't there. What I did notice was that the litre bottle of Teachers was nearly empty with about an inch left in the bottom. I saw him in the bar after the show as we celebrated our first night triumph and he seemed perfectly OK and quite sober. He was downing large whiskys and I realised then that he had a serious drink problem but I genuinely felt that it wasn't my place to preach to him about it. On hindsight, I realise it's exactly what I *should* have done.

The last panto we did together was the longest runner the Crucible ever did, seven weeks of Babes in the Wood. It did wonderful business and was to be the last panto ever at the Crucible because the Lyceum was opening the following year. Before we'd started rehearsals for it, Mike had been told that his contract wasn't being renewed in the new year and that he was out. I felt desperately sorry for him but his drinking was becoming obvious to all around him and the boss, Clare Venables felt she had to let him go. The drinking was never mentioned as a reason, it was said they felt he'd gone as far as he could "artistically" and that they thought he needed a change. This was the first nail in the coffin of what was to become the most tragic chain of events which defy the imagination.

I'd noticed over the preceding couple of years that on the odd times I'd met him, Mike's son Dominic had become increasingly strange and withdrawn. He'd gone from shiny, hair- parted school uniformed twelve year old to spiky haired big booted weirdo sixteen year old. No one knew, because Mike had kept it a secret, but Dom was doing drugs. Mike was a real family man and his parents who lived in Bradford were very dear to him, he adored his father and they were extremely close. While Mike was serving his notice at the Crucible in the spring of 1990, his father died suddenly. I know what he went through because I lost my own beloved father in similar circumstances in 1979. None of Mike's friends, even close ones knew that Dominic was having councilling and treatment for his drug addiction. Very shortly after the death of his father, Mike's son committed suicide by jumping from the top of the Park Hill Flats. If you sat in the bar of the Crucible and looked out of the big picture window over the valley, the massive Park Hill Flats dominated the skyline. They were a chillingly constant reminder to Mike of his son's death. It's impossible to comprehend what this

Me & Mike Kay

gentle sensitive man was enduring as a result of these two appalling tragedies coming so close together. You will find it almost impossible to believe as I describe what happened next.

Two weeks after the death of Dominic, Mike's wife Veronica killed herself. She had apparently, unknown to Mike, been having an affair with Dominic's drug councillor and the stigma must have driven her to her dreadful decision. In the short time of two months, this poor dear man had lost his father, his only son and then his wife. I suspect that if you presented the scenario which I've just described as a fictional subject for a play or a book, it would be speedily dismissed as too far fetched and bizarre.

Mike's daughter Gemma was like a rock to him during this unimaginable time in his life and she grew into a woman almost overnight. His countless friends rallied round to support and comfort him and must have made him realise how much he was loved by all. Alas, his alcoholism followed him through the few short remaining years of his life and his liver eventually gave up on him. I saw him very shortly before he died; I went to visit him in hospital with Stumpy. His skin was exactly the same colour as a banana due to the jaundice and the dear man passed away not long afterwards.

I often look back to those wonderful pantos which Mike and I did at the Crucible and the many laughs we had, God rest him.

The Unexpected Guest

In 1998 Donna and I decided to sell the cottage and go for a new house. We finally found a lovely new estate in Deepcar near Sheffield and chose a four bedroom detached house with lots of space for all my stuff. The builder had got the horn to sell Bobby Knutt a new house and he gave me a massive discount plus he fitted out the whole kitchen. He also put in carpets and curtains of our choice and landscaped the garden. I absolutely loved it, three toilets and two bathrooms plus I converted the smallest bedroom into a workshop for my model ships. I've always been a keen modeler and I still have some beautiful Napoleonic miniature lead soldiers which I made years ago before my right hand started shaking. I'll tell you about the shakes later on.

My profile was still quite high as my Emmerdale character was well remembered by the viewers and I was getting sick of folk asking "When ya coming back in Emmerdale?". Of course, I would have given my left bollock to have been back in the soap so I could be sleeping in my own bed instead of tearing all over the bleedin' planet on cruise ships. The ships are a chapter all on their own and I'm saving them till last.

In the spring of '99 I got a call from Tim Scott to say I'd been offered a touring stage play, starting the end of August for a producer called Ian Dickens. It was a well known Agatha Christie murder mystery called The Unexpected Guest and I was offered top billing as police inspector Thomas. It was eight weeks work and I was to join the play half way through its run in Swansea Grand Theatre. The guy topping the bill had been Steven Pinder who I'd done panto with in Southport the previous Christmas. He was playing the part of the murderer but he was going back into Brookside in September so Ian needed a replacement. When I got the script, or the "book" as it's called, I nearly shit myself. It was like soddin' Hamlet. Once I made my entrance at the beginning of scene two, I was never off. I thought I'd never learn it in time but I worked really hard on it and had a minimum of two hours a day on the lines. I set my stall out at a page per day and each day I'd go back over the previous pages that I'd learnt to consolidate them in my memory. As usual, Donna was playing all the other parts when I had a read through. Thomas was a Welshman so I gave him a nice gentle South Wales lilt, not the singy-songy valleys accent that I adopt if I'm doing a welsh gag in my act.

The plan was for me to go down to Swansea on the Monday when the play opened there and rehearse it all day with the rest of the cast. Steven Pinder was being replaced by David Callister in the murderer's role and he was an absolute sweety to work with. He was one of Ian's regular jobbing actors who could turn his hand to anything. Another chap who joined the cast was Howard Leader, he used to be one of Esther Rantzen's regular panel on "That's Life". He was playing the slime bag butler whom everybody suspected as the killer and we had a memorable scene together during the play, we became the very best of pals.

Sharing the billing with me was Anna Karen who was famous for her role as Olive from "On the Buses". It seemed strange to hear her playing the posh old matriarch instead of the cockney Olive, she was wonderful in the part. We did the first run through and thank God I never missed a line, Ian was very impressed at me having learned it so thoroughly plus he liked the Welsh accent. I watched the play every night of the week so as to take in the moves and positions and spoke the inspector's lines as the other actor said them. Ian sprung a pearler on me on the Thursday morning, he'd decided that I should go on and do it on the Saturday night so as to get one performance under my belt. It was a good idea but my arse cheeks were really twitching at the thought of doing this huge part live for the first time. I also had a terribly serious personal problem at home, my lovely sister Helen was dying from cancer.

She'd had it for about four years and initially she'd had her breasts removed and undergone the chemotherapy and all the other painful and intrusive treatments. She was given the all clear but in the late spring of '99 it came back with a vengeance. I loved her so very much, she was quiet mannered and softly spoken just like our father. If you read my first book, you'll remember how much I loved my father and how it devastated me when he died so suddenly in 1979. Helen had fought all the way but was now on the last lap and not expected to last the week. I'd gone to see her at home the week before Swansea and I ended up sobbing my heart out at the sight of her agony. I was now nearly three hundred miles away and prayed that she'd last out until I got back home on the Sunday morning. It was a cruel irony that I was away when my Dad died, away when my mum died, and now here I was, away from my beloved Helen as she lay dying. I'd told Donna not to let me know if she died because what with the stress of doing the play on the Saturday night, I wasn't sure that I could have done it.

On the Saturday afternoon, Helen's husband Graham rang me to say that she'd passed away, he meant well, but I wished he'd not told me. I went back to my dressing room in the theatre and I broke down, crying uncontrollably. David Callister must have heard me and came in to ask me what was wrong. When I told him he immediately went and found Ian Dickens who was really sympathetic and said that I needn't go on that night. I realised that going on was what I needed so I told him I'd be OK and that I would do it. I don't think that at anytime in my whole career have I been so desperately nervous about going onto a stage. I was praying to the God of actors that I would remember my lines. The first scene finished, the curtain came in while the second scene was set. It saw me sitting at a desk in the drawing room while my sergeant was nosing around for clues. Just before the curtain flew out I had a terrible attack of the "Sweats", I was literally wringing wet through with nerves but I made it through that scene with flying colours. I was fine after that, although it was very uncomfortable being wet through on that already well lit and hot stage. The play ended and the three new members of the cast were called forward for an extra bow for which we received a very satisfying ovation.

After the show, we were all invited to the bar for a drink with the "Friends of the Theatre". All theatres have these type of people who form their various little groups to raise funds via coffee mornings

Cast of The Unexpected Guest

253

which the resident cast of whatever play is being shown that week is required to attend. They are basically nice people, but sadly they are mostly obsequious anoraks who are all founder members of the Gt Britain Boring team. I recall that night very well indeed for obvious reasons, I was having a well deserved large port and brandy while at the same time being cornered by this rather overweight Welsh lady who was complimenting (in her opinion) the high quality of my portrayal of a policeman. I was chatting back to her in my normal Yorkshire accent when she raised her hand to her mouth and exclaimed loudly "Oh my God, you're not a Welshman are yew". I said that I was a proud Yorkshireman and she said that my welsh accent was so convincing that she thought I was a local lad. I was quite chuffed at that.

So, I had conquered my first night nerves and my grief over Helen's death but now I had to wait another ten days before the next performance which was in Peterborough at the Key Theatre. There was a blank week which the other cast were grateful for but I had to run my lines every day to keep them fresh in my mind. I stayed with my dear old mate Finetime Fontayne at his home in Stamford. Here's an example of his wonderful sense of humour. In his living room by the side of an armchair was a life size carved wooden animal with a sort of saddle on its back to place drinks on. It had two small horns so asked him if it was a goat. He replied "No, it's an impala, his name's Vlad".

We had a bit of a disaster that second week on the Thursday night's performance. During the third scene in which my character was interrogating the members of the household I was grilling the butler. It was a very wordy quick fire speech which needed all my concentration. He was sitting in a high backed armchair and I was circling it in a sort of stalker-like fashion as I fired the questions at him. Half way through this deeply probing interrogation, the phone rings for me and as I annoyingly answer it I'm aware that the interruption has given the butler time to compose himself for the rest of the questioning. The phone would ring on a direct cue as I said the words "Did you at any time?"- - - . I said the line and guess what, no telephone ringing. It was the ASM's job to press a button in his corner thus making the bell ring. The twat forgot didn't he. I looked down at little Howard in his armchair and did another circuit of it but still the phone didn't ring. Now you cannot ad lib in an Agatha Christie play because similar to Shakespeare aficionados, most of the Agatha anoraks out there in the audience probably know the script better than the actors on the stage. By now I was starting to feel a right silly bugger, I'd got no lines because the next course of action was my sergeant picking up the phone and saying "It's for you Sir". By now the audience had sussed that something was amiss so I just said "You know, I'm sure that phone should be ringing now", which got a titter from the crowd. I then said "I'd better answer it anyway". I went and picked up the phone and carried on as if nothing had gone wrong.

The ASM was full of apologies in the interval saying he'd just forgotten to press the bell button but I told him that it wasn't him out there looking and feeling an absolute cunt in front of a full house. He didn't do it again.

Donna and I had another bereavement shortly after I finished the play, we lost our lovely dog Ben. He was fourteen and a half which is old for a golden retriever. We'd had him since he was ten weeks old and he was like a child to us. His back end just went one Sunday morning and he couldn't raise himself up off the floor. I waited until Donna got back from her Sunday morning fitness class and we called the vet who only lived four doors up the road. We reluctantly agreed that his time had come and Donna cradled his head in her lap as he gently passed into doggy heaven. We cried like babies, even the vet cried because his own retriever used to play with Ben. We swore we'd never have another dog and have to endure this misery again, but we did. We adopted Dylan, a border collie, when he was seven. He's now fifteen and I suppose in a short time we're going to have to deal with *his* demise.

British Broadcasting Corporation Television Centre Wood Lane London W12 7RJ Telephone 0181 743 8000

Last of the Summer Wine
Teddington Studios
Broom Road,
Teddington,
Middx. TW11 9NT
Tel: 0208-614-2590
Fax: 0208-614-2863

5th August, 1999

Dear Bobby,

'LAST OF THE SUMMER WINE'

Thank you for such an excellent performance in our 'Magic and the Morris Minor' episode. I had no idea that there was such an excellent actor within a stone's throw of our locations.

It was a fun episode and it was certainly great fun working with you. It was also an extremely rewarding experience for me and the show.

Best wishes,

Yours sincerely,

ALAN J. W. BELL
Producer, 'Last of the Summer Wine'

Bobby Knutt,
51 The Rookery,
Deepcar,
Sheffield, S36 2NA.

256

Tony Capstick

I couldn't possibly write a book about my life and the people who've crossed my path without including Tony Capstick. I've loved very few men in my life but because I grew up without any brothers, there have been the odd few with whom I became so fraternal that I loved them like real brothers. Capstick was one of that minority. I never called him by his Christian name; it was either "Capstick" or "Antoninus". I'd known of him because of his work on radio 2 in a programme called "Folkweave" which he presented but I didn't get to know him properly until he started to do the working men's clubs around 1980 time.

I'd seen him billed to appear at Smithywood WMC on their regular Thursday night big show. I didn't know that it was his first ever appearance in a WMC. He was very popular in South Yorkshire thanks to his regular show on Radio Sheffield and the club was full. I introduced myself and he was, in his own words, over the moon at meeting me as he knew I was {in his own words again}a legend in the clubs. OK, I'd won the clubland awards comedian of the year for six consecutive years before retiring so I guess he was about right on that score. We had a drink and a chat before he went on and I knew there and then that we were to become firm pals. I quickly gathered that we were on the same wavelength intellectually but I conceded to his amazingly quick wit and observance of all around him as a subject for his humour. He went on that night to do his first spot and I knew I was watching a master of his craft. I was absolutely pissing myself laughing at his act which didn't have one single joke in it. He just rattled on about everything and anything in the style of a raconteur rather than a comedian. I must confess that quite a bit of it went over their heads but he still did very well. He came straight up to me after that first spot and asked me for my opinion. I was really chuffed that he even valued it but I did, after all have vastly more experience as a club comic than he had.

I told him that all he needed to do was speed up a little as there had been little lulls in his act when a less responsive audience would have lost their interest. He was a child of the folk clubs who's audiences were a lot more attentive and usually more intelligent than your average WMC's crowd. I told him that he had to become a chameleon that could change from one style to another at the drop of a hat. We became firm friends and our favourite pastime was to ring each other with the latest gags that were going round. Tony was an intellectual giant with a mind that soaked up knowledge and information like a huge sponge. His ability to ad-lib and come up with a clever retort was limitless and I soon realised what a genius he was. He had one serious weakness, booze. He was a very heavy drinker and occasionally he'd consume so much as to make a twat of himself. All his mates plus some of the general population knew of his passion for alcohol but all forgave him when he drank too much and usually made sure he got home OK.

Everyone had a "Capstick" story, he left an impression on everybody he met, I could fill another book with them. I remember a charity show which I organised for the Weston Park Hospital sometime in the early eighties. It was held at the Colley Road WMC on the Parson Cross estate in Sheffield. I'd got all my mates in the comedy world to do a spot as I'd billed it as a grand comedy spectacular. It sold out and I'd scrounged a lot of very valuable raffle prizes from my many rich businessmen friends plus the club was donating the proceeds from the bingo to the fund and providing a free bar for the entertainers.

I went up at lunchtime to set up my own sound system so as to ensure all the comics would be heard loud and clear. The show was due to start at 8pm so I got there at seven to welcome all my mates who were working for free. As I entered the foyer of the club the doorman said "Yer mate's in't lounge waitin' fothee". I walked into the lounge and there was Capstick with his ladyfriend sitting at his table downing shorts. I forgot to mention that his other weakness was a love of the ladies; he was a certified fanny rat. He came and put his arm around me and gave a big sloppy kiss which was his usual way of greeting me. "Have a port and brandy dear boy" he said. "Dear boy" was one of his expressions when he'd had a few and believe me he'd had a few. I asked him as diplomatically as possible to cut back a bit until he'd been on, then he could get as pissed as he liked. I knew his vast capacity for drink far exceeded most mortals but I'd seen him drunk before and he just used to collapse in an incoherent stupor.

I was compering the show and had arranged the running order which had Capstick closing the first half; this was always a plum spot in any show. I knew he'd never last till then so I quickly rearranged the bill so as to get him on straight after the opening overture from the organist and drummer. I got him into the dressing room and helped him change into his stage suit and I literally had to tie his shoes for him. I'd got my old pal Colin "Fingers" Henry to stand by in case of an emergency. I looked at Capstick who was in a right state and said "Look Mate, you don't have to go on you know, I'll tell 'em you're ill with the flu or something".

He looked at me, took a deep breath and then said in a perfectly coherent voice "I'm alright Knutty, get me on, I'm fine".

I couldn't believe that he could recover so quickly, but there he was, seemingly sober as a judge so I decided to put him on. I went on and did five minutes after Jean the organist had finished her opener then gave Capstick a massive build up, I even hedged my bets by telling them that he wasn't too well with a bad cold but had insisted on coming to do the show. He got a huge round of applause when I introduced him after which I went to the back of the room to check the sound was OK. By the time I'd got there, Capstick's moment of sobriety had passed and he was mumbling any old bollocks into the mike. I could hear the stage whispers buzzing round the concert room, "He's pissed". I sped down to the front and went onto the stage and stood next to him at the same time putting my arm around his shoulder at which time he rested his head on mine like a little trusting puppy, I said "Ladies and gentlemen, as I told you, Tony's not very well tonight and the medication he's on has made it worse so"...... I was just about to ask for a round of applause and take him off when he looked up at me and said "Why don't ya just tell 'em I'm fuckin' pissed". The mike picked up every word and most of the audience fell about laughing as I gently guided him back to the dressing room and another night of oblivion. Sadly for the audience, they missed out on a comedy feast as when he was on song there was no funnier man than Tony Capstick. Billy Connolly once said he was the funniest man he'd ever seen and I fully agree. When Capstick had had just a few drinks he was still hilarious but on the odd times he went on the wagon, he was a serious threat to every comic in the world.

At one time in his life he decided to take up pistol shooting and joined a proper gun club with a firing range. He'd bought a couple of expensive handguns and quickly became an expert on all things to do with armoury and ballistics. He did this by merely reading about it. He was an avid reader of all books on all subjects and he seemed to remember everything he'd ever read. I admired his intellect more than anything but I never told him, although he did pay me a huge compliment one night when we were having a few jars together. He just said "I've got you sussed Knutty, you try to make out you're a rough spoken typical Yorkshireman, but you're not are you, you're a lot bloody cleverer than you make out to be and you miss nowt". I've never forgotten those instinctive observations from my dear departed friend.

One night when he was returning home from the gun club in a taxi the taxi driver asked him what was in the shiny wooden box that he had on his knee. "It's a gun" replied Capstick.

"Is it one of those replicas?" he enquired. At this, Capstick took it out of the box and said "No it's a real one". He then wound down the window and fired the fuckin' thing up into the sky. Having fired a hand-gun myself, I know what a huge bang they make, which is why all the people on the firing ranges wear ear defenders. The sound from a high calibre pistol fired within the confines of a taxi cab must have been deafening and it frightened the living shit out of the poor driver. He dropped Tony off then immediately rang the old Bill who came out and arrested Capstick and took him into custody charging him with a firearms offence. It obviously made all the papers and he ended up being fined a thousand pounds by the courts but even worse he was suspended by Radio Sheffield. His job at the BBC was his sanctuary and his reason for getting up in the morning. He was the best broadcaster I ever heard, his bright entertaining chatter would light up anyone's day and his ability to interview anyone from aristocrats to down and outs with equal skill and alacrity was his great forte. The bosses at Radio Sheffield knew what an invaluable asset he was but I feel they must have realised a short sharp warning was what was needed to try and get him back on track.

Every one knew that Tony had a built-in self destruct button but no matter what he did to blot his copy book, he was always forgiven because people accepted that that's how he was. There was no badness or malice in him; he just had this flaw which occasionally sent him off the rails. It all blew over eventually and became just another chapter in the life and times of a lovable wild man with his own demons.

Tony had been married to Carol for as long as I'd known him and I reluctantly admit that it can't have been easy for her. I always found her to be a little gloomy in her disposition and often wondered how two people who seemed as different as chalk and cheese could remain together. They split up for good after he met another woman who I met but who's name I cannot recall. She was a teetotaler which wasn't a very good start for a guy who could drink Windermere dry. Apparently he walked out and left all his stage stuff at his old home, this included his sound system and the most beautiful Martin acoustic guitar. Guitars have been my great love since I was a teenager and I like to think I'm a bit of an expert on the subject. The guitars which are favoured by the folk singer types are nearly always the big bodied acoustics of which there are many makes and their values differ greatly. The big Gibsons from America offer a large range of wonderful acoustics but possibly the best and most sought after are the Martins. They are very expensive to buy new and the second hand ones are sometimes even more expensive as they improve with age like a classic violin. Tony had a 1950s Martin D28 with elaborate mother of pearl and ivory inlays and it was worth a fortune.

This was how he told it to me. Apparently, Carol wouldn't give him back his stuff so he had to buy a new guitar and sound system which my mate Glen from the Spare Tyres had let him have at trade price. As time passed I think the acrimony after the initial split was abating and Carol was becoming less hostile which led him to hope of a return of his beloved Martin. Now I've already described my pal's incredible intelligence, but like a lot of clever people, it doesn't necessarily mean they have the same amount of common sense. He moved into a little house just a few doors away from his old house and this really upset the applecart. In a severe fit of "Hell hath no fury", Carol dumped his precious Martin on the front garden after first jumping on it a few times. It was smashed to bits and when he told me I could have cried for him.

I told him to take it to Glen's shop where an expert guitar builder called Steve Gaines had a part time job. Steve could fix anything within reason but when he saw the job that had been done on Tony's Martin he told him that it was virtually impossible and if it were, then the man-hours involved would cost a small fortune. Tony accepted the bad news and gave the wrecked guitar to Steve saying he could salvage the neck if he liked.

There's a sort of happy ending to this little story. About three years later I was in Glen's shop having a cuppa when I noticed Steve playing a lovely old Martin D28 which sounded like a well tuned bell. I asked him where he'd got it or was it a customers in for repair. He told me it was Capstick's old one which he'd managed to repair after over a thousand hours of intricate fiddling and filing and glueing and measuring and sanding and polishing. He'd left it in his workshop for about a year then one day he was inspired to have a bash at trying to restore it back to its original condition. He did a fantastic job which was a credit to the fine craftsman that he was. Apart from a slight seam on the front of the instrument, it was indistinguishable from its old condition. He made me promise not to tell Capstick as for him to buy it back would involve an astronomical price in labour costs.

Capstick and I shared a great mutual friend in Stephen Smith, the local solicitor who also writes very funny books and was kind enough to write the foreword to this very book. Smithy is another one of the very few men that I love as a brother; he's a great wit and amazing company. He puts on shows at local theatres with a chosen comedian as his guest and they are billed as "An Evening with Stephen Smith and Bobby Knutt", or whoever is his guest of the night. I've done a couple with him and they are so rewarding for an entertainer. He spends the first hour or so interviewing you, then there's a beer break, then you go on and do your act. The interviews are always hilarious as he knows exactly which bullets to fire to get the laughs. One of the funniest intro's I ever heard him do was when he had Capstick on one night. He said "Ladies and gentlemen, it gives me great pleasure to introduce a man who I've known for many years, in fact I've known him for so long, I knew him when he had a driving licence". The fun behind this intro was the fact that Capstick had been banned *five* times by the courts and on every occasion it had been heavily covered by the press.

On the last and fifth case, Smithy was as usual defending him and even though he could have got David Blunkett a driving licence, nobody, not even Smithy himself was expecting anything but a custodial sentence. I'd rung him and asked him what he reckoned Cappo's chances were and he said they were very slim. On the day of the case which was at the Rotherham Magistrate's Court, I went down to hear the case and give Tony my support. I used to make military models so I'd got a whole bunch of modeller's miniature tools in my garage. I chose a very small rat-tail file and shoved it in my top pocket. When I got down to the courthouse, the copper on the door recognized me and asked if I'd come to see my mate. He showed me down to the interview rooms and I found him sitting with Smithy looking very morose indeed. I could imagine what was going through his mind as he thought of clanking keys and incarceration with no chance of a large Bacardi anywhere in the loop. He was glad to see me and stoically tried to appear cheerful. I then went in my top pocket and said "Here, There's a present for you" as I handed him the file. Both he and Smithy pissed themselves and I was so glad to have broken the miserable atmosphere which had previously pervaded the room.

His case was called and I had every finger crossed as I looked at him in the dock across the court. He looked like a little lost lad who was standing before the headmaster waiting to be caned after the customary admonition. The prosecutor read out the charge after which Smithy stood up and began his most eloquent defense for years. The magistrate listened and eventually spoke saying that even though a custodial sentence was usual in this case, he was taking into account the amount of charity work and goodwill that Tony had accrued over the years as a well loved personality and that no good purpose would be served by sending him to prison. I could see old Capstick visually relax and come down from a place which he desperately didn't want to be in. Smithy had done it again, champion of the underdog and saviour of the oppressed.

We met a joyful Joseph Anthony Capstick outside the court house; the time was about 11am. He said "Come on lads, let's go for a drink", Smithy declined because he had another case coming up and I declined because it was too bloody early and I didn't want to get into a session with the wild man because once you got to the bar with him he would never let you go.

Tony was a monster talent who'd even enjoyed pop notoriety with his number three hit "Capstick Comes Home". He also had a semi regular appearance in Last of the Summer Wine as a village policeman. Sadly, his Achilles heel was to be his downfall. We all thought he'd be OK when he unexpectedly married Gill in 2000. She was a check-out girl at Morrisons but she liked a drink as much as he did and their relationship could be sometimes a bit volatile. His drinking got worse and he was eventually axed from his show on Radio Sheffield. He'd worked there for thirty years and it broke his heart, it also signalled his demise because his drinking got worse. In early 2003 he was rushed into hospital and after a spell in there he was warned by the doctors that if he carried on drinking he would surely die. I think this frightened him as he went on the wagon although he still frequented his favourite hostelry The Rockingham Arms in the village of Wentworth, but he just drank coffee. I often called in to see him but I always seemed to miss him.

I sadly saw little of him in the final stages of his life as I was always away on the bloody ships. The last time I saw him I was sitting outside the Rocky Arms with Donna on a lovely sunny autumn lunchtime. We'd been out for a spin in the MGB and had called in for just the one. As we sat there, a taxi drew up and out got this little old man, the taxi driver helped him out of the cab and when he saw me he cried out loudly "Knutty dear boy". It was Tony and I hardly recognized him. He was smartly dressed as he always was and he came up and hugged me then he grabbed Donna and gave her a big squeeze and a kiss, he'd always adored her. I told him to sit between us and asked him what he wanted to drink, expecting him to say a coffee, he asked for a large glass of chardonnay. I said I was surprised at him being back on the sauce but he said he only drank wine now, never spirits. I got him and Donna a large glass of chardonnay each and as I placed it down in front of him he picked it up and downed it in on swallow. He said it was his round but I declined as I'd got a full pint of Old Peculier and I was driving. I couldn't help but notice his physical demise. In his hey day he'd never been big but he was a well muscled wiry little bugger and quite powerful. His legs were like sticks now and his physical being was that of someone way older than his actual age, he was fifty nine.

We parted with another hug and a kiss and I was never to see him alive again. A few weeks later in October 2003, I was sitting in a tapas bar in Cadiz with a couple of shipmates when my mobile rang. It was Radio Sheffield wanting to know my comments on Tony Capstick's death. I was shocked beyond belief and told them I couldn't speak as it was the first I'd heard of it. My mates could see I was very upset but they got me out of it and I ordered a bottle of wine for myself and drank it all down in Capstick's memory, he would have liked that.

I missed his funeral as the ship didn't get back in time, it was a grand affair with everyone singing his praises and Wentworth church was packed to the rafters. His death had a huge coverage in the local newspaper with the dramatic headline "TRAGIC END OF FLAWED GENIUS". I suppose that put it in a nutshell really because that's what he was, a genius with a few flaws. We're all entitled to have a few flaws aren't we? For all his flaws, old Cappo was loved by all and will always be remembered with warmth and affection. I still miss him terribly, sometimes when I hear a new gag, I'll subconsciously think to myself, "I'll ring Capstick up with that one, he'll piss himself".

He's buried in Wentworth churchyard in a lovely well kept grave. His wife Gill who was much younger than him, passed away in late 2009 and her ashes rest with him. I often walk Dylan through the grounds and never fail to visit him to pull up the odd weed on his plot. As it says on his headstone, he was a remarkable man.

Tony Capstick & Rex Bacon from the 'Discoes'

A Life On The Ocean Wave

In the February of 1996 I did my first ever cruise ship. A great mate of mine Mike Ryal had done years on the ships before he became dependant on his thrice weekly dialysis sessions to keep him alive. He knew the main booker for P&O, a bloke called David Llewellyn and he persuaded him to come up to Sheffield and see me performing at Big David Baldwin's Omega. It was a private function and I was on my own patch so I expected to do well, which I did. Mike knew I always worked clean but on this occasion he said I must be squeaky clean, not even a "Bloody" must pass my lips. Not long after I was offered a leg of the Canberra's world cruise from Sydney to San Francisco. Mike had even arranged for Donna to come with me free of charge. I rang all my mates who'd performed on the ships and without exception they all told me the one same vitally important thing, keep it clean.

I knew I had to do three forty five minute spots so I planned to take my guitar and sing a few of my comedy ditties. I had three new stage jackets made and Donna was busy shopping for posh frocks for formal nights. There are three different dress codes on most ships, formal, informal and casual. I was a complete new boy and had a lot to learn about this new avenue of work into which I was venturing. I bought two new and very expensive suitcases from John Lewis for the trip. I didn't know at the time, but cruising was going to keep me solvent for the next thirteen years and I've gone through more suitcases than I care to count thanks to that vandalistic species known as the baggage handler.

We flew from Manchester to Amsterdam then on to Singapore and finally down to Sydney. A taxi was waiting to take us to the ship and I couldn't believe the size of her as we drew up on to the dockside. Canberra, the White Whale as she was nick named, had been built for the ten pound immigration trips to Australia and was launched in 1960, her maiden voyage being a year later. Owing to ever more popular jet travel and the decrease in immigration to Oz, she was converted into a cruise ship in the mid seventies. Of all the cruise ships that have ever sailed the seas, she was undoubtedly the most popular. She seemed to have a soul and although she was quite primitive compared to the luxurious leviathans which sail the oceans nowadays, she'll always be remembered with unbelievable fondness. Quite a few of the cabins didn't even have a toilet so you'd often witness the early morning trips of old ladies in dressing gowns parading down the corridors, tooth brush in one hand and toilet roll in the other.

We were both completely knackered from the length of the flight plus the jetlag but we were determined to try and stay awake until bedtime. I went to see the cruise director, on a ship he's the man who's in total charge of all the entertainment and activities on board. He was a guy called Nigel Travis and he made us so welcome. He's one of the nicest blokes who ever walked in a pair of shoes and we're close pals to this day, I was so lucky to have him as my first cruise director. We got to our cabin which was an inside one, this meant that it didn't have a porthole so there was no natural light at any time but at least it had a shower and toilet. It took me many years to get an outside passenger cabin in my contract but I finally managed it.

When we'd unpacked we decided to go ashore and explore the shops and stalls along the waterfront. As I mentioned earlier, I've always been a bugger for cowboy boots and hats and we passed a shop that sold nothing else but boots and hats. Smack in the middle of the window display was a crocodile skin hat with crocodile teeth all around the hatband. It was identical to the one Paul Hogan wore in the film Crocodile Dundee and I fell in love with it. We went in and I tried it on, it fitted perfectly. Donna quietly said "Darling, could you really walk round Tesco in that hat, it's beautiful but it's a bit over the top". She wasn't trying to put me off it or deter me from buying it, but she was making a sensible observation which I considered and finally agreed with. I was still determined to buy a hat so I tried on nearly every bloody one in the shop. Nothing came close to my original choice so I finally went back and tried it on again, we both agreed it was unique and I had to have it. I told the storekeeper I'd buy it and he cheerfully said "Great choice Sir, that'll be eight hundred and ninety five dollars". I suppose that's the first time in his life he'd heard the Yorkshire war cry "HOW MUCH?" It was four hundred and fifty quid in sterling and I nearly passed out. I politely told him that I wasn't going to spend that much on a hat and we left.

We got back on board Canberra and I met Alan Randall who was also appearing on the ship, he'd been cruising for years and over the next three weeks we became close pals as he filled me in on all the aspects of shipboard entertainment. He was travelling with his wife Mary and she and Donna got on like a house on fire. We dined with them every night in one of the two fabulous restaurants; we had our own personal table with the same waiter who looked after us like a slave. The staff on board cruise ships are the best anywhere in the world, mainly because they're working for their tips at the end of the voyage. They are very poorly paid and their wages are considerably enhanced by the gratuities which they hope to receive. The best job on the ship is cabin steward, he's the one who makes up your cabin twice a day and gets you anything you ask him to, including morning tea and coffee at any time you request it. It's like having your own personal genie that seems to sense your every need. I often do the gag when I'm praising the stewards in my show, "I went to go to the toilet at three O'clock this morning, when I came out of the bathroom, he'd made the bed".

I realise now how green I was as a ship's comic on that first memorable cruise but I still did very well on each of my three spots and Nigel gave me a glowing report which resulted in lots more work. It really was a wonderful cruise and we stopped at two ports in New Zealand one of which was Littleton. It was like turning the clocks back seventy years, it was so quaint and unspoiled and we loved it. We then headed across the Pacific to Fiji where Donna and I had our first go at snorkeling followed by lunch on the beach in a palm roofed open plan café bar with grass skirted maidens serving pina coladas and fresh cooked crayfish. We were in paradise. As we crossed the Equator the whole ship celebrated with the customary

269

King Neptune's fun and games which always ends up with all the participants being chucked in the pool.

The next stop was an overnight stay in Hawaii; Alan had been before so he acted as our guide. He took us to the biggest shopping mall I've ever seen followed by a visit to the Arizona monument at Pearl Harbour. It was one of the most moving experiences of my life. They show you a film first of all which describes the attack on Pearl Harbour and how the Arizona went down with all hands when it literally blew up. The next part of the visit is a boat ride out to the actual monument which was built directly over the hull of the sunken battleship. As you stand on the platform above the ship, you can actually see the gun turrets and decks as it sits forever like a shrine on the bed of the harbour. The monument itself is a huge marble wall with the name of every dead sailor engraved upon it, I found it to be quite eerie as probably did every one else, for nobody was speaking at all. What I couldn't get my head round was the number of Japanese present, they far outnumbered the other tourists and I've often wondered what they were thinking during their visit. Their inscrutable emotionless expressions revealed nothing whatsoever of their feelings. Having read "The Knights of Bushido" by Lord Russell of Liverpool when I was a young man, I doubted whether they had any feelings at all. It was a vivid account of Japanese atrocities on foreign POWs during the war, it revealed them to be a barbaric, savage and sadistic race which leads to the reason why many can never forgive them for the abominable cruelty they inflicted on our lads.

Hawaii was our last port of call before the voyage ended for us in San Francisco. It took six days to cross the vast Pacific Ocean and we never saw a ship or a bird or any living thing, we just saw the sea. When we arrived at San Francisco, a new group of entertainers would come aboard to do the next leg. About a thousand passengers were doing the whole cruise, all the way round the world. Over the years I've done all the various legs of the different world cruises and they are a different animal to your normal two week hop around the Canaries or the Med. On a worldy (as a world cruise is known), the ship becomes a small village with everyone of the full distance passengers getting to know each other as the weeks pass by. The first Captain's cocktail party is where they all meet and size each other up. They all get dressed in their best formal evening wear and drink free champagne with the captain and his officers. Some of these people arrive at the gangway as Mr and Mrs Brown, but by the time they're on board, they are Lord and Lady Brown. They converse in nautical terms and boast that they know the captain personally and this is their forty ninth cruise. They invite each other to their cabins for private drinkies on the balcony and talk about all the ships they've been on, sad bastards. On the last leg when they've all been together for nearly three months and they're bored to fuckin' death of each other's company, that's when the daggers come out. You can hear the catty, overweight, over made-up harridans bitching to each other in the cocktail bar, saying things like "Look at her, she's had that frock on eleven times this cruise, she reckons it's designer but it looks like Primark to me".

Then you get the old widows going all the way round in a balcony cabin. It's about thirty five grand to do the full cruise but the old biddies don't give a shit. They sit there on their balconies drinking champagne as they pass through the Panama Canal saying things like "It's what he would have wanted".

I recall one famous true story about an incident on the Canberra. It was the night of the first world cruise cocktail party and this particular lady passenger had a complete wardrobe of new designer dresses and evening gowns tailored just for the cruise. Around teatime she took her chosen dress down to the ironing room to press it for the night's soiree. On arriving at the laundry she realised she'd left the sash for the dress in her cabin so she left the dress on the ironing board and nipped back for the sash. Upon returning to the laundry she found her dress was missing, presumably stolen. She immediately reported it to security, showing them the sash which was of the same material as the dress, which was the only one of its kind. She obviously chose something else to wear for the party and as she mingled with the other guests, she saw a woman wearing her dress. She stormed up to her and angrily told her "That's my dress you're wearing", to which the other woman calmly replied "Prove it", and walked away. She called security who reluctantly told the lady that there was nothing they could do as indeed there was no concrete proof of the woman's guilt. It's common knowledge among us ship's entertainers that you *never* leave anything unattended in the laundry rooms 'cause they'll walk.

I have met some wonderful people on the ships but I've also met some of the biggest wankers on the planet. The species known as the cruise ship passenger is one on his own. Firstly there are the virgin cruisers who are genuinely bowled over by the service and hospitality offered on board these floating palaces. The food is invariably second to none and you can stuff yourself for just about twenty four hours a day if you want to. There are two types of diners on the ships, first there are the ones who insist on taking every meal in the dining room and would never dream of joining the hoi polloi in the self service and their snobbery is infinite. They stubbornly insist on being waited on by the obsequious dining room staff who pamper their every pedantic whim. The others are the greedy bastards that eat at every opportunity because it's there, and they've paid for it. Breakfast usually starts at 7-00am and goes on until 10-00am. The variety of food available is unbelievable from every type of fruit and cereal to the full display of cooked breakfast ingredients. This is followed by mid morning snacks from 11-00 till 12-00, then it's lunchtime. There are usually seven or eight hot main courses with all the accompaniments and veg plus an amazing array of salads and desserts. There is always a curry dish on at lunchtime and they are the best you'll ever taste as they have a lot of Goan and Indian chefs on board. Lunch usually ends at 2-30pm to be immediately followed by afternoon snacks of pasta and cooked meats plus pies and sweets. Dinner is two sittings, 6-30 and 8-30 and is always a five course extravaganza with wine flowing copiously and vintage ports and cognacs to finish. I've always thought that the main problem with these overweight gluttons is that they've only got one arsehole.

Next you get the professional complainers who moan about absolutely everything in the hope of getting a free cruise or perhaps a large discount off their next one. There is *nothing* you could possibly complain about on a well run cruise ship. It's a five star floating hotel which caters for your every desire. There are so many things to do on a ship to keep people occupied. On good weather days there are deck games like quoits and shuffleboard and there's always loads of deck walkers doing their laps to burn off last night's over indulgence. There are golf nets and a tennis court plus two or three swimming pools, table tennis and a jacuzzi. There are lecturers on so many different subjects and arts and crafts classes where passengers can do pottery and painting, jewelry making and wine tasting. The various chefs usually give cookery classes and sometimes they have very famous chefs on board as guest speakers. P&O book famous footballers, golfers, cricketers and athletes plus politicians who are always popular as they sometimes divulge their secrets on the lecture stage. I've met Martin Bell and that dour old Yorkshireman Sir Bernard Ingham but my favourite was Betty Boothroyd, what an absolute sweety. I did a far eastern trip with Angela Rippon who I used to fancy like mad, she still looks well and I trained with her every day in the gym. Her lectures were informative and very funny.

Then of course there's the actual entertainment which can be seen in either a hugely luxurious theatre or a cabaret lounge. The resident theatre company is always made up of very talented all singing all dancing youngsters who are the backbone of the revue shows which pack the theatre for twice nightly performances. They are always backed by a minimum six piece orchestra of supremely talented musicians led by a musical director who has the job of keeping these geniuses in order as they are mostly all dedicated piss artists. The crew bar, or "The Pig", is their dark domain where the booze is ridiculously cheap and plentiful. The visiting cabaret artistes vary from big name TV stars to the regular group of comics, male and female singers, magicians and speciality acts. They constantly travel the world joining ship after ship and hardly ever go home. They are mostly all, just like me, institutionalized as ship's entertainers. It happens to you without you realizing it and you reach a stage where working on land based venues is a problem. You get used to the superb backing musicians, the professionalism of the sound and lighting lads and the backstage crew who'll bend over backwards to give you what you want. The cruise director always gives you a massive and eloquent build up before he or she puts you on. The audiences are invariably excellent and *want* to be entertained. Having said that, if they don't like an act, they'll just get up and walk out leaving some poor struggling act in a half empty theatre. They *never* heckle a comic so he gets used to these well mannered and receptive audiences and he loses his ability to fight. There's another problem with doing the ships, people at home forget you, "Is Bobby Knutt dead?"

"No, he works on the cruise ships".

I've had some great and not so great experiences on P&O ships. I remember I was booked to do four cruises back to back in the Caribbean starting just after Christmas 1997 on the Victoria. It was a lovely ship with an intimate atmosphere due to its being much smaller than the Canberra or the Oriana. I'd been working for P&O for nearly two years and I'd really got used to the set-up. I got on famously with all the cruise directors whom I'd encountered and was even becoming friends with the various ships' captains on the fleet. The only CD I kept well at arms length was a guy called Ross Howard, he was a raving queen with a very effeminate manner. He was a failed entertainer and he put himself into every revue show that the youngsters did and if I compare him to the other CDs on the fleet, he was fuckin' hopeless. I boarded Victoria on 27th December and he told me that my first show was on New Years Eve out on the deck by the Riviera pool. He went on to inform me that I'd be going on at exactly 11-45pm for an eight minute spot before the Captain went on for Auld Lang Syne. The two impossible things about this arrangement was that comedy very rarely works outdoors and I wasn't an eight minute comic. It needed a quick fire patter comic or a Butlins type compere to do an eight minute spot in that situation. I begged him not to put me on as I knew I'd die on my arse. I told him the reasons but he insisted and even quoted the rule book about breaking my contract if I didn't obey the CDs instructions.

Allow me to digress and tell you something about Christmas and New Year cruises. They are mostly full of old people whose ages range from eighty to dead. They are usually the ancient relatives of rich people who can't be bothered with them over the festive season so they stick 'em on a ship. They know that they'll be fed, watered and well looked after and if they snuff it; they'll pop 'em in the freezer till the ship docks back at home in Blighty. You can imagine how hard it is to entertain these old folk, most of the poor old sods are deaf and their favourite pastime is sleeping. There was a luxurious lounge on the old Canberra called the Meridian. It had a magnificent Bechstein grand piano and the classical musicians would appear there on most evenings with their very high brow repertoires. The only two noises in this room were classical music and snoring. They'd hobble in after dinner, find an armchair and immediately disappear into the land of Nod.

On that fateful last night of 1997, I went on after a prayer that God ignored. I couldn't raise a titter from this doddering bunch of old fogeys and the normal passengers were hard work so I came off to the sound of my own feet. The only thing which cheered me up was the fact that even the Captain couldn't get them up on their feet to link arms for Auld Lang Syne. They were a right bunch of miserable bastards but I thought that I'd be able to crack 'em when I got into the cabaret lounge which was a dream of a room for a comic. Alas for me that didn't happen either, that fuckin' raving shirtlifter of a CD put me on a week later in the night club at the ungodly hours of 10-45 and 12-30pm. Nobody ever went into the night club and the poor DJ was regularly arrested for talking to himself. There was about forty people in for the first show and I struggled through. There was an audience of ten for the second one and the twat made me go on. It was embarrassing for both me and them and I cut it short. Gossip goes around a ship like wildfire and it soon went round that I'd died again. Donna was with me and she was distraught for me, trying to cheer me up but it wasn't working. The problem with a cruise ship comedian's life is this; if I die at home in a club or a theatre, I jump in my car, drive away and I never see 'em again. If I die on a ship, I'm having breakfast with the buggers the next morning. You can't get away from them and their acid comments are always uttered just loud enough for you to hear.

My final show on the last night that cruise *was* in the main cabaret lounge and I just went on and took the piss out of 'em, it worked a treat and I did really well. Sadly for me they'd already filled in their comments forms and they'd had a field day pulling me to pieces. All I wanted was for them to fuck off home and let the next compliment of passengers embark so I'd have a new start.

The next three cruises were heaven; I tore the bollocks off 'em every single show and Donna was elated for me. She loves me just as intensely as I love her and if one of us hurts, so does the other. My triumph on the last three cruises made no difference to the vindictive twat of a CD; he gave me a bad report which seriously affected my P&O work for a couple of years. I tried to explain to David Llewellyn that it was just one bad cruise owing to the ridiculous times of my spots but he wouldn't budge even when he agreed I'd stormed them on the other three cruises. I ended up telling him to stick his ships up his fuckin' arse, probably not a wise move, but I really enjoyed saying it.

On the second cruise of the four I met a man who was to become one of my greatest friends when he joined the ship in Barbados, Stuart Gilles. He won Opportunity Knocks for about six or seven weeks when it was in its heyday and went on to have a major hit with a song called "Amanda". We became very close pals and over the years we've worked together on many cruises. I love to watch his act, it's the epitome of class and the utmost in professionalism, his baritone voice and his faultless choice of songs wows the audience every time. He's around seventy now and looks forty five with a slim figure and a voice that's never aged. He's one of nature's pure gentlemen and without doubt the kindest man in the whole of the show business profession.

Stuart is a Scotsman and he'll forgive me if I say he's not tight or miserly, he's just "careful". Whenever he does a ship, he always puts himself forward for the duty of tour escort looking after the passengers who've all paid maybe a hundred quid each to go on an exotic full days coach trip to some Inca temple or Greek ancient monument. I've done it myself and I must admit I've seen some magnificent sights and visited world famous places like the Hermitage Museum in St Petersburg, I've seen the cliff divers in Acapulco and the Temple at Ephesus.

All a tour escort has to do is keep an eye on the coffin dodgers and count them on and off the coach trying at the same time not to lose one. This might not seem too difficult but when you stop at a place where they can go off and do their own thing, you've got to insist that they be back on the bus for a certain time so you can set off for the next point of interest. There's always one that either gets lost or just turns up late. Stuart has been cruising for many more years than me and subsequently he's virtually been everywhere, done all the trips and all free. I remember one cruise we did on the Black Watch, a Fred Olsen ship; we were doing the Baltic and Russia run. On board was one of the strangest passengers I'd ever come across, and believe me, there are some bleedin' nutters allowed on board ships This geezer was a skinny little bloke, travelling alone, who went around the ship with a clipboard in his hand. He'd go up to a doorway or a lifeboat and start writing and ticking off things on his board with a knowing smile. He had the same pair of shorts on every single day and he looked like a bath wouldn't have done him any harm. He'd been warned once by the purser about his behaviour around the bars as he was a very heavy drinker and in my opinion, not quite a full shilling.

St Petersburg is the most popular place for tours as there are so many palaces and museums to visit. I've been there over a dozen times and I must say that in my humble opinion, the place itself is an absolute shithole. It's a monument to communism not working but it still remains one of the most popular tourist destinations in the world.

Most of the Russian tours take in about seven or eight stops including the midday lunch so it's vital for the tour escort to stress the importance of being back at each allotted return time. Sadly for old Stuart, he got the clipboard nutter on his trip. He'd come back late on the first three stops and Stuart had to warn him on each occasion that he was delaying the tour and they were already thirty minutes late overall. About two stops into the afternoon itinerary, he vanished so Stuart told the rest of the very annoyed passengers that he was just going to try and find him failing which they'd have to leave him behind. He set off to look for the nutter and soon found him sitting alone by a fountain with his clipboard; he also noticed that he'd shit himself. He'd still got his mangy old shorts on but now they were covered in shit which was also running down his leg. I can't imagine how my dear mate could have felt at the predicament which befell him. He *had* to get this bloke back to the ship but to ask the other passengers on the bus to endure the disgusting sight and smell of this strange fellow was practically unthinkable. He had no alternative so he guided the shit-encrusted numpty back to the coach and nervously explained to the very pissed off passengers that they'd have to move down the already full bus so as to allow this gentleman his own space sitting on a newspaper on the back seat of the bus. You can well imagine how traumatic was the journey home to the ship, the poor twat at the back ponging like an old tramp and the delicate senses of the tutting passengers being invaded by his obnoxious odours.

Upon arriving back at the ship, Stuart told the nutter to stay where he was while got the rest of the people off the bus. He'd warned security of the incident and they allowed him to take the man straight down to the medical centre via the crew quarters and not through the passenger areas. When Stuart had got the bloke settled he seemed to have calmed down and resigned to the fact that he'd shit his pants. He thanked Stuart for looking after him in such a kindly and compassionate way and held out his hand for Stuart to shake. It's a natural instinct for any man who has a hand held out to him; he goes to shake it, which Stuart did. It was then that he discovered that the man had shit on his hands as well as his trousers. When he told me the story later that day, I absolutely pissed myself laughing and we always reminisce of that event whenever we get together.

My best mate on the ships, Stuart Gillies

Camembert, Bouillabaisse & Peril At Sea

I remember one cruise around the Adriatic and the Mediterranean on the Oriana. It's a fabulous ship but I'd been allocated a really bad cabin. It was number E101 on deck six, an inside cabin right in the bow and directly underneath the theatre so the noise from the shows was unbearable if you fancied an early night. Because it was situated in the bow (the front end) the movement was very noticeable and if you suffered from sea sickness it was a nightmare. I, thank God have very rarely been afflicted with it, but on the rare occasions that I have, I felt like I wanted to die. There's a pecking order on P&O ships among the entertainers and despite my excellent CV and TV track record, I couldn't get them to guarantee me an outside cabin. Some of the acts who in my opinion had nowhere near my standing in the business were given balcony cabins as part of their deal. I later learned that they had very highly placed managements to fight their corners while I had nobody as I booked direct.

We were on our way back south down the Italian coast of the Adriatic when an announcement from the captain over the ship's speaker system told us all that he was going to the aid of a sinking cargo vessel after having received an SOS. He kept us all informed that the ship would soon be within viewing distance off the starboard side. I can't believe how the Oriana stayed upright as every single passenger and a lot of the crew were all leaning over the ship's starboard rails for a sight of the stricken ship. He told us that there was a crew of nine aboard her, eight of whom had managed to get into a life raft but the ninth man was in the water and the Italian coastguard helicopter was searching for him. Soon the cargo ship could be seen, she was settling down by her stern and her bow was slowly rising from the surface. She'd been carrying a few thousand tons of timber in the form of long planks and it had moved suddenly causing an instability which the ship couldn't handle and she capsized. Apparently, (we learned all this later on) the crew had only about ninety seconds to abandon ship because as on all cargo vessels, the bridge and crew quarters are always situated at the stern end and that's how long it took the stern to disappear beneath the sea.

We saw the bright orange life raft bobbing around among the thousands of planks which littered the surface like giant matchsticks. One of our lifeboats was launched and she carefully edged her way through the mass of wooden boards, each of which could have pierced her fiberglass hull with ease. She took the eight survivors on board and as the last one left the raft, a huge cheer went up from the two thousand observers on board Oriana. She blew her huge siren which rattled the eardrums of anyone near the funnel and the rescued sailors were brought on board.

The captain then informed us that the coastguard had located the lost seaman and our rescue dinghy sped out in the direction of his position which was off the port side. It was amusing to see two thousand people scrambling for position on the opposite side of the ship so they could witness his liberation from a watery grave. He was brought aboard and taken straight to the medical centre as he was suffering from hypothermia. It was even more amusing to see them all rush back to the starboard side to see the final moments of the cargo ship as she slipped beneath the waves to join Davy Jones. I felt a tinge of sadness as I watched her sink, I know she was probably only an old scruffy rustbucket but she was a home to the men who'd sailed in her and now she was no more.

The remaining eight crew were fed and watered, given new clothes and toiletries and made a grand fuss of by everyone. They were Turks who spoke no English except "Thankyou". A collection was held and over four thousand pounds was raised for them by the generosity of the passengers and crew. I was actually on that night doing my show in the magnificent theatre and I obviously couldn't ignore the events of the day which were now the sole topic of conversation for everyone on board. My opening gag was "Do you think P&O will give those sailors a discount for joining half way through the cruise?"

One of our last ports of call before we sailed back home up

through the Bay of Biscay was Marseilles. I'd been dying to go there for many years as it was the world capital for the famous French dish, bouillabaisse. I'd only ever made it myself, admittedly from authentic French recipes and cook books, and the results had been very satisfactory. The secret of the authentic dish is the abundance of different fish around the Med which are available to use as ingredients for this expensive delicacy. I went ashore and made straight for the waterfront where all the open fish stalls sell their fresh catches of the day. I was amazed at all the many different varieties of fish and shellfish which were on sale. Many years later I was watching my favourite TV chef Rick Stein doing a programme from exactly the same spot on which I'd stood on that memorable day. I then went to the area where all the restaurants were situated and every single one had its own bouillabaisse advertised in varying price brackets according to which ingredients you chose to have in it. I saw one for about seventy quid which was full of crab, lobsters and scallops. I thought to myself "Fuck that for a game of soldiers, I'm not paying seventy quid for what is basically a bowl of fish soup". I finally chose a nice looking corner café right on the seafront whose bouillabaisses ranged from about fifteen to forty quid a portion. I was quite shocked at the exorbitant prices charged by these Froggy cafes but I was in Marseilles and I was adamant about having my dream dish in the place where it was conceived. I chose a mid range variety at about thirty quid plus a chilled bottle of chardonnay to wash it down. The waiter eventually brought a steaming tureen of this incomparable fish soup and placed it in the middle of the table. It had in it a lobster, some spider crab legs, langoustines and prawns plus an abundance of different white fish. It was floating in a delicious bouillon of aromatic flavours; I could taste fennel, thyme, oregano and a hint of Pernod. It was accompanied by a large plate of crusty French bread along with a rouille which is a fiery sort of dip made from mayonnaise, garlic and mashed red chillis. I'd died and gone to Heaven, I sat there for well over an hour slowly savouring this culinary orgasm until I was totally full. I'll never forget that wonderful meal and to this day the only thing wrong with it was that Donna wasn't there to share it with me.

On my way back to the P&O shuttle bus which ferries all the passengers back to the ship, I saw a very appealing looking fromagerie and seeing as I'm a sucker for any type of cheese, I wandered in. I was feeling like a world class gourmand after my exquisite lunch so I decided to buy some French camembert. I chose three different types which were all highly recommended by the fat little man who owned the shop. He had on a striped apron, a bow tie and a moustache exactly like Hercule Poirrots; I wished I'd had a camera so I could have shown him to you. I also chose a couple of bottles of Rose de Anjou to enjoy later that evening. He wrapped the three discs of cheese which were sealed in their little round wooden boxes and bid me Au revoir. I got back down to my gloomy E101 cabin and put my stash of cheese and wine in the fridge.

The next morning I awoke and as I made my way to the bathroom I could smell something really bad. I opened the bathroom door and it seemed to get worse, ships toilets are notorious for blockages and I called my cabin steward who was equally nauseated when he entered my cabin. The obliging little Indian chap said "Do not be worrying yourself Mr Bobby, I will be calling the plumber gentleman very smartish like when I am getting out of your cabin. He will be here like very quickly when I am telling him of your smelly bathroom so do not be worrying". His little head was nodding from side to side as he assured me of his undying efforts to rid me of my pongy cabin.

It was only about half an hour later when my lad reappeared with the plumber who in turn pulled a face when he entered the cabin. "See how quickly like I am bringing you the plumbing gentleman, he will be sorting you out in a couple of jiffys with no problems. You go enjoy good breakfast and all will be not smelly when you are coming back". Bless him; he was really working hard for his tip. When I got back the smell was just as bad and the cabin boy was waiting for me to say that there was no problem with my plumbing and there was no blockage. He said "I am putting in a chitty for chief engineer to be looking at your cabin when he is getting the time". Later that afternoon I settled down to watch a film on the crew channel and decided to have a glass of wine. I opened the fridge door and the smell was fucking staggering, it was the camembert not the toilet. The stuff we buy at home doesn't have the same pungency for some reason but this was the real McCoy. I went and cadged a roll of gaffer tape from the stage manager and put the cheese into two plastic bags which I then sealed completely with the tape. When I was satisfied that it was totally sealed I put it back in the fridge but the pong still lingered till the end of the cruise.

The camembert was delicious but it did the same thing to our kitchen as it had done to my cabin so Donna put it in the garage. Within a couple of days the garage stunk bloody awful so we decided the only thing to do was have a little cheese and wine party between ourselves and eat it all at once. I still adore camembert but I now have an airtight Tupperware box in which to keep it. The next time I saw the little cabin steward he said to me "It is being most strange and mysterious Mr Bobby, when you are leaving the cabin the bathroom was cured of the smell all by itself, most mysterious indeed". I suppose the poor little guy was suspecting that I had a severe case of BO and to be honest I wouldn't have blamed him. I didn't have the heart to tell him about the cheese after all the trouble he'd gone to.

Barracuda attack

Lost Luggage

In late March 2000 I received a call from an agent called Jonathan Blackburn. His father, Alan Blackburn was a well known booker of big stars and was based in Monte Carlo so I automatically surmised that his son was also a big hitter. It was a Wednesday morning and I was busy preparing a coq au vin for that night's dinner. Jonathan told me I'd been recommended to him by a chap at the Openwide agency for whom I'd done some Airtours cruises. He asked me if I was free to fly out to Papeete on Friday morning and join the Victoria on its world cruise. I asked him if he meant the P&O Victoria and he said it was, at which point I told him that I'd told David Llewellyn, their chief booker to fuck off three years previously. He said that it didn't matter as he'd left the company and a new man called Anthony Radford was now in charge. They had obviously been let down by someone at the last minute and were desperate for a suitable replacement. I told him my fee and he said he didn't think they'd go to it so I told him that's what I got last time I worked for them. He came back about ten minutes later and said the deal was done for me to fly out to Tahiti and sail up the Pacific, through the Panama Canal and disembark in Barbados twenty one days later. I then told him to check who the cruise director was because if it was the vitriolic shirtlifter Ross Howard who'd given me a bad report and got me fired from P&O, I wouldn't do it. He patiently rang P&O back and finally reassured me that it was a guy called Ian Fraser. I had thirty six hours to pack and prepare myself for this monster journey across the world to the South Pacific. My schedule was faxed up to me which was British Airways from Manchester to Amsterdam, then an Air France twelve hour flight direct to Los Angeles. I was to have an eight hour wait in LA then another eight hours on down to Tahiti.

You can well imagine how utterly knackered I was by the time I arrived in Tahiti, my legs were aching, my arse was numb and I was desperate for a shower. The queue for passport control seemed never ending as the 747 disgorged its sweaty passengers into the hot, cramped waiting area. As a matter of interest, standing immediately behind me in this slow moving snake of pungent people was the American actress Jeri Ryan who plays "Seven of Nine" in Star Trek Voyager. I was amazed how tiny she was but I didn't make any attempt at conversation as I didn't want to seem like a fawning fan. It took two hours for the dozy bastards at the passport booths to finally pass us through to the baggage area. The bags had been going round endlessly on the ancient old carousel so they'd obviously all been offloaded from the Jumbo. I looked for my large green case and my guitar case but couldn't see either. Gradually, the last few people collected their bags, the carousel was empty and it stopped going round. There were about thirty irate passengers including me who hadn't got their bags. We were told to wait in *another* queue so we could report our lost luggage to the man who was dealing with it. Miss Star Trek was one of them and she seemed to take it all rather calmly, unlike most of the other passengers. They were all Yanks and all very loud in their protestations to this poor man who was trying to take all their details. The two people in front of me were particularly obnoxious and their language was atrocious. This guy was merely trying to help them yet they seemed to be blaming him for their losses.

I finally sat down in his office and immediately reassured him that I wouldn't be raising my voice or blaming him for my lost bags. He was a smashing bloke who must have weighed over twenty stone but he wasn't fat, he was a typical Polynesian giant. He told me that my bags would definitely be on tomorrow's flight from LA but I explained that that would be no good as I would be on board a ship hundreds of miles away. He was very understanding and tapped away on his computer keyboard for what seemed ages. He then gave me a printed sheet and told me to give it to the port agent who was looking after the ship on behalf of P&O. The taxi driver who'd been sent to pick me up was miraculously still there when I came out of the terminal. He was sitting on a bench holding up a board with my name on it, I could have kissed him. I finally got to the ship about four hours later than I'd been expected and went to look for the CD Ian Fraser. He took me to his cabin and I told him of my predicament, no luggage, no anything, no clean clothes or underwear, not even a toothbrush. Now ship's shops are always closed when the vessel is in port because of customs laws but he rang the shop manager and told her to report to his cabin. When she arrived he told her to take me down to the shop and give me whatever I needed and put it on his account. I have never ever forgotten that great kindness which he showed to a complete stranger in his hour of desperate need. I was fixed up with a shirt, trousers underwear, shorts, T shirts and any toiletries that I needed. We had a few beers in his cabin and he told me I wouldn't be on for about four nights so I could get over the jet-lag. He became my best pal on the ships and I worked with him many times over the years. He was one of the wisest cruise directors on the fleet and definitely the best when it came to the welfare of his acts.

I'd heard nothing from the port agent and I went to bed that evening feeling so miserable and despondent. I couldn't sleep for worrying about my possessions and especially my beautiful Washburn country guitar which was irreplaceable. I awoke at about 3am thanks to the jetlag and I proceeded to make a list of all the things which were in my case and tried to work out their estimated worth. There were all my stage clothes and music plus my formal and informal clothes for evening wear, three pairs of shoes, camera, binoculars and all the incidental things which make up a travellers luggage. I walked around the promenade deck feeling very stressed out and watched the sunrise as we approached Bora Bora, the most expensive island on the planet. At 7am I went to the breakfast buffet just as it was opening and as I sat devouring some Barnsley muesli a man approached me and introduced himself as the port agent. He was a Frenchman with an accent just like Maurice Chevalier and he said that he had some good news and some bad news. The good news was that he'd traced my bag and it was being flown to Bora Bora that day and would be delivered to Victoria before she sailed at 6pm. The bad news was that they hadn't found my guitar yet but he was working on it and giving it first priority. I was over the moon in the knowledge that my bag was on its way so later on I had lunch and a bottle of Frascati to celebrate. I'd got a bottle of ready mixed port and brandy in my rucksack which was my hand luggage so I had a couple of nips in my cabin that afternoon. My bag arrived about 4-30pm and I was a very happy bunny to be able to unpack at last and square away my cabin. To top it all, the port agent said they'd found my guitar but it wouldn't turn up until Acapulco seven days later, at least I hadn't lost it.

I went down to dinner, the artistes had their own table on that particular ship so I chewed the fat with the other acts and had another bottle of wine. I have a very high tolerance for alcohol so I never get drunk but I have a strict rule about not drinking when I'm working. I wandered into the cocktail bar at about 8pm and the deputy cruise director came up looking very flustered. She said "Ian has been looking for you, the pianist that backs the two sopranos who are on at 8-30 has been taken ill and he wants to know if you can stand in tonight". I'd had a drink, I'd had no band call and I had nothing prepared so I said "Of course I can, but I'll need a bit longer than half an hour to get myself sorted, can I go on at 9pm?" After all he'd done for me; I wasn't going to see him in the shit so it was a pleasure to help him out.

The cabaret room on the Victoria was one of the best I've ever worked in, either on land or sea. I was called The International Lounge and it had a thrust stage so they were all around you, a comic's dream. They'd announced that the classical couple would not be appearing but there would be a cabaret at 9pm. This caused a few of the punters to drift off so I went on to a room about two thirds full. I ripped 'em apart, from the opening gag they were with me, the compere had told them that I'd agreed to stand in at a few minutes notice and I'd had no rehearsal. They genuinely thought that I was adlibbing the whole way through and they loved it. What they didn't know was that *any* decent comic could get up at a minutes notice and ramble for an hour without any problem whatsoever. I tore the bollocks off 'em and Ian was absolutely over the moon. By the time I came to do my second show I'd got my guitar back so I could do my full act and I went even better than the first show to a packed house. The word had gone round the ship and they closed the room fifteen minutes before I was due on. When I went on, I shouted to the folk who were trying to listen to me outside to come in and sit down on the edge of the stage so I ended up with about another thirty or so posh people sitting round the stage like kids in school assembly. It was one of the best nights I've ever had on a ship and Ian sent a glowing report back to head office, before I'd finished the cruise they'd put five more jobs in the book.

When I got my guitar back in Acapulco, the case was damaged, it was a specially made Hiscox flight case, you can drive a lorry over it and the guitar inside will still be unharmed. It looked as if someone had been hitting it with a hammer as there were actual holes in the plastic casing. The guitar was seemingly undamaged but ever since that time I've had problems keeping it in tune for more than a couple of performances. I vowed never to put a guitar in an aircraft hold again.

Airport Security

The worldwide clampdown on airport security after the New York twin towers disaster drastically affected my journeys to and from cruise ships. It's easily understandable and equally acceptable as to why these strict measures are applied before you're allowed to board a plane. The problem is that when you fly as much as I have to do, it becomes a right royal pain in the arse. The American airports are by far the worst when it come to either arriving or leaving and I've had some awful experiences with their rude and pedantic immigration staff. As a man who works on ships and is not classed as a passenger, I have to have in my passport what's known as an American C1D visa. All crew members have to have one and for some unknown reason, as soon as an American passport official spots it, they hoist you off for an in depth interrogation which usually delays you by at least an hour.

I remember once arriving at Miami airport which incidentally is the worst and strictest airport in the USA, if not the world. Three jumbo jets had arrived within ten minutes of each other and there were over a thousand sweaty people queueing to go through passport control. It took me just over three hours to reach the passport booth and as soon as he saw the C1D visa he told me to go and wait in another queue with all the other ships crew. I knew from experience not to question him as they are like robots with their rules and if you start getting awkward they'll haul you off to a bare holding room for an hour or two for no other reason than that they are a bunch of utter wankers. No matter how pleasant you try to be with them, they never ever smile or ever try to reciprocate your amiable manner. They must have to take an intelligence test before they're employed and if they are found to have the IQ anywhere near that of the average Weetabix, they get the job. It took me another ninety minutes to get out into the baggage hall where my bag had been taken off the carousel and put in a corner for safe keeping. The P&O pick-up taxi was long gone and I had to pay for a cab from the airport to the docks.

When I started to play Shadows instrumentals on my shows I naturally took on board my beautiful Fender Stratocaster, identical to the one Hank Marvin plays. It's my pride and joy and after the Acapulco episode I've always carried it on as hand luggage which has caused me more than enough trouble. I've sometimes had to beg and cajole a jobsworth check-in man to let me take it on to the aircraft along with my small hand bag, their swan song is "You're only allowed one piece of hand luggage". I remember one occasion when I was boarding a BA 747 back to Heathrow from San Francisco. I'd gone through two stringent security checks where they searched me, my bag and my guitar case. When we arrived into the actual departure gate where you walk down the tunnel to board the aircraft, there was a third security check with about one in four passengers being stopped by these two very fat uniformed security geezers. There were two tressle tables onto which the unlucky chosen passengers had to empty their bags for a third time of asking. By now I was getting very ratty and I just knew I'd be stopped, I was right. The guy who I copped for was a very fat Hispanic type of bloke with a huge gut around which was strapped his gun and his beat-the-fuck-out-of-you-stick. He roughly searched my small rucksack then he pointed to my guitar case which was by now on the table and said "What's in there?" I thought to myself "What a fuckin' moron". It's a guitar case; it's *shaped* like a guitar, its bleedin' obvious to anyone with a glimmer of intelligence that it contains a guitar. I felt like saying "I've got a fuckin' hippopotamus in there with a herd of wildebeest you fuckin' intellectual dwarf". I chose the wiser option and just quietly said "A guitar". He then said in a very curt and abrupt manner "Open the case". By now I was getting ready to blow, he was a rude obnoxious and impolite arsehole and I'd had enough. I said "I'm very sorry but I can't open the case".

He glared at me and repeated "Open the case".

"I'm very sorry but I can't open the case until you say the magic word".

He now looked at me in a totally perplexed manner as if I'd just arrived from another planet.

"I told you to open the case".

"Yes and I'm telling you that I can't open it until you say the magic word which is PLEASE. Have you not got any manners?"

He hesitated for a moment then said "Open the case,......please". I could see that he was fuming inside at being chastised by me but I then defused the moment by saying "Thankyou", and opening the case. It contained my shiny red Stratocaster and the shoulder strap plus two spare sets of strings and the tremolo arm. As you probably know, the tremolo arm is the metal arm which screws into the bridge of the instrument and when you pull or push it, it makes that sweeping wah-wah effect so common with Shadows music. It's about six inches long with a right angle bend at one end. He picked it up and examined it then said to me "You can't take this on board the aircraft". I was flabberghasted, I asked him why and he said it could be used as a weapon. I said "Don't be ridiculous, it's a part of the guitar and I can't play without it". He was really enjoying the moment and no matter what I said to try and convince him that it was a harmless guitar component he insisted that I couldn't take it onto the aircraft. I went ballistic and told him that if the tremolo arm can't go on the aircraft then neither could I. I said "Get my bags off the plane, I'm not flying". Now the plane was due to leave in fifteen minutes time and the delay involved in searching a packed 747 hold for my suitcase would have taken a good two hours. By now the fat bastard's supervisor, who was sitting in the corner of the departure gate, had noticed the commotion and came over to see what was amiss. I swear to God she was a good twenty stone and about five foot two in height. She was as wide as she was tall, another Hispanic and uglier than the bloke who was hassling me. She came up and said "What's the problem here?" She had a deep rasping voice like Jimmy Durante's and looked like she'd just stepped out of an American comedy film. I mustered every ounce of dignity I could, smiled at her, held up the tremolo arm and said in my best Oxford accent, "Madam, forgive me, but your minion here is attempting to forbid me from taking this implement onto the aircraft, it's an essential part of my instrument and if you don't object, I will demonstrate what it's function is." I quickly screwed the trem into its socket and played a chord for her at the same time, jiggling the arm to get the desired effect. She looked at the other fat bastard in a contemptuous manner as if to say "You useless cunt" and then said to me, "That'll be OK sir, sorry to have troubled you". I closed the case and gave the security bloke a scathing, scornful look before triumphantly striding down the tunnel onto the Jumbo.

Stormy Seas

Many people who are contemplating going on their first cruise are usually a little irked at the thought of raging seas and acute sea sickness. They are sometimes comforted by well meaning but ignorant people who tell them that the ships are so big that you can't feel any movement at all. This is a load of bollocks because a hundred thousand ton vessel is just as susceptible to the sea's moods as a little fishing coble out of Bridlington. If there's a twenty foot swell, which means that the top layer of the ocean is rising and falling by twenty feet, then whatever is floating on the surface will rise and fall with it. The two movements which affect a moving ship are pitching and rolling. Pitching is going up and down, and rolling is going from side to side. Sometimes the ship pitches *and* rolls at the same time which is hell for anyone who suffers from "mal-de-mer" as it's like a corkscrew motion. I'm very lucky as I don't suffer from it yet if I go on a bus or coach I go green after ten minutes.

You can hit a storm any where in the world in any sea but some places are more likely to be rougher than others. The Bay of Biscay can be a right bastard but I've crossed it probably over a hundred times and it's nearly always been kind to me. Having said that, I've seen first time cruisers puking all over the ship at the slightest movement and you've got to feel sorry for them. It's the worst feeling in the world as I described in an earlier chapter when I was sick on a hovercraft.

Probably the worst storm I ever experienced was on the Canberra as we were sailing up the Med towards Barcelona. It's a notorious stretch of sea which can be unusually rough for the normally calm Mediterranean. Apparently, it's got something to do with the currents and the contours of the sea floor in that area. The captain warned the passengers of the approaching storm and closed the promenade deck which is open to the elements. I was on with a great mate of mine, a Welsh singer called Leo Andrew. He's as camp as a box of frogs and he's wonderful company as most gay men are. The CD was a guy called Phil Raymond who's nickname was

On The Black Prince

'Just like that' in Casablanca

"Voodoo Vera". He was another gay guy but it was rumoured that he dabbled in the black arts, hence his nomme de guerre. I never liked cruising with him as he'd work you to death on a voyage. I once did a three week crossover to the Caribbean and back and he made me do six spots. I was really scratting around for gags by the final show. He'd also go on and do twenty minutes patter before he introduced a comic which was bang out of order.

On the night of the storm, poor old Leo was scheduled to do a spot of Ivor Novello songs in the Meridian lounge for the dead people. I kid you not, the Canberra was being tossed around like a cork in a maelstrom and walking upright was becoming increasingly difficult. I got a call in my cabin from a very irate Leo who said in his lovely Welsh valley's accent, "Knutty, you'll never guess what that cows done, she's making me go on tonight, I'll have nobody in and I'll die on my fekkin' arse. The ship's like a fekkin' roller coaster, there'll be nobody coming out to play tonight I can tell you". To top it all, the keyboard player from the orchestra had been stricken with sea sickness and they'd told the Australian cocktail bar pianist to back him. Now she'd been on the Canberra since the year dot, she was a tall, scrawny hard drinking chain smoking woman with an irascible nature and took no shit from anybody. She had a really broad Aussie accent and sounded just like Crocodile Dundee. She was an excellent pianist though, so Leo had no worries in that direction but the problem was that the grand piano wasn't tied down to the floor.

I reassured Leo that it'd be a laugh and I'd be there to support him. We met at the Meridian bar and had a snifter then along came the Aussie lady whose name was Diane Jarrett. She ordered her usual poison then said "How the fackin' hell does he expect us to fackin' play in a fackin' storm with no fackin' audience to fackin' play to?" There were about ten old codgers in the room who'd braved it down to the lounge for their dose of Ivor Novello. Not long before Leo's introduction, the ship rolled violently and about six or seven bottles of booze smashed onto the bar floor along with quite a few glasses. Voodoo Vera didn't even have the decency to come down and put

Leo on, he sent one of the entertainments team to do it. Old Leo went on like the trooper he was to no applause from the indifferent and apathetic bunch of wrinklies in their armchairs. The storm was getting worse as more glasses hit the deck behind the bar. Halfway through Leo's third song the ship pitched forward into a deep trough and the grand piano went with it. It was one of the funniest things I'd ever seen and the look on the face of the pianist was priceless as the Bechstein glided away from her leaving her alone on her piano stool with her fingers tinkling away at thin air. The two Indian stage lads tried to reach the piano in time to stop it from colliding with a beautiful gilded sort of sideboard but to no avail. Whack!!! It came to a halt as it hit the antique dresser with half the audience none the wiser as they were asleep. Leo was nearly in tears, the Aussie pianist was storming up to the bar cursing loudly, I was in absolute hysterics and had to sit down in an armchair to compose myself. The most famous showbiz phrase about the show *must* go on went tits up that night, the show *didn't* go on so Leo and I went and got pissed in the Pig and Whistle.

The other memorable storm which I can recall happened in the year 2000 as I was crossing back from New York to Southampton on Oriana. The cruise director was my old mate Ian Fraser and the captain was in my opinion the best on the fleet, a taciturn Sheffielder called Richard Fennelow, who like me, was a staunch Sheffield United supporter. Unlike the other loquacious P&O captains who loved to be on the intercom reporting information from the bridge, Richard was a shy man who was uneasy at being on the microphone. His voice sounded uncannily like Max Wall's and I used to get a huge laugh in the theatre when I did my impression of him doing an announcement. He only ever came onto the intercom if it was an important matter.

We were about half way home and the third day was foul weather with high winds which rocked the ship. Even though she's a big old girl of 70,000 tons she was rolling like a duck in a bathtub. I've always found rough seas to be very exciting and I was out on the prom deck watching her plough her way through the oncoming waves which were smashing against her prow with tremendous force. I was surprised that Captain Fennelow hadn't closed the decks but he must have thought it unnecessary. A little later he announced that we'd received an SOS from a yacht in trouble south of our plotted course and we were changing course to go to her assistance. He'd been sailing *into* the storm which is what any mariner will do to maintain stability. It's better to have the waves crashing against your bows than your sides for obvious reasons. Now that we were heading in a southerly direction the wind and waves were battering our port side causing her to list to starboard and every one was walking with a similar list. As I was looking out over the ship's rail into the mist I could have sworn that I saw a thick cloud approaching the ship but as it got closer I was horrified to realise that it was a wall of water much higher than me and I was seven decks up. I ran for one of the doors which led back indoors and just made it as it struck Oriana. The Poseidon Adventure was flashing through my mind as this massive shockwave shuddered through the ship but she took it like a good'un. It reminded me of the Mayor of Hiroshima's famous last words, "What the fuck was that?"

The wave was over seventy feet high and its force took it right over the top of the ship. The sundeck, or deck 13 is well over a hundred feet above the waterline and its got cricket and golf nets, deck chairs and games equipment, none of it survived. The lot was washed overboard into the Atlantic. The ship sustained damage with five cabin windows on deck five being smashed, injuring a junior officer and one poor old lady who was nearly sucked back out into the sea by the swirl of the water in her cabin. I went straight up to my cabin high up on deck eleven and found my life jacket. As I arrived there the Captain announced that we'd received minor damage and to avoid taking on water through the broken windows he was changing course very quickly which would cause the ship to list but that it was a perfectly safe manouevre. He then instructed everyone on board to sit on the floor, or the bed if they were in their cabin. You can imagine that if a Captain is going to change direction

My pal Ian Fraser, Cruise Director

Winner of the 'Sleeping with your mouth open' competition

299

in a ship as big as Oriana, he does it in a grand arc over a distance of a mile or so which causes absolutely no listing of the vessel. If, however, he yanks the wheel over hard to port the ship heels over drastically owing to her sheer height and weight. As he undertook the manouevre, I looked out of my cabin window and she'd gone over that far that all I could see was the sea, no sky, just sea. The ship righted herself but she didn't just come back perpendicular and stay there, she then heeled over in the opposite direction so now all I could see was the sky. I was thinking "Come back working men's clubs, all is forgiven". The story of the freak wave had hit all the national daily papers and the Oriana enjoyed her five minutes of fame. We limped home a day late into Southampton with a hoard of reporters waiting on shore to snaffle a story from anyone willing to talk to them. We'd all been warned that any ships company talking to them would be dismissed.

I was just thinking how lucky we were to have been in the capable hands of a highly experienced seaman like Captain Fennelow who calmly and professionally overcame the danger with ease. The sea never fails to make me feel small, human and vulnerable, it can be warm, tranquil and welcoming but when it's got a paddy on, it has no equal for ferocity.

I Have A Stroke

What I'm about to describe happened in late March 2002 but I think the build up to it started quite a time before. 2001 had not been my best year and yet as usual the bills keep rolling in and my overdraft was slowly creeping upwards. I hadn't suddenly stopped being funny and become a crap comic, the whole business was suffering and every one of my comic pals were all saying how bad business was. The work just wasn't there and I was beginning to feel stressed out at the constant battle to keep my income greater than my outgoings. I had all the normal bills which we incur for our everyday living expenses plus a pretty hefty mortgage on the Deepcar property. When I look back, it wasn't hefty at all compared to what most people are paying these days, but it still had to be paid every month. I was now pretty well doing all my work on cruise ships and I was living out of a suitcase. My life totally revolved around taxis, planes and ships. My home life was a constant cycle of packing, unpacking, washing clothes and repacking for the next trip. I was missing Donna more and more with every cruise that I took but the alternative was having no work and no income. I was working on land once in a blue moon but the fees people were offering were an insult, less than I was getting twenty five years ago.

My casting agent Tim had fallen out with me because he said I was never available for castings as I was always abroad. The funny thing about that was that if I had a few weeks off, thus making myself available, the castings didn't come anyway so it was a catch 22 situation. I was becoming very unhappy at my general circumstances and started drinking more wine than was good for me. I really don't know whether the scenario which I've just described had anything to do with my having a stroke but I have come to realise that stress is as real as a broken leg and I was having more than my share of it.

I was on board P&O's Victoria with a lovely lady cruise director called Christine Noble. She was a New Zealander who'd been with the firm for years. The cruise was a ten day jaunt round the Canary Islands and we'd just tied on alongside the dock in Tenerife at about 7am. No matter where I am in the world, I ring Donna at least twice a day, she fills me in on what's happening at home and it's just good to be able to talk to her. On the morning in question I awoke feeling rather strange. The only word I can use is the word "strange" as it fits perfectly how I felt. The cabin seemed to be going round as if I was drunk and my head was slightly swimming. It was a very odd feeling which I'd never experienced before. I'd not had a lot to drink the previous night so it couldn't have been a hangover, I didn't feel sick nor did I have a headache. I let it go and thought I'd ring Donna for a chat. I'd recently acquired a new mobile phone with a speed dial so all I had to do was press 2 and the green button and I was through. I switched it on then after a few seconds it requested me to enter my pin number. *I couldn't remember it*; I tried and tried yet I could not for the life of me remember it. I've changed it now but my pin at that time was 2512, which is Christmas day, an easy number to remember. In my confusion, I still remembered that my pin was Christmas day, but I couldn't remember the date on which it fell. I sat on the bed and concentrated intensely until the date came into my head and I punched it into the keypad. I somehow knew that the speed dial was 2 plus green so I tapped that in and in a couple of seconds I was through to Donna. She picked up the phone and I tried to speak to her, nothing but gibberish came out. I could not say the name "Donna", all I could manage was a garbled "Do- - -h". After a couple of attempts to say her name she was saying "Bobby, are you alright, what's wrong?" I immediately realised that something was seriously wrong so I rang off. I didn't want her listening to me trying in vain to say her name like a gibbering imbecile. I sat there in my cabin wondering "What the fuck is wrong with me?" At the back of my mind I suspected a stroke but there was no numbness of a left or right side, my face wasn't contorted or drooping. My ability to reason and think wasn't impaired but still I couldn't speak a coherent word.

I sat worrying for an hour and a half then at just before 9am I went to the medical centre just as it was opening for crew visitors. When the nurse came and asked for my details I mumbled that I couldn't speak and managed to communicate to her that I thought I was having a stroke. She fetched the doctor, an overweight young female who had been overdosing on ugly pills. On finally understanding what I was on about and hearing my self diagnosis she said in a very pompous manner, "Of course you haven't had a stroke, you're just overtired, you need some rest". I hadn't got the vocal ability to argue that I'd just had a good nine hours kip and that I wasn't the slightest bit tired. She prescribed me some seasickness tablets which also make you sleep and sent me away.

I took the tablets and sure enough, I slept for about four hours and woke up feeling no better and no different to what I had felt earlier on that morning. I rang Christine and I still could hardly get a word out although I was slightly more coherent than I had been earlier on. She could tell something was very wrong and came straight down to my cabin with the stage manager, Irish Dave. I was supposed to be on stage doing my first show that night but it was obvious that I was in no fit state to appear before an audience. As the day wore on my speech improved very slowly and when I could string a sentence together I rang Donna. She had been out of her mind with worry and I reassured her that I was physically OK but I'd had this speech glitch which was improving by the hour.

The next morning came and I was back to normal, well, I say "Back to normal", I could speak perfectly well but I still had a strange sort of feeling which as much as I try, I cannot describe for the life of me. Donna had contacted our doctor Jacob, who had immediately sussed what had happened to me and had made the necessary arrangements for me to see the stroke councillor at the Sheffield Hallamshire hospital. I'd had a T.I.A, better known as a transient ischaemic attack, or mini-stroke. Two nights later I went on in the cabaret lounge and tore the bollocks off 'em as though nothing had happened. I have always been eternally grateful to Christine Noble for her kindness and understanding in allowing me time to rest after my attack. As for the doctor's diagnosis of my potentially life threatening situation, the incompetent cow is probably still plying her trade on the oceans of the world and dishing out seasickness pills for heart attacks, constipation and piles whilst charging a hundred quid a throw for her expert and useless diagnosis of an ailment.

When I got home on the Monday lunchtime I was booked into the hospital first thing Tuesday morning. They gave me a full five thousand mile service plus this geezer had me on a bed with all this blue jelly on my neck. He ran this metal gadget over my neck for about twenty minutes while he dictated all this medical jargon non stop into this tape recorder. Later that day when I'd finally finished and the test results were made known, I had to visit the stroke councillor. She was a very pleasant lady who told me in detail what had happened to me on the ship. The test results showed that I'd had slight furring of my left carotid artery and a tiny piece of debris (a tiny clot of blood) had broken free and floated up into my brain and had got stuck in my thinking department. This is why I couldn't speak properly and my gradual return to normality was due to the fact that the clot had flushed its way through my brain and dissipated into my system. She also told me that because I'd been taking small doses of aspirin every day for many years, it had saved me from having a major stroke. I'd revealed this to the first doctor who, during the questionnaire, asked me what medication, if any, I was on. I'd been taking 75mg of aspirin for 25 years as I'd read in one of my weight training manuals that it was good to have slightly thinner blood. The one thing which upset me about our discussion was that she told me I couldn't train with weights any more. The strain of heavy weights would be too much for my vascular system to take so I had to reluctantly pack it in. Not being able to go in the gym any more gradually made me lethargic and lazy and I started putting weight on. I now try and console myself with the fact that fat comics are a lot funnier than thin ones.

The day after the hospital visit I went up to our caravan at Whitby for a rest and a total chill out. It was our little Shangri-La and Donna and I have had some wonderfully relaxing times in that delightful paradise that is Whitby. It was Donna's idea that I go so I packed the MGB with culinary goodies and a dozen bottles of Mateus Rose and set off. When I got to Pickering I noticed the fuel gauge was a bit low so I thought I'd stop and fill up before I got to my destination. The petrol stations in Whitby are all run by the descendants of Dick Turpin, the robbing bastards charge up to ten pence a litre more than anybody else. I filled up my beloved classic car and went to pay the man. He said "You don't see many diesel MGBs do you?" I said "It's not a diesel".

He replied "Well you've just filled it up with diesel".

I thought "YOU FUCKIN' TWAT, YOU STUPID FUCKIN' TWAT".

Luckily for me, it wasn't just a petrol station, it was a garage as well so I pushed the 'B over his pit and we proceeded to drain off a full tank of diesel into a scrap oil drum. When the tank was empty I put the seal back in and pushed the car back onto the forecourt for a proper fill of unleaded. It was the dearest bleedin' tankfull of petrol I'd ever bought and I began to wonder if my silly mistake had anything to do with my little stroke.

As a precautionary measure, the hospital prescribed me pills for my cholesterol and some more for my blood pressure. I've been taking them ever since and although I'm a big fat bastard, apart from a few old man's aches and pains, I've been right as rain ever since. Whenever I start feeling a bit low or depressed I console myself with the fact that I was once the fastest and most victorious little sperm out of millions.

What's Round The Corner?

After my T.I.A, Doctor Jacob told me I'd got to slow down and not work so hard. That's all well and good but in my game if you slow down you don't earn as much so you have to cut your cloth accordingly. After a long and heart searching discussion with Donna, we decided to put the house up for sale and downsize so I could pay off all the incidental debts and also the mortgage. It was a decision we both hated because we absolutely loved the place. We'd got it exactly how we wanted it and the space we had for our everyday living was enormous. I had my office and a music room downstairs with all my guitars on the wall. Donna had her own dressing room and en suite off our main bedroom. I was beautifully decorated in a way so that all the colours co-ordinated with the furniture and fittings. Alas, my health had to come first but it was a decision which really upset us both and on the day that we drove down our road to find that the estate agent had been and put up the "For Sale" sign in our garden, we were near to tears. Our two best friends Mick and Pat Ward suggested that we sell as quickly as possible and then move in with them till we found a suitable home.

We sold it in three days, put all our possessions into storage and moved in with them for two months. They've got a beautiful big house in Wharncliffe Side near Sheffield and there was an empty granny flat downstairs which we moved into. Pat was an optician and Mick was a paramedic in the ambulance service. We looked at all sorts of houses but nothing seemed to turn us on until one day I got a call from Mick who said he'd seen a bungalow for sale in Elsecar, a village on the coast of Barnsley. I made an appointment to view it and found it was owned by a little old lady of 82 years who'd recently lost her husband. It was on the periphery of a very rough estate and I was a little reluctant as I drove up to it. The old ladies daughter was there to show me round and I could immediately see great potential in the place. The décor was bleedin' awful; it was decorated in "Early Pensioner" with woodchip wallpaper and a vomit green bathroom suite. It had three bedrooms and a detached garage which had an L shaped extension with a full size carpenter's bench in there which she said she was leaving behind. It had gardens back and front and a drive long enough to accommodate six cars. I realised that it would only take a few thousand quid to turn the place into a beautiful home. I'd made a lot of tax free profit on the house which enabled us to pay off the mortgage, buy the bungalow for cash and still have more than enough left over for the renovations.

Donna also saw the potential in the place and we got cracking ripping out all the kitchen and bathroom furniture plus new doors and windows. It's so easy to do with an empty house as you're not trying to work around fixtures and fittings. The wood chip wallpaper was a right bastard to get off but I finally managed it with the aid of an industrial steam stripper. The last things to go in after it had been decorated were the carpets and we were ready for moving in.

All the time we'd been living at Mick and Pats house, Donna had been bonding with one of their two dogs, he was a seven year old black and white border collie named Dylan. He absolutely adored Donna and would whimper outside our bedroom until we let him in; he wouldn't leave her side and followed her everywhere. He's the cleverest dog I've ever known and immediately obeys every command he's given. About three days after we moved into the bungalow, I had to fly off and join a cruise ship for a three week stint. Donna was worried about being on her own in a new district, especially with all the rag, tags and bobtails that lived on the nearby Welland estate. There are some really nice folk on Welland but there's also a minority who are the scum of the Earth, they live totally off the state handouts in their filthy houses and have never done an honest days work in their lives. It was Pats suggestion for Donna to take Dylan for the duration of my cruise so he could act as a guard dog. He would protect her and give her confidence in the knowledge that nobody would come near the place while he was there. Within a week of being together they had become inseparable and Pat could see that he would pine for Donna if he had to go back home so she said we could have him if it was OK by me. Donna had remembered what I'd said when Ben died in 1999, I swore we'd never have another dog and have to endure the pain of losing him.

When Donna told me during one of our ship to shore phone calls what Pat had said, I couldn't refuse her as I knew how much she loved the dog. He's fifteen years old now and still like a bloody puppy, he never stops pestering us to throw him a soft toy which he catches in his mouth and drops straight at our feet to be thrown again. We love him like the child we never had yet I know we'll have to go through the agony of losing him one of these days.

It Doesn't Get Any Easier

As I said, nobody knows what's round the corner, for the past few years I've muddled along and survived like most pro comics of my age group. We're a bit anachronistic and we sometimes find difficulty in adapting to the modern times in which we live.

In March 2009 I did the fifth leg of the Arcadia world cruise for P&O. They'd already had six comics on before me and a lot of what I do had been done already. The audience was at that stage of a world cruise where they'd seen and done it all and the entertainers were no longer a major attraction. I went on for my first show and really struggled for laughs and my second show about five nights later died on its arse. It's like I said before, if you die on a ship, you're having breakfast with the bastards the next morning and you can actually *hear* the acid comments flying round in stage whispers just loud enough for you to hear them. I got a bad report and you can imagine what the more vindictive passengers were putting on their comment forms. I'd worked for the company for thirteen years and 99% of my cruises had been received with rapturous applause and in a lot of cases, standing ovations. The phone stopped ringing and eventually I contacted Anthony Radford, their head of entertainment who was the overseer of everything that constituted stage shows on the fleet. He had always been straight as a die with me and he said that owing to the bad report he was reluctantly "resting" me for a further twelve months.

I had no work in the book for 2009, absolutely zilch, I was in front at the bank but that would soon change after a few months of earning fuck all. Thank God Donna was working, it was a bit of a cushion, but it wouldn't solve my immediate problems. I had no alternative but to put my beloved MGB roadster up for sale. I took it back to Adrian at the Spinning Wheel garage where I'd bought it nine years before. It was in immaculate pristine condition and he sold it for 13,000 pounds and took a grand for his commission. I now had 12,000 quid to bolster my current account but my heart was broken at having to lose my pride and joy.

A good mate of mine called Steve Walls who I'd met on the ships told me to contact a firm called TED UK, he said they booked all the Thompson holiday hotels. I googled them and I was delighted to discover that their managing director was none other than my dear old pal Nigel Hudston. I rang him and told him the truth that I'd been shit upon by P&O and I had no work in my book whatsoever. I'd never done the Thompson "Fly Backs" as they were called so I'd not known that Nigel's company booked them. He was an absolute diamond, he told me that if I'd have rang him a month before, he could have filled my book, but whatever was left I could have. He was as good as his word and within 24 hours, his chief booker Steve rang me and put in a couple of gigs in Madeira at a gorgeous four star hotel in their "Thompson Gold" range. The Gold hotels are all adults only and are chiefly patronized by the over fifties who want luxury, peace and quiet, and no noisy little bastards running round causing mayhem and pissing in the pool. I was the first act that had ever gone to work for them in this newly acquired hotel so a lot was riding on my success. I did two shows and absolutely paralysed them, I got two standing ovations and my future success with TED UK was assured. Anytime they had a cancellation, they put me in and during 2009 I did quite a few of their gigs in Cyprus, Rhodes and the Costa del Sol. The wonderful thing about these gigs from my point of view is that I'm only away for five days maximum so I've got the weekend free to spend with Donna.

I know that 2010 will be a whole lot better once the fly backs start in May, they go right through until November so I'll be able to keep my head above water.

For the whole of my professional career, which has now spanned forty eight years, I've been like Wilkins Micawber, waiting for something to turn up, and you know what, it always has. I've never been rich, but I've lived comfortably and always paid my way. Now that I'm in the twilight of my years I look back on what a rich and exciting life I've had, even though I've had both joy and sadness in equal measures. I've visited seventy one different countries and sailed every ocean of the world. I've made some wonderful friends whose company I cherish on the rare occasions that I see them. I've met six different members of the Royal Family, the First Sea Lord, Admirals, Generals, miners, furnacemen, bus drivers and bingo callers and got on with them all.

The 20th of January 2011 will be my twenty fifth wedding anniversary, so the gypsy fortune teller's prophesy was true, Donna changed my life completely in so many different ways. She's the light of my life and spending my remaining years walking by her side is all I could possibly wish for. I'm a wiser man thanks to her and I've finally realised that "love" is what's left over when being "in love" has burned away.

I love her so very much

It's Goodnight From Me......

That's all folks as they say in the cartoons. I never thought there was *one* book in me, let alone two. It's been a wonderful journey for me to delve into my memory banks once again and record it for what hopefully will be your enjoyment. I want to sincerely thank all you people out there who bought my first book, especially the ones amongst you who took the time to put me a review on the Amazon customer's internet sight. I was proud and humbled by your kind comments. I know this book is different in a lot of ways to the first one. Book one saw me evolving into what I more or less was at the start of book two.

As we grow older we see a lot more sadness in our lives and seem to go to a lot more funerals, hence the subtitle of this book, Comedy and Tragedy. Still, even counting for some of its sadder sections, I hope I've managed to keep you entertained as much as I did the first time.

A thousand thanks my old Darlings, and may you all live long enough to see the end of the DFS sale.

God bless you all,

Knutty.

More Knutty Recipies

The recipes which I stuck into the back of book one proved to be extremely popular and I've had some lovely feedback from my readers. One chap stopped me in Asda last year and said the recipes were the best bit of the book, the cheeky twat. Here are a few more for you to try, follow them to the letter the first time you cook them, then if you fancy changing or adding something, be my guest. You'll note I still work in pounds and ounces so if you're a metric person, you'll have to convert accordingly.

THAI RED CHICKEN CURRY

INGREDIENTS:

Four chicken breast fillets cut into strips about the size of your little finger.
A bunch of spring onions finely chopped, green bits as well.
A good cup full of cashew nuts
2 tbs Thai red curry paste.
2 tbs golden caster sugar {or whatever sugar you have}
Half a cup of Thai fish sauce.
Half a pint of tinned coconut milk.
A few drops of liquid orange food colouring. Don't use the powdered stuff from the Chinese supermarket; it's full of dangerous E numbers.
2 tbs groundnut oil.
Sharwoods Chinese medium noodles

Heat the oil in a wok until it smokes then add the chicken. Stir fry until it starts to colour then add the spring onions. Cook until the onions give off their aroma then add the fish sauce, colouring and sugar. Continue cooking for another two or three mins then add the coconut milk. Simmer for about 10 mins then add the cashews and let them warm through for about a couple of mins then serve with the noodles.

It's quick, delicious and highly fattening but Hey! Life's for living so enjoy it.

KING PRAWN THERMIDOR

I cooked both this and the above recipe on my cookery show on Central TV and I was delighted at the way the crew descended on them like ravenous gannets at the end of the show.

I buy my king prawns at the Chinese supermarket; they are frozen headless fresh water prawns and are very reasonably priced at about eight quid for a kilo. Thaw them thoroughly and take out the black line which runs down the back of the prawn.

INGREDIENTS:

1 kilo frozen king prawns
2oz butter
2 tbs finely chopped shallot
1 tbs chopped parsley
2 tsps chopped fresh tarragon
1 medium size glass white wine
Half a pint of béchamel sauce, {see below}
3 tbs Parmesan cheese
1 tsp mustard powder, 1 level tsp salt and 1 tsp paprika

BECHAMEL SAUCE

Half pint full cream milk
1 shallot, sliced
Half a carrot coarsely chopped.
Half stick of celery coarsely chopped
A bay leaf and six peppercorns
1oz butter and 1oz flour
Salt and pepper.

Put the milk vegetables, bay leaf and peppercorns in a saucepan and bring slowly to the boil. Remove from the heat, cover and leave to infuse for about 30 mins. Strain the liquid and use this with the butter and flour to make a roux sauce. Do this by melting the butter then gradually adding the flour until you have a golden paste, then slowly add the milk stirring constantly to get rid of any lumps.

THERMIDOR:

Melt 1oz butter in a large frying pan then add the shallot, parsley and tarragon. After a few mins add the wine and simmer for five mins. Add the prawns and cook until they start to turn pink. Add the béchamel sauce and simmer until reduced to a creamy consistency. Next, add the parmesan, salt, mustard and paprika.
I serve this with extra creamy mashed potatoes that have lots of milk and butter in them. If you want it to be really special you can put the mashed potatoes in a large gratin dish, make a hole in the middle into which you pour the thermidor mixture, sprinkle it all with more Parmesan and stick it under the hot grill for about five or six mins until the cheese starts to brown.
This is another of my calorie free dishes, it tastes delicious and Donna and I have it every Christmas Eve for a special supper treat.

MY SECRET BOLOGNESE SAUCE

This is Donna's all time favourite dish which I *have* to cook for her at least twice a month. She reckons my Bolognese sauce is the best she's ever tasted and I must admit myself that it's pretty orgasmic. You can always use what's left of it the next day for assembling a very tasty Lasagne Verdi. I always make a huge amount of this so the ingredient amounts are quite large. I have the biggest size Le Creuset cooking pot which I've had for over twenty years and it's ideal to cook a great dollop of Bolognese.

INGREDIENTS:

3 lbs of lean steak mince
3 large Spanish onions halved and finely sliced

8 fat garlic cloves finely chopped
Half a cup of extra virgin olive oil
2 large carrots coarsely chopped
3 sticks of celery
Half a pound of smoked streaky bacon, diced. Or better still a six inch length of Polish Vieska smoked sausage skinned and diced. Morrison's deli counter sells it
3 tins of chopped tomatoes
1 whole tube of tomato puree
1 large bottle of Dolmio Bolognese sauce
1 tsp smoked paprika for background heat
1 large handful each of dried oregano and dried Italian seasoning, don't skimp on these, be bold.
2 tbs brown sugar
Spaghetti, lots of parmesan and butter.

Heat the pan and add the oil, fry the bacon or Vieska until crisp and remove from the pan. Add the garlic and fry till it starts to colour, don't let it burn. Add the onions carrots and celery and sweat them down till they soften, about ten to fifteen mins. Add the mince and break it up with a wooden spatula as you stir it into the vegetables. It must be broken up and browned before you proceed with the next stage. Add the dried herbs and stir in then add the tomato puree. Stir the puree well in then add the Dolmio and the tinned tomatoes. Season with salt and pepper then add the sugar. Bring up to a simmer the place it in the oven for two and a half hours on gas 4. Don't ask me what that is in electric as I've no idea.
I like my spaghetti well cooked, I'm not one of the "Al Dente" brigade. I serve the spaghetti with butter and parmesan stirred well into it before spooning on a dollop of the sauce. I've got to say, it's bloody delicious and every one of my mates who have tried it have all said the same.

SHIREGREEN MOCK FERRET ON TOAST

Whenever I'm asked to contribute a recipe to a charity book or something of that nature, I send them this one.

First of all take one fresh ferret. To determine the freshness of the ferret, stick a pin in it, if it bites your thumb, the ferret is fresh. You will note the title of this delicacy is "Shiregreen Mock Ferret on toast", so you must obtain a Shiregreen Mocking Barrel.{a bucket will not do as the zinc content impairs the flavour of the ferret}. These Mocking barrels are now exceedingly rare and are much sought after by gourmets all over the world. However they can still be purchased occasionally from Hiram and Minnie Mousetrouser's barrel emporium on Hatfield House Lane in Sheffield.

The barrel is about three feet deep and once the ferret is placed in the barrel, an effective escape is virtually impossible. Place the ferret in the barrel and begin to mock it by saying things like "Oh, what a silly ferret you are". This will demoralize the once proud ferret who should now willingly co-operate.

Next, place the ferret on the toast, you may find at this point that the ferret will keep walking off the toast. Should this occur, affix the ferret to the toast with some Ellisdon's Ferret Toast Staples which can be purchased at any branch of the Albanian Bugatti Owners Club.

Simmer the ferret, {in its jacket} in the River Don for three days, if it does not have a jacket you may use your own. Sprinkle with Henderson's Relish and garnish with Cunningham's Piccalilli. Serve immediately.

THE BEST FRUIT CAKE EVER

INGREDIENTS:

1 cup butter
1 cup sugar
4 large eggs
1 cup dried fruit
1 tsp baking powder
1 tsp baking soda
1 tbs lemon juice
1 cup mixed nuts
2 quarts of aged whisky.

Before you start, check the whisky for quality. Good isn't it, now go ahead.

Select a large mixing bowl, measuring cup, etc. Check the whisky again as it must be right. To ensure the whisky is of the highest quality, pour 1 level cupful into a glass and drink it as fast as you can.

Repeat!!

With an eclectic mixer beat 1 cup of butter into a large fluffy owl. Add 1 tsp of sugar and beat the hell out of it again. Meanwhile, at this pasnicular point in time, wake sure that the whixey hasn't gone bad while you weren't looking by shecking it again.

Open second Quart if nestessary. Add 2 large eggs, 2 cups fruid druit and beat till high. If druit gets shtuck in peaters, jusht pry the mousters loosh wiv a drewscriver. Example the whikstey again, shecking confistancy then shift 2 cups of salt or destergent or whatever.

Chample the whitchey shum more. Shift in slum lemon shoosh. Fold in chopped sputter and shrained nuts. Add 100 babblespoons of brown booker or whushevers closest and mix well.

Greash ubben and turn the cakey pan 350 degrees. Now pour the whole mesh into the weshin' machine and set on sinsh cycle. Check dat whixney wunsh more and pash out.

....